THE GOO
FO

The Good Computing Book for Beginners

All you need to know about computers
(and nothing you don't)

THE COMPLETE INTRODUCTION
with a practical glossary of terms

by Dennis Jarrett

ECC PUBLICATIONS
in association with
HUTCHINSON
London Melbourne Sydney Auckland Johannesburg

Hutchinson & Co. (Publishers) Ltd

An imprint of the Hutchinson Publishing Group

17–21 Conway Street, London WIP 6JD

Hutchinson Group (Australia) Pty Ltd
30–32 Cremorne Street, Richmond South, Victoria 3121
PO Box 151, Broadway, New South Wales 2007

Hutchinson Group (NZ) Ltd
32–34 View Road, PO Box 40–086, Glenfield, Auckland 10

Hutchinson Group (SA) (Pty) Ltd
PO Box 337, Bergvlei 2012, South Africa

First published by ECC Publications 1980
Second edition published by Hutchinson 1983

Typeset and printed by Elanders AB, Sweden

ISBN 0 09 152261 7

The first edition of this book was for Carol and Kay, who could have used something like it when they were getting started with computers. This one is for Janice, who liked the first version and then changed her mind when she met me; and also for Lyn, whose comments on it were the most pleasant yet the least sycophantic.

CONTENTS

About the author

Dennis Jarrett is a writer on computers but it goes further than that. If pressed for a short but fuller description he would probably have to settle for some pompous phrase like "consultant in information technology".

Like many people in and around computers, his participation was largely accidental. Having left university in the late '60s with many West Coast albums and a degree in a collection of subjects, none of which had any relevance to his future career, he found himself writing user manuals for a computer company because that offered more money than a management trainee course with BOC.

From a short and inglorious career as a technical author, he moved subsequently into computer journalism via a now-defunct weekly which was given to investigative reporting and bad puns. That was followed by a long spell as a freelance writer, working for anyone who could afford him, until he joined the small group of people who were planning to set up *Which Computer?* magazine in 1977. He was the first editor of that publication and later became editorial director of the independent publishing group which grew around it. Its titles included *Business Matters, Which Word Processor?* and the *Computer Guides* series.

He left to establish his own company in 1980 with a small band of what might legitimately be called fellow professionals. The Paradox Group gets its name because a paradox is something which works in spite of itself. The work in question includes publishing a few journals of its own and supplying editorial services for other publishers. There is also much one-off writing of individual articles, some lecturing, the provision of consultancy services of various kinds for users and for office systems marketeers, and an involvement in a range of handbooks on computer systems for specific industries and professions.

Dennis Jarrett is also the author of *The Electronic Office – A Management Guide* and an as-yet unpublished introduction to microcomputers in business and about eight volumes of uncompleted/unpublished/-downright bad plays, novels and poems.

PREFACE TO THE FIRST EDITION

I found out about computers the hard way. It has taken me ten years to realise that the best way to look at computers is the same way you would think of a motor car or a washing machine or a Kleenex.

A computer is primarily a functional object – it *does* something. You don't necessarily need to know anything about how or why it works, or how it was made; all you really need is a list of instructions about how to use it.

On the other hand it's dumb to pass up the opportunities open to us now. Computers today are small enough and cheap enough for a great number of people to get their hands on one – from schoolkids to businessmen, from radio hams to typists. As with a car or a washing machine, you'll be able to get more out of it if you know just a little about its potential – and its limitations.

What's more, you might even get interested in the subject. Once you realise how easy programming really is, and how easy it is to hand the computer a new program to beaver away with, there's really no limit to the kind of things a computer can do.

That's really why I wrote this book. Nobody told *me* all of this when I was getting started in the computer industry. But then I'd been in the business for five years before I even sat in front of a real computer terminal. How times change.

As you can see, this book really comes in two parts – a textual overview followed by a glossary. There are hundreds of introductory books on computing, of course, and dozens of dictionaries. I've nothing against them and, in fact, there's a short bibliography at the back in which I recommend some.

Very few of them are really *practical* enough – they tend to be written by academics or technical specialists or academic technical specialists; they are generally dull and boring; the U.K. ones in particular have many outdated concepts, the American books quickly go out of date because they dwell a great deal on specific products (there's one excellent 1978 book which I would recommend, except that every single photograph in it refers to a superseded product or a company which has gone bust).

Above all, I feel that most of those books simply have too much information in them. What you're holding here is a starter book and a ready-reference; it's not an encyclopaedia of computer science, so don't expect the earth. Besides, at this price what can you expect?

I assume that most of you are new to computers, in which case your first forays into the muddied field will probably be via a small computer – perhaps one labelled a 'microcomputer' or 'personal computer'.

That's why this book concentrates on small, cheap systems in explaining the basics. But you'll also find the principal terms and ideas of large-scale computing covered in the glossary.

Who is the book really for? What kind of beginner am I writing for?

Well, I expect you to belong to one or more of these groups:

- teachers
- schoolchildren
- enlightened parents
- trainees in data processing
- people who might have to buy and/or use a computer for business functions

- people who think they might be generally interested in computing as a kind of hobby
- anyone going on a medium-length train journey with nothing else to read
- anyone who just wants to know what all the fuss is about.

Parts of this book appeared in an earlier form in the magazine *Practical Computing*, which began life with me as managing editor. Carol Gourlay contributed to the Glossary.

PREFACE TO THE SECOND EDITION

It is amazing to think that 30,000 people have bought this little book in the last two years. Well, 30,000 copies were printed, anyhow, but then I have lost, or given away, or poured coffee over about 60. So I don't suppose there are really so many copies in daily use, especially as I have not seen 30,000 royalties.

Still, a fair number of people must have bought – borrowed? stolen? – *The Good Computing Book*. Leaving aside all implications as to its quality, I think the level of sales is a fair indication of the appeal of a modestly-priced and relatively non-technical introduction to computers.

It is also an expression of the new interest in small, cheap computers; and that's one of the principal differences between this 1983 introduction and the original 1980 version. There are cheap, powerful computers available now; you can buy them for the same price as a decent hi-fi system, schools can get them for the same price as one electric typewriter, businesses can get them for the cost of one or two percentage points off the contingency allowance.

Small, low-cost computers mean more people are getting their hands on the things. More and more people are becoming 'computer literate'; more than 300,000 Sinclair ZX-81s have been sold now. That kind of acceptance for computers raises the public consciousness generally; people are becoming less unhappy about computers.

They are also demanding more sophistication, which can't be bad. Why settle for an unsatisfactory keyboard just because that is what the manufacturer has decided you shall have? Why put up with elliptical jargon-filled command sequences like POKE and

PEEK when easy-to-understand alternatives like DRAW or PAINT are by no means difficult to implement?

The pressure of competition is forcing the vendors to recognise those arguments and to make the extra effort, very little of which is usually required to improve the appeal of the product.

The other significant change between 1980 and 1983 is the arrival at modest cost of 16-bit microcomputers. As it happens, the two prominent examples of the current ready-to-go 16-bit business microcomputers both exhibit a good deal of work on fitting the machine and its operation more closely to the user – excellent keyboards, good-quality displays, sensible and comprehensible screen messages – by and large.

In theory, the 16-bit microcomputers will be able to run larger and more sophisticated programs, probably operating more quickly at the same time. In practice, promise may take a time for full realisation – but it will happen. So will the low-cost 16-bit home computer.

This edition of the book retains the same structure of introductory chapters plus glossary but for the latter especially, the revisions – and additions – are substantial.

In addition, the book includes two new chapters, neither of which can be counted essential reading. The history of microcomputers is there to expand the background and to provide something of an historical context; the 'bluffer's guide' is intended as entertainment, though I do not mislead when I say it is based on practical experience.

Both of those chapters appeared originally, in a much less mature form, in *Microcomputer Printout*, whose editor, Richard Pawson, receives my appreciation for his permission to re-use the material.

1 INTRODUCTION TO THE INTRODUCTION

There are too many myths about computers. Too many people hold too many rigid and unsubstantiated beliefs about what computers are, what they can and can't do, how and why they work.

This book will change all that.

For a start, let's summarise the myths:

- computers can think
- computers are large
- computers are bureaucratic
- computers are expensive
- computers have flashing lights
- most computers are run by government bodies
- most of the rest are run by large companies
- computers are electronic brains
- computers are basically incomprehensilbe unless you're some kind of genius
- computers are best left to someone else
- computers go wrong all the time.

They are all fundamentally WRONG. Computers aren't *necessarily* like that, though some people would like you to think so. It's worth looking briefly at how the myths evolved before deciding what's wrong with them.

The Emperor has No Clothes

The whole computer business – like most other businesses – is driven by what you might call technological and economic forces. Twelve years ago the technology was at a stage where all the components were expensive, so not many people could afford computers; but for those who could bear that much outlay, there were considerable benefits of scale to be had – so computers tended to be complicated, expensive, and big.

That's one of the main props of the computer myth. The other is the presumed need for dedicated acolytes, people in pebble glasses and baggy jeans or white coats who are paid a lot of money for preventing anyone else getting their hands on the computer. While computers were complicated, it's true that to understand, organise and manipulate their complexity a bunch of specialised jobs had to be created. That meant a need for special computer training; it also created a new jargon, a kind of shorthand which helped computer people talk to each other – not an easy thing for them to do, it seemed. The training and the jargon both served to fence them off from the rest of us.

Today some computers are still big and complicated; they still require specialised staff, they still cost a lot of money to buy and to run, they still need their own jargon, they still have lots of flashing lights and they still operate at unimaginably fast speeds.

That kind of computer is now in the minority. They are bought for only two reasons — one, to solve gigantically complex problems, or two, to allow a large number of people to get at a little bit of the computer all at the same time. Weather forecasting or space exploration are obvious candidates for the first category. The second is called time-sharing, and it is an alternative to giving the same number of people a small computer of their own; it's especially useful when you need occasional access to the kind of complicated calculation or modelling functions you couldn't fit on to a small computer, but to some extent a small computer of your own is what this book is all about.

That mixture of technology and economics has worked to produce a breed of computer which does not differ in *kind* from the multi-million-dollar megaliths with their over-qualified ministering minions, their impenetrable forests of new and mis-spelled words, their general inaccessibility. Technology has provided us with a cheaper and more compact type of computer. The economic factors dictate that more people can afford them, more individuals want them, more businesses need them, so they can be produced and sold cheaply. Computers are becoming ACCESSIBLE.

What is a computer?
A computer is a fast rule-following idiot machine with the ability to remember things.

It's fast because it is electronic; and electrons are pretty speedy. It follows rules because that is all a computer does. You can alter or replace the rules more or less at will, you can add rules, you can complicate rules. And it's an idiot because it simply can't think for itself – not in terms of original, creative thought, anyway. It just follows those rules.

This applies to all computers, irrespective of their size, shape, colour, capacity, nationality or the uses to which they might be put.

The essential element is that you provide rules for it to follow – and that you can change them. All this talk of 'rules' is a little abstract, so let's give the business a name – *programming*. A program is just a set of instructions for the computer to follow. It will try to follow them blindly, typing errors and all. If you change the program, or substitute another one, the fast idiot will chug through the new instructions as coldly and as logically as before.

Remember this – the freshly-arrived computer is blank; it has no intrinsic purpose until you give it one.

And the word 'computer' is actually incorrect – an historical accident; it doesn't necessarily do computations at all. It's just that the first computers spent all their time doing calculations – initially for shell trajectories in the second world war and Census returns just after it.

It's helpful to start calling the computer a 'system'; most computer people do, and for a change this is a meaningful use of a jargon word. A system is a set of components which can be combined to produce effects which none of the individual bits could manage on their own.

The components of the computer system are a mix of *software* (which is a group name for all the programs) and *hardware* (all the bits that you could stub your toes on – literally, everything which is hard, tangible, visible).

You can relate that to what a computer does when it is computing. In essence, four things happen when a computer computes:

- information (or words, or data, or instructions, or whatever) goes in; this is *input*
- it gets decoded, acted upon, massaged, manipulated according to the rules laid down in whatever program is in there at the time; this is *processing*
- the information may be *stored* for future use; so may whole programs, and any results of the processing
- alternatively (or subsequently) the results of that processing may be displayed, printed, or in some other way proclaimed to the outside world (usually you); this is called *output*.

A conventional computer, then, has facilities for:

- input
- processing
- storage

• output.

So what happens is that you (or someone else) writes a program and inputs it, to be stored in memory until it is needed. Subsequently some data is input as well – data is just something on which the rules in the program can work. The program is activated and processes your data, and the results are output somehow.

2 WHAT GOES ON INSIDE

This chapter will tell you how a computer works — and why computers have to look like they do. This may be a little technical but try and persevere; if you can understand how and why things happen in the computer, you should be able to understand what a computer can and cannot do.

In the event of confusion, irritation, depression and/or general technofear, go straight to Chapter 4 and return to this one when you're feeling more like it.

The Idiot in the Middle

Obviously the bit in the middle of all this computing will be the processing component. It will not come as a shock to discover that this is called a **processor** (or central processing unit, or CPU).

Time for technology. What happens inside a processor is that electricity moves down one circuit or the other. The complexity of the alternatives – how fast the choice can be made, how quickly the electrons can get along the chosen route, how small the whole thing can become – is what distinguishes one processor from another.

There are dozens of processors being made, incidentally, and there are hundreds of products for the end-user (you and me). In fact, them; numerous companies have found ways of incorporating the same processor into identifiably different computer systems.

Computers are really a whole series of electronic switches. Like most switches, these can be ON or OFF. There isn't really any other possibility. As it happens, there's a neat way of expressing this ON/OFF business; it's called binary numbering.

Now don't get worried by this, but there are many numbering systems other than the one we use – which is called decimal, because it uses 10 digits. The binary system uses only two digits, which for the sake of argument are '0' and '1'. If '0' corresponds to 'off' and '1' to 'on', you obviously have a neat way of representing the internal operations of the computer.

The electronics can decode a string of 0s and 1s as a series of off/on combinations. And *voila!* you have a way of communicating with the electronics. You can tell it that certain types of 0/1 patterns will be program instructions; other binary patterns will be information to be processed by programs.

Suspicious Characters

It is possible to write programs for any computer which gives instructions encoded as 0s and 1s. Provided you and the computer both know what the binary sequence means, it is possible to hold *any* information in this form – even alphabetic characters.

You just make sure that you and the computer both know what binary patterns correspond to which alphanumeric characters – as with any other code, like Morse or semaphore or naval flags, both sides have to know what the codes mean.

It is extremely tedious to communicate with the computer in this way, though, not least because any normal person would have to keep checking on the precise binary codes for the alphanumeric characters – you couldn't remember them all, you'd go out of your mind.

So the vendor gives the computer a special manufacturer-supplied program which will convert a series of 0s and 1s into a more intelligible way of expressing information into the binary digits a computer can use. This way you can give the computer a number or a letter, and with a quick piece of internal transformation it can understand what you mean.

Most computers translate characters according to an eight-bit code – a 'bit' being a binary digit, one of those 0s and 1s. An eight-bit code comprises a string of eight digits, each of which can be 0 or 1. With a choice of 0 or 1 in each of the eight positions, that gives a total of 128 possible combinations; and 128 different bit patterns is enough to give unique patterns for each letter of the alphabet, each number, and a few punctuation marks and arithmetic symbols, too.

So when you key-in a sequence of alphanumeric characters at your computer keyboard, it will decode them speedily into a group of eight-bit codes – and these are the binary patterns it can understand.

It can hold those in its memory, too. The storage capacity of a computer, the amount of information it can keep in memory, is usually expressed in characters – or bytes. A 'byte' is eight bits, so generally one byte is the equivalent of one character.

You'll also come across the cryptic symbol 'K', This is shorthand for 1,024 (don't worry about why K means 1,024, it's just one of those things). So '8K' means $8 \times 1,024 = 8,192$ characters.

Chips That Pass in the Night
Electronics these days is all about switching streams of electrons (which is what electricity consists of, really) and it's only 60 or 70 years old.

In the early days a kind of switch called a relay was used; they were comparatively slow to operate, though. 'Slowness' here means a few thousandths of a second, which sounds fast; but even a simple internal operation looks complicated when you reduce it to a number of switches opening and closing. For one operation, that typically means several thousand, maybe several *million* switchings. They all mount up.

So the advent of vacuum tubes in the 1950s pleased everyone; as electronic switches, they operated rather faster. Transistors followed a few years later, faster still and more reliable. The major breakthrough of the early 1960s was the **integrated** circuit, and that's where we are now.

Even faster and even more reliable, integrated circuits were also considerably cheaper and much more compact. They used the newish technology of semiconductor materials to cram an increasingly large number of electronic switches on to a diminishing silicon chip.

Ah-ha, so you've heard of silicon chips, have you? Silicon materials happen to be the best way at present of getting the maximum number of circuits – at least 100, more usually several thousand – on to a really small area of crystalline material (which, let's face it, is basically a bit of rock).

This is the famous chip. It is encased in a block of plastic with metal legs – you've probably seen them, they look like mechanised cockroaches. Each leg corresponds with and is connected to one of the circuit ends on the chip.

This little lot plugs into (or is soldered into) a socket on a printed circuit card – which for no good reason is sometimes called a printed circuit *board* and abbreviated to PCB.

These PCBs are fibreglass or plastic rectangles with circuit lines printed on to them and holes drilled to take the legs. The lines are gold or silver or some other electrically-conductive metal, and they run between the socket holes; put the proper semiconductor packages into the correct holes and the chips can pass among themselves electronic signals which mean actual data to each other.

The processor part is not the only chip in the computer – it may need three or four chips to itself. Other chips do other things – more of that later. Generally the computer manufacturer can't get all the chips you need on to a single PCB, so the chips on one board need some way of communicating with the chips on another. They also need some way of getting information to and from the rest of the system; and they need some electrical power to work in the first place.

So a PCB has a line of 'circuit connectors' along one or more edges. These are the other end of the printed circuit lines which connect the socket holes. The circuit boards are usually plugged into slots in a kind of metal skeleton called a chassis or a frame. This has built-in wires connecting one slot with another. This thin cabling also connects all the slots to the electricity supply – and eventually to the other parts of the system as well. Then, the connectors along the edge of the PCB mate with connectors in the frame, so there's a way of passing signals to and from the PCB via the wiring in the frame. Clever, isn't it?

Processor Power

A processor isn't a computer; it's just one of several components which together make up a computer system. But it's an important component because it largely decides exactly what your computer can and cannot do.

A *microprocessor* is just a small processor. That description doesn't do it justice – by comparison with previous processors, though, a microprocessor represents a major technological advance; on one or two chips the designers have managed to cram all the circuits for which conventional computers have several chips.

There are three important implications of this; microprocessors are cheap to mass-produce, they are very small, and (for various technical reasons) they can't be as powerful or as fast as their upmarket brethren.

You might come across names like the Zilog Z-80 or Z-8000, Intel 8080 or 8085 or 8086 or 8088, MOS Technology 6502, Digital Equipment LSI-11, and Motorola M6809. All of these are widely-used microprocessors and all have spawned numerous siblings with family resemblances – *but none of them is actually a computer*. They are just the processors used in computers.

As it happens, all the companies named put their microprocessors into computers and sell them under different names; but the bulk of microcomputer sales come from other manufacturers, who buy the processors as they buy any other component and build a computer with them.

Thanks for the Memory

A particular arrangement of particular chips will provide the functions of a processor. A different selection of chips is needed to provide other parts of the computer system – including the **memory**.

There are various ways of storing information (especially programs) for future use. They differ primarily in speed of access, how long it takes you to get at the stored information.

You read information fastest from internal memory – which consists of chips on one or more PCBs. The fastest type of internal memory is the so-called read-only memory or **ROM**; it has that name because you can't 'write' new information on to it.

ROM is physically one or more of those plug-in semiconductor packages. Its contents are usually fixed by the manufacturer and generally they consist of frequently-used programs without which your system couldn't really operate.

Then there is read/write memory, whose contents you can alter by writing new information on it (in practice you're over-writing what's already there). More often it's called random-access memory or RAM. This is the main 'user' memory of the system, just waiting for you to fill with your own programs or the data on which your programs will operate.

These are the two basic types of internal memory. Apart from ROM and RAM, there are various 'external' methods of storing programs and data. These are connected by cable along which the information is read from or written to the storage device. External storage is much slower than internal memory, in that it takes considerably longer for the computer to get at information, but external storage is considerably cheaper. Besides, for technical reasons there are practical limits to how much RAM can be provided before things get horribly complicated and expensive. Small computers generally have no more than 64K bytes of user memory, which is tiny compared to what a cassette or a floppy disc will store.

What happens is that your computer system makes the most of things, capitalising on the virtues of internal memory (fast access) and external storage (cheap and lots of it). Programs and the data to which they can be applied are held externally and they are read into the internal memory only when they are needed. So they remain accessible to the computer – but they don't clutter up all that expensive RAM.

The two external storage media you will encounter

are magnetic tape and disc; the slowest and cheapest versions of each are cassette and floppy disc.

Cassettes as used with computers are much the same as ordinary audio cassettes – and on the cheaper computers they *are* audio cassettes. Certainly the cassette units are sometimes off-the-shelf portable tape recorders.

The recording is done by magnetising spots on the tape in a particular pattern, such that one collection of spots is read as the code for one character. An average cassette can store about 300,000 characters in this way.

Cassettes are obviously a cheap form of storage – you can get one of those recorders for less than £30, after all, and the cassettes aren't expensive but they are limited.

You can't read from or write to cassette at anything like the speeds possible with disc. More important, cassettes store data serially. That means (would you believe) one piece of data is stored after another; and if you want to get at a particular item you have to pass over everything which precedes it on the tape.

You don't have that disadvantage with **floppy discs**. These are in three sizes. The biggest is about the size of a 45 rpm record; there's a popular alternative, cheaper and less capacious, around two-thirds that size; and in the last year or so the industry has produced an even less expensive mini-disc with a diameter of 3in.

All of these really are discs, and they really are floppy – though to give them at least some rigidity and some protection they are in cardboard envelopes. Some people call them 'diskettes' or 'mini-discs' or 'flexible discs'.

The disc inserted into a box called a disc drive; they have slots cut in them to expose the disc surface so that the read/write head inside the drive can get at the information stored on it as they rotate inside the cardboard sleeve.

Discs are much faster than cassettes at getting data to and from the processor. They also allow what's called 'random' access to data stored; this isn't really random – it just recognises the fact that you can tell the read/write head to move over the disc before it does any reading or writing.

The alternative term is 'direct access'. It is much more appropriate, since you are going more or less directly to the information; the read/write head just has to get at the proper track, so the disc never has to go more than a single revolution before the information on that track gets below the read head. It's something like moving the record arm over an LP to the correct point for the music you want to hear.

With audio tape, there's no simple and quick way of getting straight to the start of a particular taped song on cassette; by and large, the same applies to data on a cassette.

The data on disc is held in more or less the same way as for cassette, with tiny magnetised spots on the tracks. One of those small floppy discs will store at least 50,000 characters per side. A single side on the larger floppy disc should be good for at least 200,000 characters, and some go up to 500,000 or more.

You can pay more and get a disc drive to cope with double-sided floppies, which obviously doubles the capacity; the discs themselves also cost more.

Another increase in your budget might allow for double-density floppies – special discs and more expensive drives again, for these discs use technological tricks to get twice as much data in the same space.

In fact, double-density with around 300,000 characters per side is becoming the norm for mini-floppies now. Likewise the 8in. floppies these days typically offer 600,000 characters per side in a double-density format.

So floppy discs can be single- or double-sided, and single- or double-density. The top limit for storage on a floppy disc used to be about a million characters – that's a double-sided double-density large-size floppy – but someone has recently managed to squeeze a whopping three million characters on to one disc.

You can buy floppy disc units one at a time but usually they come in pairs. There are three good reasons for this.

For a start, some computers require you to have one disc permanently loaded. This is generally called the 'system disc' and it will contain the basic manufacturer-supplied control programs for your computer. These are read into memory to be acted upon as and when required, so that the whole internal memory doesn't have to be filled all the time with control programs which aren't being used.

There may be some room left on this 'system' disc for you to store your own programs and data, but if you have a second disc drive you'll have much more space to play with.

Even if your system doesn't need a special system disc, it can be very useful to have the second drive available. Perhaps your system could keep all its programs on one disc and any files of data on the other. Or perhaps you just want a lot of storage because you've a lot of things to store. Bear in mind, though, that you can swop disc in and out easily enough, so you can have a whole library of files – you just load the one with which you want to work at the time.

The third reason is the best of all – it goes under the sonorous heading of 'back-up' or 'security'. It's really easy to mess up the contents of a disc; you can spill coffee on it, the dog can chew it, you can leave it on top of a radiator. You might scratch it or scrape it as you put it into the disc drive. Some slight internal electrical hiccup can also cause a misread or contaminate your lovely files.

So you take a copy of disc contents, usually as the last thing you do at the end of the day. You put the copy disc in the second drive and just read to it the entire contents of the disc in drive number one – and for that you clearly need two drives. You then make sure the dog doesn't gnaw *both* discs.

Past and future

These aren't the only forms of external storage but the others are outdated. The Glossary deals at length with punched cards; they've definitely had their day and were never really used on or suitable for small computers.

Paper tape is still fairly common, particularly in schools because it's cheap, fairly reliable, fairly long-lived, and very donatable. Paper tape stores data in a form you can see; a reel of paper tape contains holes punched across the tape; there can usually be up to eight of these corresponding to the eight-bit binary code, and each hole denotes a '1' position in that code – no hole means a '0'. Paper tape is very slow to read and slower still to punch, and the special reader/punch unit which does all that is not cheap; it's also fairly noisy. Still, it is a clear and simple method of storing data – and if you already have the reader/punch mechanism, it might be worth considering.

The only other external storage medium worth mentioning is the **ledger card**. This is found on some office computers; it harks back to the old non-mechanical and non-electronic days, when every record in a company's files (for each supplier, product, employee, customer and so on) was kept on a separate card in a ledger file. Transferring this idea to the computer meant inserting a ledger card into the machine, typing new information on to it, and adding the results of any calculations – like prices with VAT or how many items are still left in stock. A clever development put a magnetic strip on to these cards as well, so basic information could be encoded on the card in a form which was machine-readable as well as the human-readable typing.

As for tomorrow's options, there is an outside possibility that we will see floppy discs being displaced by some version of the **solid-state** all-electronic memory technologies (like semiconductor chips, which you'll recall are used for the *internal* memory in most computers now).

Such chips are a compact way of storing information; you can store a good deal of it in the average cubic inch this way. Certainly it's a very quick way of getting the information into store and then reading out again. What's more, there are no problems with moving parts. It is one of the inescapable truths of designing things that as soon as you incorporate anything which *moves* you have problems of wear, tear and general break-downability. To circumvent them, devices like disc drives, which have more than a few moving parts, have to include highly-engineered components and that increases the price.

On other hand, despite the built-in problems of reliability and engineering expense, the floppy disc drives can easily beat electronic memories on a cost-per-thing-stored basis. Sadly, chips are relatively expensive.

They aren't particularly easy to incorporate into biggish external storage devices, either; the cheapest solid-state devices lose all their contents when the power is switched off, remember? A bunch of chips packed together in the same box can also generate a good deal of heat, which has to be removed somehow; no, it's not as simple as just opening a window and there are other technical problems, too.

So while solid-state eletronic 'thingies' may be the obvious method of storing information, it seems likely that they won't displace the disc as the usual means of holding programs and data. The disc itself might not stay the same, though.

My money is on a newish type of disc – the **digital optical disc**. Since this is a hobbyhorse of mine, I shall be riding off into the sunset for a few paragraphs now – skip to the next section if you wish.

The digital optical disc is a development of the domestic video disc, which started to appear in the shops in 1982. Video discs record video pictures and play them back on your TV, just like a video cassette recorder. The video disc eventually should be cheaper than video cassettes; the picture is supposed to be somewhat better; and because you can move the read head across the surface of the disc it is quick and easy to get to a particular point – much quicker and easier than having to skip through a reel of video tape, anyhow.

Most video discs are really similar to ordinary LPs. A detectable pattern is impressed into the disc surface at the factory, you play it (but can't record on to it), and it works serially (which is, after all, what you need to watch a movie or some other video entertainment, just as it's the way to listen to music).

The key difference is in the read head. An ordinary LP works by physical contacts; a stylus makes mechanical contact with the grooves in the surface and detects the tones encoded on it. The video disc instead has a laser which picks up the presence or absence of tiny pits in the surface of the disc, and the electronics inside the thing translate them into a video picture.

How's that again? Well, a picture need not be entirely solid; it can, for instance, be made up of closely-spaced dots, which is how newspapers do it. A picture on your TV is made up of horizontal lines (625 of them, in theory) with varying shades of light and dark along the line; stacking-up those lines gives a pattern which you recognise as a picture, and altering the combination of light and shade on the lines makes the picture move. Now that kind of information can be stored as a wavy signal pattern in terms of those little pits burnt by the laser.

From this has developed the digital optical disc, or the video data disc, or whatever you want to call it; no-one seems agreed on a common term yet, so your guess will be as good as that of anyone else. It uses a digital method of recording, which means those little pits correspond to data bits. Unlike the consumer product, the digital video disc can be written on by the user.

At present it's a technique which has one really major disadvantage; because you're burning holes in the surface of the disc, it is not possible to re-write or write over the first lot of information you store. You would need some means of filling-in those tiny pits and starting again with a smooth surface. So you can write only once on to video discs.

So what's the big deal? Well, when production gets going the video disc will be reasonably cheap. It will also be able to store a great deal of information; one 12in. disc contains plenty of room for those laser-burnt pits, because they are only one micron or thereabouts in diameter (that's one-millionth of a metre). So one 12in. disc could replace, say, 50,000 pages of A4 typing; beat that.

Because they include very few mechanical components, video discs are unlikely to break down too often. They work fairly quickly, probably about the same speed as floppy discs for getting information to and from the disc.

There is also the spectacular claim for total accuracy. Now no disc or cassette or semiconductor chip can guarantee that everything you try to write into memory and read from it will make the journey safely all the time; there are always electrical and electronic hiccups which can cause a bit or two to be lost in transit but the pioneers of the digital optical disc say that, in practical terms, this recording system is completely error-free.

The video disc will not be a replacement for the kind of high-capacity, fast-access magnetic discs which are used in really big computers, even if they crack the problem of producing a re-writable disc. They just won't be fast enough to compete but in the early days, at least, the write-once-only limitation will not be a problem. The storage capacity will be high enough and the discs cheap enough simply to write a new and updated copy of the same disc when information changes. You'd then just throw away the original.

So for now the obvious uses are applications where you need to store things for a time, the kind of 'archives' for which the existing data storage options would usually be magnetic tape, microfilm, or even paper records.

Where does the small-computer user come in? More to the point, *when?* There are two key developments. One is obviously the provision of a re-writable digital optical disc and that's happening now. There are clever ways of re-coating the surface being developed.

The other will be the arrival of a microcomputer-sized version, and again that's on the way. The people working on the baby brother video disc tend to call them things like 'the optical floppy'. They will be video discs of four or five inches in diameter, about the same size as a contemporary minifloppy. Amazingly, they will store about 100 million characters of information on each side and the cost will be equivalent (in terms of pence per byte stored) to the price of floppy disc units.

What about timing? They won't happen tomorrow but I'd guess we should see plenty of them around in 1990. Keep watching this space.

I/O (it's off to work we go)

I/O is input/output, getting information to and from the computer, and the two are usually bracketed together because the one device often provides both functions – it's easier to build it that way.

The visual display unit or VDU is the classic example. It comprises two separate devices – one for input (the typewriter-like **keyboard**) and another for output (the television-like **screen**) – but a VDU manufacturer finds it convenient to provide just one cable for connection to the processor.

In fact, of course, that cable contains some wires specific to the input function and some for output – and since the computer knows which is which, the VDU isn't really a single device at all.

In any case, most of today's smaller computers make a physical distinction between a display and the keyboard – the Apple II, for instance, has a keyboard built into the box which holds all the electronics, with a screen as a totally separate element.

Of course, the current crop of less-than-£300 home computers make the points very explicit; machines like the BBC Computer, Commodore Vic, Atari, the Sinclairs and the Atom all require you to provide your own screen in the form of your TV set. On larger computers, another 'all-in' device for I/O which may be encountered is the keyboard/printer terminal, basically an alternative to the VDU but with a printer instead of a screen.

In addition, you will probably have a totally separate printer with no keyboard. You will certainly need one if you intend to use your computer system for any business work; but even if you are using a computer only for your own entertainment, edification and delight, you'll appreciate being able to print-out copies of any programs you write. It is extremely difficult to revise and amend programs without a printed copy, in fact.

There are other more esoteric forms of I/O. One which appeals particularly to technology buffs is **speech**; the computer recognises what you're saying, and it replies vocally, too. The voice output part is more or less possible now, though it's not exactly BBC quality; voice input is proving more of a problem. See the Glossary for more on voice I/O.

Another promising area is **hand-written input**. There are character recognition units which can detect typewriting, and some can even pick up handwriting (see *OCR* in the Glossary) but they are very expensive. Prices, however, are falling on the technically much less sophisticated digitisers. Some of these are sensitive pads on which you place your paper. You write on the paper and the pressure you exert is sensed by the digitiser pad; it converts the shape you make into a series of X-Y co-ordinates, which are a doddle to represent and manipulate digitally. The computer figures-out which shape you're making and decides what letter you've written.

A different type of digitiser allows you effectively to input **graphic** material – maps originally, but these days just about anything which comes as lines. The principle is the same, converting specific points on a figure or shape into digital X-Y co-ordinates; but this time you do it specifically by marking the positions yourself, either by pressing through the existing paper or plan on to the sensitive pad, or by using some other way of telling the computer where exactly the point is in relation to other points.

3 PROGRAMS AND PROGRAMMING

There is one big mistake most people make about computers. They assume that the hardware – the kind of things you can see and get your hands on – *is* the computer. The truth is that the programs which run inside the computer are much, much more important in giving the computer its capability and its personality.

So why does this book put a chapter on the hardware before one on software? Because that's the way most of us approach computers in the first place; because it's sometimes convenient to describe the way things work before you talk about the work they do; and because this way around it is easier to make the point about the relative importance of hardware and software.

Bearing that in mind, let's talk about programs and programming.

There are many things which can be expressed in some kind of formal manner which basically constitutes a collection of rules.

If such and such is the case, then do this; otherwise do that. Do this first, then that, then the other. If it's raining don't go to Harrogate – stay in bed. If the Klingons appear, take evasive action. Check budgets against actuals: if they don't match, sack yourself. Have you finished yet? If not, carry on.

Get the idea? It's all about selecting appropriate courses of pre-determined actions according to what options are presented.

Computers follow rules blindly and quickly; and since most things can be expressed as rules and alternatives, computers can be made to do most things.

The trick is in getting the rules correct. You have to

make sure you are covering all the options – and that the procedures you are covering are the correct ones. And 'correct' does not merely mean the existing rules and methods: it means the *appropriate* rules.

The 'rules' are the formalised methods and procedures which you – or someone else – lay down for the computer. Individually, they are called programs. Collectively they are called software; and software is in two flavours – what we might call 'systems' software and 'applications' software. One does something for you; the other type does something for the system.

Sitting in the system

You need never be aware of it but beavering away inside your computer is a bunch of manufacturer-supplied programs. The principal item of system software (sometimes it's the only one) is the **operating system**.

All computers have one of these. An operating system essentially runs the computer for you. As an example, let's look at one of the most popular – it's called CP/M, and it is in four parts. One is concerned with 'handling' disc drives; that means sending information to discs, organising the layout of data on the disc, remembering what's where, and fetching the proper bit when a program requests something.

Another section does a similar but less complicated job for the other less complicated things which can be plugged in, like directing information to a printer.

A third section looks after you, figuring-out what it is you're typing and what you're trying to say; it also directs any error or status messages to your screen, and lets you shuffle files around on disc with commands like delete a file or create a new one.

The fourth part of CP/M is used to hold programs

which have been transferred from disc into memory because you've requested them.

CP/M is a comparatively simple operating system but those four basic functions will be found in any other example of the genre.

A much more complicated operating system would be needed to run multiple terminals. That would mean, for instance, that it would always have to decide which of them was sending information, which should be getting some, and in what order they should each get a few microseconds of the processor's attention.

So far as you're concerned, though, the operating system will manifest itself only as a few messages which might appear on the screen and a few special commands you can use at the keyboard.

There are many other examples of system software – check *utility* and *database manager* in the Glossary, for example. System software usually is supplied by the manufacturer but you can also buy helpful system software packages off the shelf. They are supplied on a disc or cassette and loaded into memory, or as plug-in ROM chips.

Speaking with tongues
The other critical examples of system software all concern programming languages. Remember all that decoding being done by the computer is to save you having to communicate with it in binary notation, all those 0s and 1s? Well, that conversion and decoding process can be relatively simple for the computer – in which case the progam instructions you type-in are fairly cryptic, because they aren't all that far removed from binary.

Or the decoding can be much more complicated, with English-like program commands which don't have to relate particularly closely to the functioning of the computer.

The first is sometimes called low-level programming and it uses a type of programming language called an **assembly language**. Nearly all computers have one of these languages, and no two are alike. They are damned difficult to learn to use, and unless you've no choice or unless you enjoy complicated puzzles, I advise you to avoid them.

Or perhaps that's something of a cop-out. Many people love this kind of programming (not me, you may have gathered) and it has some important plus points. Because assembler programs are nearer to the binary form computers use, they don't take so long for the computer to decode – so programs perform much faster than the equivalent in a high-level language; but it's hell trying to get to grips with an assembler, unless you're being paid for the effort.

If you want to write programs, use what old-style computer people would call a high-level language. That phrase just means that programs for several different computers can theoretically be written in the same language.

There are more than a dozen of these high-level languages – but the one in which you should get interested is called **Basic**. This is straightforward to learn and it's easy to get the hang of it; in general, the syntax and vocabulary of a programming language like Basic are simpler to grasp than the rules of a foreign human tongue.

It's well worth getting to know. Basic has become so popular partly because it was devised from the start as a beginners' language. It had little competition; and the business of translating it into binary digits for the computer (the so-called 'machine code') didn't require as much space or effort from the computers as other programming languages.

A number of good introductions to the Basic language are listed among the books in Chapter 8.

Today you might also hear about **Pascal**, a good-looking language with similar aspirations; it's just starting to appear on small computers. The only other serious contender is **Cobol**, a long-winded language for business use which really scores only when you are already familiar with it – for example, if you've used it previously on a big computer.

The equivalent of the assembler, the system software which decodes high-level programs, is either an **interpreter** or a **compiler**. The difference is that once you've written your program, you push it through a compiler and this decodes it into binary for you; it is then stored on disc or tape, ready to run. So when you want to execute the program subsequently, it will run very quickly because no more conversion is necessary. What's more, you no longer need the compiler software cluttering-up memory – but you still need that pre-execution decoding phase.

That's not required with an interpreter; this is a piece of system software which is permanently there in memory, and every time you run your program it is decoded on the spot.

So compiled programs run faster and use less memory but interpreted programs don't need a slow and laborious pre-execution phase. Basic is usually interpreted, Cobol is usually compiled.

An application a day

When you've written a program – using assembler, compiler or interpreter – you have an example of the second type of software. It's called **applications** software, and it does something for you rather than for the computer.

Examples are games, payroll, word processing – anything which does what *you* want your computer to do.

There are three ways you can acquire some applications programs. First, you might contemplate paying someone to do it for you – and if you're looking for business applications this is an option you should consider. The people who do the work will probably be called a software house – that's a service company, typically small, which sells programming skills on a per-job basis.

More likely you'll buy a few software packages. These are pre-written programs on a tape or disc with some instructions on using the package. You just load and go.

Make sure the package in question will work on your computer. Just because all floppy discs look the same doesn't mean all computers can read anything on all floppy discs. That's because the way information is organised on disc is entirely up to the operating system in the computer at the time – which may not be the same as the operating system which happens to be in your computer.

What's more, the computer manufacturer may think of some more facilities which could go into the operating system. So a new version will be put out; and though you get the extra goodies, there's no guarantee that programs written for the earlier version will still run happily on the uprated model.

In general you'll be reasonably safe, though. Games are a sure bet; if you specify Pet or TRS-80, nominate which model you have, and get the proper programs – they ought to work.

Similarly if you buy business programs on floppy

disc, they will probably work. Provided you stated correctly what computer and what operating system you have, you will have a good case for kicking up an aggrieved stink if off-the-shelf programs like these don't perform.

On the other hand, they may not be exactly what you were expecting. User instructions with packages are frequently unsatisfactory, written by illiterate programmers just before going to the pub. The program may be poorly written, too, so that it operates inefficiently inside the computer – and in practice that means it's deadeningly slow, with you waiting long seconds or even minutes before anything happens on the screen. On top of that the program may have some quirks in it – like it doesn't do the kind of things you were taking for granted.

All that happens because there are unprincipled sharks and well-meaning buffoons in the computer business, just like any other. One way to avoid it is simply to pay only when you're satisfied – or in the case of postal orders to use only those suppliers with a watertight money-back guarantee. Another method is to buy only from reputable and established vendors, or to get programs from a dealer where you can try them before you part with the money.

Do-it-yourself

Or there's the third alternative – you can write programs yourself. This is nowhere near so difficult as it sounds, provided you don't try anything too complicated until you're ready for it; the technical side of programming is really very simple and relatively easy to learn. Many novices find it a lot of fun. I don't, but then I like the results so I'm prepared to undergo the mental effort required.

In theory, there are three phases to writing a program, and if you're going to try your hand at it you'd better get used to them.

They are fairly obvious; first you plan what you're going to do, then you write the program, and finally you key it into the computer and try to run it. Note that you shouldn't get your hands on the computer until the final stages.

In practice, most non-professional programmers aren't so rigorous in their approach – they often start entering program instructions straight away at the computer without much preparation. That's fine for small programs, and for some computer languages (notably Basic), but it is also the cause of much inefficient and inelegant programming, so programs take up more memory than they need and they are so clumsy that they run slower than they need.

In preparing your thoughts and deciding how to solve your problem, the Amazing Flowchart is highly recommended. This is a simple graphic way of expressing what happens – or what should happen. It's easy to spot what you need to do to cover all the options and with a little practice it becomes easy to spot alternative ways of doing things which might be neater and more elegant.

Creativity in programming and elegant solutions to problems is what sets one computer user apart from another. Fortunately computers are fast enough to tolerate some ham-fisted, long-winded, clumsy program-writing, so even if your solution isn't the best possible it may not matter.

At least you should be able to improve on the technical side, knowing what you can and can't try to do with a program.

Having passed this design stage, you then try to translate your final flowchart into program instructions in whatever programming language you are to use. At first that won't be too simple – it depends how long you spent learning the ins and outs of the language. But this is much the easiest part of programming.

The tears start at stage three. When you key-in your brainchild – this work of art, this small piece of your soul and mind – what will happen is that the screen will fill up with a forest of nasty remarks like SYNTAX FAULT and ERROR and question marks.

You then have to go laboriously through the program to find where you've gone wrong. Some people enjoy this as an intellectual exercise. Personally I hate it – but it's necessary.

4 WHAT'S A PERSONAL COMPUTER?

You can forget most of what's gone before. That's because today you can buy straight off the shelf a fully-fledged, plug-in-and-go computer complete with programs, a system which requires you to understand as much about electronics as the buyer of a music centre knows about hi-fi or the driver knows about a car's internal combustion engine.

For this reason there's a good case for using the term 'appliance computer' to describe these take-home-and-plug-in systems. Frankly, though, you'll get more out of your purchase if you know something about what's going on inside.

That off-the-shelf buy is what is usually called a 'personal computer' – the emphasis being on the individual use. Though you might buy one for your business, you, the purchaser, will also be the principal user. By comparison, larger computers sometimes occupy full-time staff who do nothing but work with the computer; but they didn't select it and they didn't sign the cheque.

Let's start at the bottom. The most basic personal computer looks like this:

● *input:* typewriter-style keyboard.

● *processor:* totally invisible, probably buried somewhere inside the keyboard on circuit boards.

● *storage:* internal memory is probably there, too, on one or two more PCBs. External storage may be a cheap cable-connected cassette unit; a more expensive system will have small floppy discs.

● *output* – a screen, possibly an ordinary TV set.

Taking some of the best-sellers in the market as examples, one can see how many different approaches there are to putting together the most basic styles of computer:

● *Home computers like the Sinclair ZX-81 and Spectrum, Commodore Vic, Acorn Atom and Atari 800*

Prices less than £300. A single unit housing all the electronics inside and containing the keyboard, perhaps typewriter-style, as on the Vic, or more like a calculator, as on the Sinclair, with connections for a separate TV or monitor, cassette, printer, joysticks, paddles, and the like. There will also be one or more sockets into which can be plugged extra user memory, or read-only memory cartridges containing games or additional programming functions.

● *Apple II*
Price from about £700. This follows the same pattern – one unit with electronics inside and keyboard outside, plug-in cable connections for cassette or disc, printer, screen, and other devices which may be used with the computer.

● *Commodore 8000*
About £850. A single unit containing typewriter-style keyboard and screen, plus all the electronics; early versions also had a cassette deck built-in but that is now connected by cable to a socket in the back, as are discs, printers, and any other devices.

● *Tandy TRS-80 Model I*
From £500 or so. Four separate units – screen, full-size keyboard (incorporates the processor and memory), cassette player, and power supply (all computers need a black box called a power supply which converts mains voltage to the current they use – in most com-

puters this transformer is invisible inside another unit).

As for software, all have an operating system of some kind (typically a ROM chip or two which contain all the low-level binary decoding functions which make things work – you won't need to know anything about it, though). You will also get a programming language, usually Basic.

Further up-market is a more crowded area, with plenty of suppliers hunting the small businessman who can afford to invest £2,000 to £7,000 in return for the promise of more efficiency and increased profitability.

Apple tackles this market with the Apple II basically by swapping the cassette unit for disc drives and plugging-in a printer – there's already a socket for it. You'll need a replacement operating system to cope with the random-access capabilities of the disc; and if you're a small business you'll probably buy some off-the-shelf programs, too, along with as much memory as you can afford.

All of that also applies to the Tandy TRS-80 – swap cassette for disc unit, load new operating system, plug-in printer, buy some packages. There is also a special businessman's version of the TRS-80 which has the disc drives and the power supply built into the screen unit, so it's less cluttered.

You can attach printer, discs and more memory to the basic Commodore Pet, but again there is a special uprated version. The Pet upgrade is a similar but different unit. It looks the same but loses the integral cassette and has a real typewriter-style keyboard instead of the small calculator-type keys. Printer and disc units are cable-connected; again you'll get an extended operating system and will probably buy some program packages for it. More relevant is the Commodore 8000, another super-Pet though it has lost the Pet label; it has a bigger, better screen and generally looks more businesslike.

What can it do?

Well, what do you want? If you're not exactly certain about computers, read this chapter for a few ideas about what microcomputers are being used for and what categories of system are available.

Peter Ustinov's biography compares TV to telephones. If someone asked you whether you *like* telephones, you'd have to say it depends who is on the line and what they are saying. The same applies to TV, says Ustinov; and it's also true of computers, says Jarrett.

A small computer can probably do something for everyone. That's an over-simplification, of course, but in practice it can probably do something for you – provided you tell it what to do. If the job you have in mind can somehow be expressed as a series of rules or instructions, and if you can somehow provide those instructions in the form of a computer program, the computer can do it.

There are two ways of getting a program in. You can key it in yourself or you can 'load' it from cassette, disc or paper tape – in which case someone else will probably have written the program and sold it to you ready for loading in that form.

So you can put in a program you've written yourself or you can load someone else's. What those programs *do* is really limited only by your imagination – within reason.

Here are some examples we've heard of:

● *Games.*
It's easy to regard computerised games at trivial and

irrelevant. In fact, game-playing can obviously be intellectually and emotionally stimulating as well as merely diverting.

● *Simulations.*

There's a cross-over point which illustrates the value of games. Simulating the economy of Sumeria or the starship *Enterprise* might be classified as games but there's little which is different about planning the future of your own company or looking at alternative ways of getting you and the family to Dubrovnik this summer.

A good example is in education, where a teacher might use the classroom computer to decide 'what-if' questions and thus bring situations to life. A prizewinner in a magazine contest some time ago did just this with a variety of simulations, including one for the Norman Conquest – the children take parts, make decisions based on the historical situation, and watch the computer decide what the outcome would be. His approach could equally be applied to geography and science subjects.

There are some first-class business modelling packages around, too.

● *Schools.*

Apart from that kind of work, the computer can also be used with obvious benefit in complicated calculations at school. Most teaching and much school administration could also gain from some automation of the more routine functions. Time-tabling is the obvious example; meal planning is another.

● *Business.*

The same applies to the administration of business, though here the returns are visible and financial. There are numerous off-the-shelf packages available for almost all aspects of running a business and, in general, we'd recommend that you look carefully (and if possible with independent advice) at what's available – there are many rip-offs in the business computer business.

Well, perhaps that's putting it too strongly. Many of the mistakes and duff systems are due to lack of skill rather than a desire to be evil. In particular, there's a shortage of systems analysis expertise in the micro game – not sufficient people who can see all the aspects of the problem and who can therefore propose solutions which cover enough of them.

There are some classic examples of how computerisation could work for you. Stock control is one; a small computer could tell the shopkeeper or a retailer what was the current stock position at any time on all items, which of them were selling quickly or slowly, which were approaching re-order levels, and how quickly your supplier will normally deliver an order. With that amount of information you ought to be able to reduce inventory levels – and save money.

You could well do the same for debtors if you have a big sales ledger, chasing bad debts and limiting credit to tardy payers. You should certainly look to save time by having the computer produce invoices with VAT analyses as an automatic by-product.

● *Word processing.*
Your computer might also print 'personalised' letters or rapidly-updated price lists if you're in business. If not, it could be used to produce articles, essays and even books. The trick is the provision of a 'word processing' program; basically this lets you enter text and stores it for subsequent editing and amendment. It prints it out at any time – and it's still stored on the computer, so you can amend it subsequently once

more, printing as many copies in as many altered formats as you want.

The personalised letter facility, incidentally, is usually provided in these word processor programs. You write a standard letter leaving gaps for personalising touches like the recipient's name and address; you set up all those variable bits separately; and when you run the program, it prints the same basic letter over and over again but with the personalised parts included in the gaps.

● *Home.*
There is more rubbish talked about computers in the home than any other area of this subject. True, a computer can run your bath, feed the cat, switch on the TV and change the record; but the extra pieces of hardware you would need could become complicated and expensive, and in any case who needs it?

If you're good with soldering irons and electronic construction there's plenty of scope there, though. Besides, there are some sensible home applications as well. Playing games on rainy evenings and doing household accounts are obvious candidates. There is a (probably apocryphal) story of a user who found that after a few months of computerising the home's bills that a brand new car would cost her less in HP payments than her old one was soaking-up in repair charges and petrol.

If you're writing a novel the computer might help, too. You need some skill to put a microprocessor into a Hoover, but surely that's one chore worthy of automation. There is some scope, too, for having the computer control your home while you're away – feeding and watering your houseplants, perhaps, or turning a video recoder on and off at longer intervals than the VCR manufacturer allows.

● *Art.*

Computer-generated art is not to everyone's taste, but at the very least you can have innocent fun persuading your computer to produce patterns, poems, animated cartoon-like sequences and even music; you might need special hardware for this. Some highly serious work has been produced with the computer, so don't take it too lightly.

As it happens, this particular category of applications exemplifies a key aspect of the computer – for 'computer art' is emphatically *not* the computer's art. It's the art of the artist, who is using the computer as a tool, just as other artists might use a paintbrush or palette knife or chisel or handprints. Computers are tools for doing things you want to do – never forget that.

● *Making some money.*

There are dozens of ways of making money from computers. If you go into it professionally, you could set yourself up as a consultant and sell advice about computers but it's a business containing charlatans already, for anyone can call themselves a consultant if they can convince someone else that they know more than the would-be client.

More likely you may be able to find an entirely ethical niche as a small, local software house – writing and selling programs for offices and shops in your area. Perhaps you'll even operate as a computer bureau, running those programs on your own small computer – the customer brings you the weekly figures, you deliver the results next day.

This is a good one for schools to explore and some are doing so. Some of the top software packages for

British businesses with the Pet are from a man who bought the computer, wrote some programs to run his own business, and now sells them very profitably to others.

● *Changing society.*
Well, just a little perhaps. One of the major social changes microcomputers can stimulate is the move away from doing office-type work in a centralised location called an office. We know of academics, designers, book-keepers, architects, lawyers, even secretaries, who are able to do all or part of their work at home using a relatively inexpensive microcomputer there. Perhaps we will compute rather than commute in the future?

Anyhow, this is a generally unexplored area. What about the housebound, the handicapped, the parents and homemakers who can't or don't want to go to an office every day?

People who can work only part of the time? People who *want* to work only part of the time?

Along those lines, there are promising technological developments, too. More and cheaper data transmission facilities are implied by British Telecom work with fibre optic cables; Prestel and other forms of videotex look even more attractive; the advent of citizens' band radio and cable may one day help to make communication between computers more feasible.

If all this comes to pass we'll be able to send information, live TV-type pictures, facsimile, and voice more or less at will. Certainly there should be nothing in the short term to stand in the way of a limited network which connects people who have similar computers, enabling them to pass information and messages and social chat among themselves. This kind of approach would combine a kind of 'electronic mail' system with a kind of electronic newsletter, a bulletin board, perhaps even an electronic newspaper.

Things have gone a long way. Enthusiasts in the States, in the Netherlands, and in some parts of Britain now have advanced messaging systems for people with the appropriate types of computer. There are two big dial-up services in the States, both of which are nudging into Europe now, which enable subscribers to call into a central computer via your micro. You can then browse through the information stored there, load and run games held on the service, receive messages from other users, enter your own. In Britain, Prestel is moving, slowly, towards this kind of facility, too.

So what price a view of the future based on the availability of clever, low-cost computers and the provision of widespread communications facilities?

Today we have the kind of system which necessitates the present agglomeration of human society in cities. That has enforced the rigidity of five-day 9-to-5 working, the unpleasantness of commuting with the other morning-mouthed millions coughing their way through the first cigarette of the day, the emphasis on everyone being in the same office block or in the same square mile or two of the city at the same time.

So let's have a big hand for the Mighty Micro and it's TTFN to old-style urban society. Now everyone can use computerised services to do much of their work and send information or messages easily to the people with whom they have personal or business contacts. That means you can have many more options about where you live and how you work. It means more *choice;* in essence, if you want to continue working in the old way, you can, but now you don't *have* to.

We could probably return to a more pleasant village-style economy, with cities which don't have to be so large and which do not reflect all the competing social and political pressures on space and services. We could lose none of the advantages of the urban civilisation and urban technology; and we could improve our individual lives and our inter-personal relationships in the process.

Ah, well, back to the real world.

Where to buy?

Nobody has to pass examinations to become a seller of computers, so there is a huge range of people doing it – apart from the mail-order business. In general, you'll come across two more or less contrasting attitudes in the computer-selling game which, in practice, correspond to the two ways of making money in the computer business.

• You can sell many low-cost items very quickly – for this you need to be in a good location in a biggish city, where you'll attract sufficient trade to make it all worthwhile. You'll have to spend as little time as possible with each customer, so you can be selling all the time; you'll need to make sure that you can get quick deliveries from suppliers, because you can't afford to be out of stock; and you'll need to have plenty of storage space to keep your stock.

• You can sell high-cost items and expect to move fewer of them – in which case you probably don't need to keep so much cash tied-up in stock-holding. You do, however, need to have a good stream of sales prospects, so advertising and other marketing will be costly; and you need to make as much money as possible out of each sale, so you'll have to be able to supply software and maintenance services – which are expensive to set up.

Most small computers in the U.K. are not sold by the people who make them. Either the manufacturer has a local subsidiary, or it appoints a distributor or agent; those middlemen get the computers on a wholesale basis and they are sold to local dealers and retailers. Those are the people who sell to you and me.

There isn't much exclusivity in selling microcomputers and practically anyone can become a dealer for practically any small computer. At least, that used to be the case; the manufacturers and wholesalers are being more circumspect these days, which keeps out some of the less-reputable vendors, but there is a air of the quick buck surrounding several of the smaller retailers.

Some dealers are unwise enough to stock a large number of microcomputers. But specialisation is one way to keep down costs and sales volume up; and those are the two ways they'll make money. Still, many sell three or four different micros at a particular price level.

That applies particularly for the less-than-£300 computers. With larger computers, say up to the £2,500 mark, the dealers will not usually take competing products in that way.

Those dealers are typically small companies which know a particular business area or a geographical region. This means they'll probably be keen to obtain your order and they will probably run a tight business operation; because of their inherently limited activities they can give a competitive quotation when you ask for a computer to use in your business.

True, those outfits might suffer just because they are small companies. Because they didn't build the computer themselves, for instance, they may not know too much about the insides of the product. The quality of their training and advice may also be somewhat speculative.

What's more, because it is easy to become a dealer, there are probably too many of them. There is certainly plenty of competition and one of the better-established dealers recently remarked that this price-cutting means that more than half of the microcomputer retailers in Britain are losing money.

This is important for the purchaser. You should expect a reasonably long-term relationship with whoever sells you a computer, particularly if you are to use it for business. This is because problems *will* arise, and you will need a convenient source of instant answers to your questions. You will also want to be told when new goodies of relevance to your needs reach the market; your dealer should be able to tell you.

The retailer who deals in the smallest computers will probably offer everything in the manufacturer's catalogue. He might also sell add-on products and ready-to-go programs made for that computer by other people. Perhaps he'll build some extras or write some programs of his own and sell them as well; in that case, he will probably try to find other retailers to take his products as well.

The dealers with larger computer systems to offer will often go further. At the furthest extreme are companies which take hardware and software from one or more sources, add a number of programs of their own, and sell the resulting system under their own name (even though the manufacturer's label still appears on the boxes).

In particular, the hardware is likely to be from at least two sources – one for the computer, the other for the printer. Most computer manufacturers don't make printers and most small computers can work with a variety of printers; the dealer thus has some choice about which printer he sells.

On the software side, the computer will have the basic systems control programs it needs; the manufacturer may also supply some other packages. To that basic complement of programs, the middleman might add a few programs which he's getting elsewhere and the dealer will probably find other applications software programs from another source, say for word processing and business planning packages. In many cases the dealer will have programs of its own to sell, too, and it will also be prepared to write new software specially for its customer, though since that is an expensive option for the buyer and for the seller alike, the dealer will try to persuade you of the merits of one of the ready-to-use packages.

The so-called 'computer store' was originally the most important way of obtaining a small computer, simply because it was the most visible – it's there in the high street, with flashing lights and gleaming metal in the window. The computer store usually sells several types of computer, several types of printers and disc drives, and just about everything you need for your computing – paper, discs, tapes, books, magazines, the lot. These places should serve as local social centres for the personal computer community, repositories of knowledge and advice and notice boards for exchanges, advice and information – or that's how it should be.

Within the last year or two, though, many computer stores which used to fit this profile have changed their ways. They decided they couldn't make enough money out of keeping a horde of rubber-necking children off the streets – and the sad fact is that the people who are most interested have the least money to spend. These days the average computer store is more interested in selling to the businessman.

Besides, there is the example of The Byte Shop chain to depress computer store owners. One of the pioneers in British microcomputer retailing, it failed noisily at the end of 1979. Its downfall was attributed to over-stocking and unprofitable business methods; like some other British high-technology ventures, it also suffered from lack of nerve on the part of a remote professional finance organisation. Now revived within the Comart group, it has cut back heavily on the numerous product lines it sold – and it is clearly aiming for the profitable small business market.

The dealers who sell to business are not so brash or even so visible as the original computer stores. They tend to operate more discreetly because that's the way to sell to business customers.

There is still an air of enthusiastic self-promotion at the home computer end of things, though. Here the vendors will generally be either a specialist computers-only shop, or a hi-fi or consumer electronics store which has added computers to a range of other similarly-priced products for the well-heeled home.

The other way to buy a computer is by mail order. This was pioneered by Sinclair and it's likely that the design of Sinclair computers is heavily-influenced by the need to minimise the costs of posting the things to you in as cheap a package as possible so that they arrive in as unbroken a state as possible.

Sinclair, of course, makes computers and it is rare among manufacturers in preferring to sell directly to you. Some of the dealers for other computers have also tried selling by mail order, notably one or two of the Vic retailers, but although the computers are well packaged they aren't designed for this (and many of them really don't like it). Mail order, however, is big business for the sale of software and hardware add-ons now; it's the cheap and simple way for a new, small company to set itself up from a front room in Ongar or Rawtenstall.

5 WHAT TO LOOK FOR

As with motor cars or hi-fi systems or sorbets, there are no hard and fast rules which do not ultimately rely on personal preference. Here are some points to consider (in no particular order of importance):

- *Processor.*

It doesn't matter much whose processor is inside your computer – unless you want to get in there with your soldering iron, in which case you probably shouldn't be reading this book.

- *Standardisation.*

Much more important is to consider what you might want to add in the future.

Some personal computers follow a standard arrangement of connectors for the slots in their metal frames; so into those slots you can put any PCB which obeys the same standard arrangement.

The best-known standard for this is called S-100. If you think you'll want to add goodies, you might well opt for a computer with the S-100 standard.

Don't be too dismayed if your favourite computer doesn't have it; the importance of the S-100 standard is put into perspective when you realise that *none* of the biggest-selling microcomputers uses it – they have their very own method of linking their internal components. Since the likes of Apple and Commodore have extensive sales, a very broad market has grown around them for products which will work with their non-standard idiosyncracies.

Another consideration in standards relates to interfaces, the plug-and-socket connections which will enable you to attach things to your computer. Here two of the key initials are IEEE and RS232.

These are alternative methods of *wiring* the plug and socket; there are also two different *shapes* of plug and socket. IEEE is found most prominently on the Commodore range, the Pet and Vic (and their derivatives).

There are many more computers which feature the RS232 connection, though, and for that reason there are many more devices like printers and VDUs which have an RS232 plug. So RS232 opens-up more options.

Again, don't despair if you don't have RS232 on your system; you can get IEEE-to-RS232 converters which enable your IEEE socket to attach an RS232 peripheral. Take some professional advice on this; some of those converters don't always manage 100 percent of the conversion required.

Another standard to look for is CP/M, though yet again its absence isn't disastrous by any means. CP/M is the most widely-used operating system among small computers. It is from an independent U.S. company, Digital Research, and many manufacturers have adopted it in one form or another rather than write their own.

CP/M is proven and well-undestood now but there's another reason for buying a system with it – there are dozens of good off-the-shelf programs available to run on systems with CP/M. Choosing this operating system opens a cornucopia of goodies.

On the other hand, the top-selling individual microcomputers do *not* use CP/M. For the smallest micros it requires too much memory; and, besides, it uses disc drives. So machines like the Atari, Vic and BBC Computer all have their own (often idiosyncratic) operating systems.

That is also true of many disc-based micros, notably the present Apple line and Commodore's other machines. There are numerous good-quality packages available for them, of course, since their widespread acceptance has made both operating systems something in the nature of alternative standards themselves.

In any case, yet again the ingenuity of computer boffins and the versatility of the micro comes to the fore; for both Commodore and Apple you can get add-on boxes or circuit boards which allow the computers to run CP/M as well as their own operating systems.

Don't get too carried away, though – you can't easily interchange files between the two operating systems (so you couldn't read existing Apple files with a newly-acquired CP/M program, for instance) and there may well be problems about buying and using standard CP/M programs (not least because the disc formats for standard CP/M programs could be slightly different from your Apple or Commodore formats).

In any case, be warned that CP/M is not an absolute standard – there's still plenty of scope for individual interpretations in how it can be used. So a program which claims to work under CP/M might not quite work under the CP/M in *your* computer. Check.

● *Read-only memory.*
ROM is generally a good thing. If you have to load the basic system software into the computer each time you want to use it, you don't have ROM in your computer. Having these functions pre-programmed and ready to go in ROM modules saves time, and you won't get any load problems either – they happen occasionally. Still, this isn't something about which you get much choice; either you have it, or you don't have it.

● *RAM.*
Read-write memory is much more important. The

pressing question is how much do you need? There's no easy answer – though in practice 8K is the likely minimum you'll need to run any but the simplest programs.

Learn how much memory you can have for your programs and data, because most personal computers put some of their basic system software in RAM, whether you like it or not.

Then you might look at what your input takes up. For instance, if you wanted to put in an A4 page full of text you would need nearly 4K of memory to store it. A relatively complicated game with many twists and turns like most of the current versions of *Star Trek* will need 7K or 8K.

There's a variant on Parkinson's Law here – you almost always use all the memory you have, whatever size it is. Go for at least 8K and try for 16K if you can afford it; you'll want to run fairly sophisticated programs sooner or later.

● *Programming.*
The first edition of this book stated baldly 'Go for Basic' on the grounds that it is something of a *lingua franca* for small computers. On many of them you have no choice, for Basic is all they will have; in any case, it is likely that Basic will have been the language used when programs are bought as packages or acquired from user groups. Besides, Basic isn't too difficult to learn and there are numerous advantages for novice users in a language which enables you to write and run programs so quickly.

Since the heady days of that first edition, however, I have modified my youthful radicalism somewhat. Everything in the preceding paragraph still holds true; Basic is quick and easy, programs printed in magazines normally will be in Basic, many packages you can buy will be written in Basic (if they aren't in assembler). So Basic is still useful.

The bug in the ointment is that Basic can encourage the production of poor programs. It is all too easy to write inelegant, inefficient, clumsy programs in Basic; the language simply gives you too much latitude. While there's nothing morally reprehensible in inelegant programming, it complicates the process – errors are more likely to be incorporated and they may be difficult to trace; amending the program will probably be more difficult; the program may not make the best possible use of the memory space available; it may operate slower than it needs to do.

There are alternative programming languages which enforce more discipline in your program-writing and objectively they may well be better for you. They include one called Pascal.

As things stand at the present, my advice is to stay with Basic for the pragmatic reasons; but consider programming in Pascal as well.

● *Keyboards.*
Unless you have a computer with a good keyboard, you can go nuts trying to type-in a program.

A good all-purpose keyboard follows the QWERTY typewriter layout; it has a solid, chunky feel when you depress keys; and it has a big, unmissable RETURN key (this you use to tell the computer you've concluded one line of input and want to start the next, so it is used frequently).

Extras on it might include a separate numeric keypad on the right (speeds the entry of numbers) and a CAPS LOCK key in addition to SHIFT LOCK (locking into capitals means only you can press all the non-alphabetic keys and still get whatever is in the lower-case position).

• *Display.*
Go for a big display if you can. A good-sized display produces more information more quickly and in more alternative shapes and sizes than a printer or a small display.

Displays are in three varieties. You ought to get the best possible results from a purpose-built visual display unit (VDU); these normally display 24 lines of 80 characters but they will generally add at least £500 to the cost of the system. A built-in screen might not display so many characters but you will get special graphics symbols and no need for cabling.

The third type is simply a converted TV, the simplest and the cheapest kind of display. It might not produce the sharpest image, however, and you probably won't be able to display many characters at once, though few micros have a restriction as rigid as the Vic maximum of just 23 lines of 22 characters per line.

• *Power supply.*
Translating the mains power into the electricity your computer needs is the job of a chunky component usually called the power supply. (In fact, it's a voltage transformer like the one used by a model train or racing car layout.)

It's possible to overload the power supply, in which case things get hot and/or frail, so look for really beefy transformers and hefty wiring. Also get some advice about how much you can plug into the system's existing power supply before it needs a hand.

• *Voltage regulators.*
Computers don't like variations in the electric current. This may result in wobbly characters on the screen, or

data being lost between the processor and cassette or disc, or (at worst) some component failing. Voltage variations are inevitable in mains electricity; and if your computer is plugged into your home's ring main you may compound the problem by having other electrical appliances switching on and off (refrigerators, stereo set-ups, irons, heaters).

For the average user, voltage regulators are probably a luxury. If you have a really wobbly, jerky display for which you can find no likely cause, or if you suddenly lose everything for a split second, it could be problems with the power supply – but it's more likely to be an internal problem.

Still, voltage regulators can't do you any harm. For an average personal computer you could get one for £25–£50; it plugs into your mains socket and you plug the computer into it. The regulator cleverly evens-out the dips and peaks in the power supply, delivering a smooth flow of electricity to your computer.

● *Printers*.
Sooner or later you'll want a printer to keep a record of your programs (you might lose or damage a cassette, after all). For some applications – like business uses or word processing – a printer clearly is vital.

The immediate problem is connecting a printer to your computer. Having specified an *RS232 interface* means you can attach practically any printer; otherwise your options are more limited.

You get the very best print quality from the so-called *daisywheel* printers but they are expensive (from £1,000 to £1,800 depending on speed, though slower, low-cost versions are now starting to appear).

You can also buy special adapters for IBM *golf-ball* typewriters, which might give you good-quality print *and* a typewriter for about £500; but you should be aware that there could be problems in using a typewriter on a job for which it was never designed.

Probably the better bet, if you want a typewriter which can also be used as a printer, is to look for the Olivetti ET121 with a similar kind of adapter; this is a modern electronic typewriter with a daisywheel print element and it is capable of trundling along at a modest 10 or 15cps without damaging itself. Still, in total you will probably find yourself paying something like £800 or more for it.

There is a cheaper possibility which uses the portable Olivetti daisywheel typewriter; you might get away with that combination for about £600, perhaps less if you shop around, but the printing will be slower and the typewriter will inevitably be less robust.

SCM recently produced what looks like the world's cheapest daisywheel printer; the TP-1 costs less than £500. For that kind of money you must expect a few limitations, though, like a very modest print speed (12cps) and only a friction-feed platen (no tractor feed for continuous forms). The cheaper, faster and more reliable options are all *matrix* printers. Dot-matrix printing is a technique whereby characters are built-up from dots and because these printers are simpler mechanically, the prices can be much lower – less than £200 for the kind of small, noisy and relatively slow printers which are perfectly adequate for use with home computers.

In the range £400 or £800 you will get a faster printer (60 to 150cps) which probably gives a cleaner print image. There is also a newish breed of up-and-coming matrix printers which get reasonably close to the solid print image produced by a daisywheel; they print their dots close together, so that they overlap to form a continuous character. The result is not quite as good as typing but it is considerably better than ordinary dot-matrix print.

● *Storage.*
Using cassette tape or floppy disc for storage gives you a cheap and easily-expanded alternative to keeping data and programs in RAM.

The cheapest kind of cassette system loads at something around 50 bytes per second and the fastest rarely exceed 300 bytes per second; it could take several minutes to transfer a complex program.

If you can afford it, choose floppy discs – their chief virtue is that they operate at much higher speeds, taking far less time to transfer information. This saves boredom but it also allows you to make better and more imaginative use of your system.

In any case, your computer may well be doing jobs all the time which involve looking-up records; you need the speed of disc storage for this.

● *Documentation.*
Personal computers generally have terrible user instructions and reference manuals. These days the accompanying documentation tends to be better-produced and some of the learner-level starter manuals are really good. Even if you are sure all the information is there somewhere, it can still be very difficult to get at it via an index or the contents page.

Quantity is no substitute for quality.

It is worth nothing that in some cases independent publishers are doing a good job of filling the documentation gap – especially in the case of the TRS-80, Apple II and Pet – all of which now have a good privately-produced 'user manuals' which out-perform the standard handbooks from their manufacturers.

● *Users.*

You should also look for an active users' newsletter, perhaps even a user group. Both are helpful media for exchanging opinions, advice, notifications of errors, and potentially useful programs. Besides, you'll make friends at user group meetings.

User groups exist for many of the small computers you'll be looking at. Some of them are run by the manufacturer but that tends to happen by default rather than design – no individual user wants the effort of setting it up. There are also gatherings of users with common applications (notably in education) and groups for people who live in the same area.

In any case, you should try to talk to some users before buying a computer or using a particular supplier – they can tell you the real strengths and weaknesses.

● *Supplier.*

There are no easy rules for picking the proper supplier. It makes sense to find if you have a local supplier and if so to go and talk. You'll probably want to be close to your supplier for a year or two at least, so make sure the two of you are compatible.

Several suppliers have joined a Computer Retailers Association. This exists primarily to promote the interests of its members but it is also trying to enforce good ethics.

If you have a complaint and are getting no redress, use the trade press. Write to the editors of all the U.K. personal computing magazines listed in Chapter 8. Try the computer industry weeklies, too – they are always keen for stories to chase.

● *Legal redress.*

In legal terms, you have plenty of protection against unprincipled vendors and duff goods. This results from the Sale of Good Act, which implies a host of conditions and warranties concerning product description, quality and general fitness for purpose.

On the other hand, there are two problems. One applies only if you've bought a microcomputer for business use. Here the vendor will probably insist on your signing a contract (in fact, *any* sale deal involving offer and acceptance is legally a contract – you don't necessarily need a piece of paper). The terms of this contract may well reduce your cover and the vendor's obligations, for commercial contracts *can* have exclusion clauses in them. What's being excluded usually are some of your rights under the Sale of Goods Act.

The vendor's contract terms aren't sacrosanct; in theory you can re-write the contract before agreeing to part with money. Any prior correspondence should include the magic words "subject to contract"; and get a lawyer to look over and re-draft the terms before you sign.

In practice, many suppliers would be unwilling to go through the hassle of negotiating terms, so they would prefer to forget your order.

The other potential problem applies to consumer and commercial purchases alike – it's the man on top of the Clapham omnibus. The law places great stress on 'reasonableness' and whole court cases frequently hinge on what that man in the bus would regard as reasonable. So though you may think some product isn't performing as advertised, the supplier's lawyers may argue that what you expected is unreasonable.

Still, the law tends to favour the buyer. If you really have got nowhere by personal representations to the vendor, and if the press has not been much help, you should threaten legal action. When the value of the goods in question is below £200, the quick and easy way is to do it yourself through something called the Small Claims Court; you'll find an excellent step-by-step booklet on how to do it available at Citizens' Advice Bureaux. Otherwise, see a lawyer.

● *The Future.*
Computers have been getting cheaper and cheaper. Will the trend continue? Is it better to wait until the prices bottom-out before buying one?

I don't think so. Some of the costs involved in making and selling computers will not fall any more – like publicity, people to write software, the people who build and sell them. So even if the cost of the hardware continues to fall, all those other people-related costs will continue to rise.

In fact, there's a case for saying that the cost of software at least will fall – as the total user population increases in size, development costs for programs can be written-off against a larger volume of sales. So the price per package can fall. This assumes that we all buy the same kind of computer and the same packages for it, though; and while software vendors are indeed reducing some prices even now because of this effect, it probably won't ever be a really significant consideration.

Anyhow, I reckon we're at or near a point where the hardware cost is relatively insignificant – all the other costs are just so big. Computers can't get much cheaper, but what will happen is that you'll probably get more for your money. If it costs as much to manufacture and market a fully-specified bells-and-whistles computer as it does a bare, boring, basic system, obviously you're going to be sold the better buy. The difference in price between soldering-in a 4K memory chip and a 64K chip is negligible; the person has to do the same job at the same salary.

So tomorrow's systems are likely to have some or all of these as standard:

- plenty of memory
- built-in language functions in ROM (so they don't have to be loaded in from disc or tape)
  - other goodies in ROM to handle quick, easy and clever file management, production and fancy formatting of reports, word processing and so on
- English-like commands
- much less physical bulk
- non-mechanical forms of storage replacing disc and cassette (and new types of disc replacing the existing media when removable storage is required)
- voice I/O built-in
- colour screens and graphics displays
- much improved ergonomics
- built-in access to viewdata and teletext
- built-in, simple-to-use methods of communicating with other computers.

The technology for all of these is here now. Such products will take three to six years to appear, though, because the bugs have to be ironed-out and the production volumes have to be big enough for the economics to be worthwhile.

Meanwhile, should you buy a computer now or wait for a time? If you want or need one, go out and look at what's available. Bear in mind that you should look for an expandable system – one which can grow with your needs but which can also accommodate easily some of those new goodies if you want them. If you're a business you should expect about four years of working life from your computer; if you're a consumer, you'll pay much less and perhaps ask for two or three.

6 BEYOND BABBAGE: AN ALTERNATIVE HISTORY OF COMPUTING

A good deal has been written on the mainstream history of computers. It's easy enough to find out just about everything there is to know on the development from the abacus though Babbage and Leibnitz and Pascal via Herman Hollerith and ENIAC and UNIVAC and EDSAC and LEO and WHIRLWIND to the computers of the 1970s.

This is an overview of a different world, of the *recent* (and perhaps more important?) history of one crucial aspect of computing. It's the story of the **microcomputer** – and especially its most energetic sibling, that brat we call the **personal computer.**

From chips to kits – the arrival of Silicon Valley

There have been two streams of development in the personal computer business. One was from electronics hobbyists, the other from education. Both were leavened and enlivened by the post-Haight-Asbury generation who were located conveniently near the cradle of the new revolution.

In general terms the **integrated circuit** must be the starting-point. It was invented in 1959 by a youthful company called Fairchild Semiconductor, which had been set up by a collection of eight electronics wizards who had left the pioneering Shockley Transistor Corp. William Shockley, co-inventor of the transistor, had founded his company in the San Francisco area in 1956: that's why Fairchild is there and it's why all the other spin-off enterprises are also in the region which came to be labelled Silicon Valley.

Fairchild included Robert Noyce and Gordon

Moore, both of whom had been among the original eight who split from Shockley. When they split they called their company **Intel** – INTegrated ELectronics – and the intention was to make solid-state memories to displace all that core everyone was using in computers.

So Intel made memories and customised integrated circuits. Noyce was one of the inventors of the IC. Then a young Intel engineer, Ted Hoff, invented the microprocessor, a miniature programmable electronic component. Or at least he probably did – Texas Instruments disputes his claim.

Ted Hoff's invention was the result of his being a good electronics designer. In 1969 Hoff was on an Intel project to produce calculator chips for the now-defunct Japanese company Busicom. At that time calculators weren't run by the kind of general-purpose programmable controllers used today; instead, they all employed custom-made hard-wired logic circuitry. In Hoff's project the Japanese designers were calling for 11 separate chips, in fact.

Hoff's Good Idea was to use some of the pioneering Intel work on memory chips and to build a fairly simple processor which could execute programs stored in memory. In the Spring of 1970, Intel acquired Frederico Faggin from Fairchild and he knew things about making chips which Hoff didn't. Between them they finished with three chips – microprocessor, memory, and I/O control.

The result was the micro which Intel announced in 1971. The 4004 contained the equivalent of about 2,250 transistors on one chip and it was roughly as powerful in computational terms as the 30-ton ENIAC, which appeared a mere 23 years before it.

Thereafter Intel really zipped along. The eight-bit 8008 followed in 1972 and was followed towards the end of the next year by the 8080. Its first competitor, the Mororola M6800, also arrived late in 1973. Meanwhile, the established giants of the semiconductor industry, like Fairchild and Texas Instruments, didn't have products until 1975.

Getting personal (courtesy of *Star Trek*)

Some people immediately started to look at micros, not so much as programmable controllers but more as general-purpose computers – very compact and reasonably cheap, but still usable. That's where the personal computer started to happen.

The **Altair** 8800 is usually recognised as the first personal computer. It was from a instrumentation company, MITS, whose previous best effort had been two rockets for hobbyists and a bulky desk-top calculator; and just to prove that not everything happened on the West Coast, MITS was based in New Mexico.

The microcomputer project appeared originally on the cover of an Autumn 1974 issue of *Popular Electronic,* an advertising come-on for MITS. The machine was described in detail in the January 1975 issue. It was an instant hit, with an embarrassingly large number of orders taken. The kit, when it appeared, sold for about $500, and in three months MITS sold as many kits as it had expected to produce in two years.

The kit had no name at the time and the editor of the magazine was casting around for one when his daughter offered 'Altair' – thus beginning a long-standing connection between personal computing and *Star Trek.* Altair happened to be the name of a planet in a current episode.

MITS wasn't the first in the field with a personal microcomputer. **Scelbi,** which majored subsequently on book publishing in the electronics/micros field, had a kit based on the Intel 8008 earlier in 1974. It didn't push it, however, and the 8008 system didn't sell too well.

The Altair 8800 didn't have the kind of built-in keyboard and/or screen we expect from today's personal computers. Instead it looked more like a minicomputer of the time, a box with two dozen switches and three dozen lights. Most of the switches were for direct addressing of memory locations and functions.

Inside was an Intel 8080 processor. The standard Altair, the 8800, was somewhat bare; there wasn't even any memory included in the price but buying or making the circuit boards and slotting them in was a major part of the pleasure for the early computer buffs.

The Altair wasn't much to write home about as a piece of engineering, either. The boards it used tended to rattle about inside the box and a small bump on the side could cause all kinds of shorting. What's more, the Altair 8800 experienced plenty of flak in the hobbyist newsletters – for late delivery, poor design, its fragmented approach to kit-building and its terrible manual.

It still sold in the thousands and it contributed a great deal, not so much in relation to how things developed subsequently but more in terms of getting the personal computer business off the ground in the first place.

For a kick-off, MITS invented the idea of a low-cost personal computer – or, to put it more formally, the idea of incorporating the new 'microprocessor' programmable controllers into the format of a usable, human-accessible computer.

Then there was the fact that the Altair used the Intel 8080, which started a real tradition. Today the heirs to the 8080 (including the Zilog Z-80) are the world's most-used eight-bit micros. That, in turn, has been responsible for the availability of some outstanding software.

MITS put **Basic** into the Altair, which again represented some pioneering. Basic was a proven, well-documented language with reasonably good facilities and not a hefty memory requirement – and it was designed for beginners. MITS customers would almost certainly fall into that category, at least so far as programming was concerned. In most respects, then, Basic was the obvious choice but the best or the most obvious route has not always been taken by those who shape the world.

MITS commissioned the Basic interpreter from two collegians, one of whom was Bill Gates. Subsequently he took Altair Basic and set up a company called **Microsoft**, which has since become the doyen of language providers.

That head start enabled Microsoft to become the first stop for any microcomputer system builder who needed a Basic, including Commodore. The money Microsoft received from the subsequent deal to put Basic on the Commodore Pet really put Microsoft on the map.

Catching the bus: the sudden arrival of S-100
The Altair also contributed a method of connecting PCBs together, a bus structure called **S-100** which used 100 possible pin connections to pass signals from one system component to another.

True, at the time the Altair S-100 bus was badly-engineered and ill-defined; there were alternatives for MITS to use – there was the Hewlett-Packard HP-IB Interface Bus, subsequently translated into officialese as the IEEE-488; and there was the widely-used RS-232C – but MITS wanted something which was better-adapted to the needs of a low-cost microcomputer design, which was complicated enough to de everything which had to be done, yet which was simple enough to be used.

So Altair produced S-100 and it, too, was an instant hit. Dozens of small companies were formed specifically to make circuit boards which could be plugged into the Altair S-100 bus to provide additional functions. Because there were so many of those standard add-in boards, other people started to make their own computers with the S-100 bus.

Altogether it was hectic time. Companies rose and bloomed overnight like flowers in the desert after rain; and they often lasted about as long. For instance, in 1977 there were these manufacturers of S-100 computers – and this is what happened to them:

Computer Power & Light (COM-PAL)	... failed
Cromemco	... still active
Electronic Tool Company	... failed
Equinox (formerly Parasitic Engineering)	... still active
IMSAI	... failed
Polymorphic Systems	... failed
Processor Technology	... failed
Technical Design Labs	... failed
Vector Graphic	... still active

MITS was taken over by Pertec, a company which made printers and disc drives for minicomputers, and the name eventually disappeared. Pertec still makes business microcomputers, incidentally.

The eager espousal of S-100 demonstrated the crucial need for standardisation and that fact alone proves to be more important than S-100 itself. Anyhow, the S-100 standard has largely been eclipsed; it is still used by several microcomputers but not by the current market leaders.

It wasn't so great even then; in 1977 Bob Stewart was having so much difficulty making the different boards in his Altair work all at the same time that almost single-handed he forced the Computer Standards Committee of the standards-making U.S. body, the IEEE, to set about a formal specification for S-100. They found more than 100 manufacturers of supposedly-compatible boards.

The effort worked and an IEEE standard emerged. As with the Altair, the importance of S-100 was its impact on the development of personal computing; the availability and the understandability of an optimised and accepted standard for system assembly encouraged many people to start building micros and add-in boards which extended their usefulness. S-100 deserves a place in the Hall of Fame.

The rash of post-MITS microcomputer vendors and other builders of S-100 things included a company called **IMS Associates Inc.** That firm won a $250,000 contract to interface an Altair to a minicomputer for some fancy instrumentation work. In the event, MITS couldn't meet the demand from end-users, so IMSAI was supplied with scarcely any Altairs to fulfil the contract. On the other hand, it had been paid the money and it decided to go ahead and build its own microcomputer.

It's interesting that, rather than spend the money on R&D and product development, IMSAI put most of the $250,000 into advertising its computer to all and sundry. So before it had been built, the company had taken a number of orders – and a good many advance payments. That enabled it to do the interfacing and also to get into the market early in a big way. Coincidentally, its product was a box containing an 8080A and using the S-100 bus, not unlike the Altair in that respect.

The IMSAI 8080 was to become one of the most popular computers of the time, selling more than 30,000 – many more than Altiar.

Cromemco was another early entrant, set up principally by Harry Garland to make S-100 boards. He had no computers at the time but he had two very good ideas for plug-in-boards – the Bytesaver (a PROM board with a built-in programmer) and the TV Dazzler (many coloured squares on the screen).

North Star was another of the notable first-stage entrants. It earned a good reputation as a supplier of floppy disc subsystems for 8080/Z-80 micros, appearing in 1977 with an S-100 mini-floppy unit of which it sold 10,000. Most micros at the time had system software which would best be described as primitive – cramming it into the minimum amount of memory was regarded as more important than giving the user useful facilities, and most operating systems could barely manage to set up ordinary sequential files on slow cassettes. So North Star had to produce a reliable operating system and, of course, it also had to find an extended Basic which utilised the disc operating system and the discs.

From that position it made good sense (and not much extra work) to develop a full-scale microcomputer around the discs. The result was a very neat package, available in kit form but more usually sold ready-built, and the Horizon is still among the best-looking 'boxed' microcomputers (it needs a terminal, of course). The box incorporated one or two mini-floppies and hides up to 12 S-100 circuit boards; the external casing is a wooden cabinet. Horizon used the Z-80A with up to 32KB RAM.

Texas-based **South West Technical Products Corp**

("Commodore will not be a big threat in the industry"
– president Daniel Meyer, circa 1977) originally made
electronics kits, including some good and very cheap
stereo amplifiers; but it followed MITS and IMSAI
enthusiastically into microcomputers with the SWTP
6800 in Autumn, 1975.

This was the first system to use the Motorola M6800
micro, though later MITS tried hedging a few bets by
announcing an impressively-unsuccessful 6800-based
system of its own as the Altair 680B.

The SWTP 6800 vied with the Altair for some time
as the most popular micro, getting a good deal of its
appeal from the fact that, unlike the MITS machine,
the SWTP system wasn't plastered with switches on
the front. There was just one ON/OFF button and one
for bootstrap loading. Since both machines required a
separate terminal for anyone to use them effectively,
the box without lights and switches didn't lose much
by comparison.

A better box was coming – the computer which
looked (and was) instantly usable.

The Good-Looking Computer

So far all the products in the personal computer
business had been boxes of electronics, not intended
for immediate plug-in-and-go use by the purchaser.
The genuinely personal computer, to be sold and used
rather as a washing machine or a hi-fi, arrived in
1976.

The **Processor Technology Sol** was launched in that
year, beating the Apple II by a few weeks. It thus
receives the applause as the first 'real' personal computer – a low-cost computer for the home, ready to use
and packaged neatly enough to be placed alongside the
hi-fi with all the visual references to high-powered

technology (like rows of bit-switches on the front) as far out of sight as possible.

At a time when most computers resembled boxes of army ammunition, the Sol (like the Apple) looked rather good – something you wouldn't mind seeing in the living room. It featured an Intel 8080 inside with up to 64KB; it used the Processor Technology mainline product, a good display driver board called the VDM which was sold as an S-100 bus component. All the electronics were mounted on a large single circuit board which was derived from the VDM.

Externally the Sol had a good-quality keyboard (IBM-like sculptured key-tops, numeric keypad to the left) in a metal housing; the side panels were real walnut. A separate cable-connected display monitor was on top of the unit; a cassette interface was provided but one or more floppy disc drives were usually sold with it. The target market tended to be businesses willing to pay something more than $5,000 for a small business computer system.

Yet it was the **Apple** which led the way into personal computing. Enter young Steve Wozniak, aged 21 in 1974, and earning his crust by designing calculators for Hewlett-Packard – where, among other things, he tried to propose something similar to what became the Apple II. About that time he became inerested in video games. He designed and built a few, including a chess display; that led him to display terminals and he had almost finished building one of his own when the Altair was announced.

That switched him on to microcomputers (the calculator chips on which he'd been working at HP were a totally different style of electronic component) and he was one of the founders of one of the earliest hobbyist clubs in California.

That was the Homebrew Computer Club, which

started holding meetings in March, 1975; they were in a garage located in Menlo Park, California. The roll-call of members from those days reads like a battle honours list for the micro; as well as Wozniak and his partner Steve Jobs, the founders of Cromemco, North Star and Processor Technology were regular attendees. One of them reckoned that those year-one members subsequently started at least 21 micro companies.

Wozniak's story was exceptional only because of the success which followed. Full of new-found microprocessor-driven enthusiasm he met Chuck Peddle of Mos Technology at WESCON, a Californian electronics trade fair. Peddle had designed a microprocessor, the 6502, and it was announced in September, 1975. Peddle was at the fair selling 6502 chips at $20 apiece and that was really extraordinary – before WESCON the Intel 8080 and Motorola 6800 cost about $170 each, though the prices fell to $69.95 when Mos Technology put up its price tags.

Wozniak bought a 6502. "It wasn't like trying to think 'Which microprocessor will make a better computer'. It was sort of like, 'Which one can you get for 20 bucks?'". That piece of serendipity is why Apple uses the 6502 rather than the more widespread 8080 or Z-80 lines.

Wozniak knew something about the Motorola 6800 at the time, as it happens, and he had designed and built a computer around it. The 6502 owes something of its parentage to the 6800. Wozniak, meanwhile, had to get his 6800-based computer to do something; so he wrote a Basic compiler for it, using a simulator written by a friend and running on a Hewlett-Packard mini. Subsequently it became Apple Integer Basic.

Wozniak put the 6502 into his video terminal but the next major step was building a PCB for single-board computers. Most people had the processor on one circuit board and the memory on another, so combining the two on to one was really innovative. His mate, Steve Jobs, sold his van and Wozniak sold his calculator to provide the capital to employ a layout artist who could do the PCB design. The aim was to sell the boards at the club but before that could happen they received an order from one of the very first local shops – could they produce 50 complete computers, not just the PCBs, but fully-stocked with chips and ready to go?

The business was worth $25,000, so they jumped at it. With some judicious borrowing and juggling of creditors they were able to complete the order and set up in business in a garage. They called the company Apple – "Steve was working at a place called Apple Orchard or something in Oregon"

It had proved impossible to get colour video on the Apple I, though. So in June, 1976 Wozniak started on the Apple II. The result was a much cleaner design, not least because Wozniak was one of the first microcomputer designers to use 16K RAM chips.

Byte magazine, then a mere fledgling, also came into the picture. The Apple II didn't have a case designed until editor Carl Helms mentioned that he was particularly interested in promoting the idea of a computer attractive enough and neat enough to take home and plug in, as you might a piece of hi-fi equipment. Wozniak designed the now-familiar enclosure.

Instant accessibility: the birth of CP/M
Something else of note happened in 1976. A company called **Digital Research** was set up. Two years earlier, Intel was learning the hard way that having the hardware wasn't enough. Its 8008 and then the 8080 were impressive enough in terms of their programming

potential but in realising that potential the micros were hampered by the lack of a versatile programming language.

Intel commissioned such a language from a consultancy called Microcomputer Applications Associates, a very young company run by Gary Kildall.

The result he called PL/M (Programming Language/Microcomputers). The exercise suggested to Kildall that as well as an all-purpose programming language, the new breed of computers also needed a good all-purpose operating system. Intel wasn't interested in paying for it, so he used PL/M to write the operating system. He called it CP/M, Control Program/Microcomputers.

As it stood, CP/M was an interesting attempt to produce an operating system which was not limited to a particular computer. The clever idea which guaranteed its success was hatched by Kildall and one of his prospective customers, Glenn Ewing of IMSAI; why not split CP/M in two? One part would then provide the functions which are not dependent on the characteristics of a particular computer, while the hardware-specific elements could be separated into another section – it was only the latter which would have to be altered to make CP/M fit different computers.

Since then CP/M has flourished. In 1978, a young Englishman, Tony Gold, set up what is probably the first software publishing house and in doing so stated explicitly that CP/M had become a *de facto* standard, an operating system so widely-used that the same programs could run under it on many different computers. His company, **Lifeboat Associates,** supplied only programs which run under CP/M – and he got rich.

The Apple crop

Meanwhile, early in 1977 Wozniak had finally left Hewlett-Packard for good and launched the Apple II. He also attracted Mike Markkula from the top marketing job at Intel. As well as his expertise, Markkula took with him some excellent contacts with the Bank of America – and a good deal of personal capital to invest; the hi-tech Silicon Valley companies like to pay their top guys partly in shares and even then Intel shares were hot.

Apple has grown into a $500 million company on the back of their ideas. Innovation has proved more difficult recently – the Apple III proved a remarkably intractable product to get on to the market, especially when you consider that techically it's a straight upgrade of the Apple II. Meanwhile, others took up the running.

Compucolor was one; it produced a logical development of the Apple theme, including a full-size screen and a movable keyboard in the package, plus a floppy disc drive built into the screen housing. This is, in essence, the configuration which many business-orientated microcomputers subsequently have adopted and it's also being used by a number of the smaller purpose-built word processors, too.

Compucolor represents an interesting exercise in micro design but it's usually characterised as trying to go too far too fast. For a start, Compucolor had a prototype up and running around the same time as the Apple II appeared in public but problems with reliability, marketing and manufacturing have hamstrung Compucolor appeal.

So has the provision of a single disc. It made the machine too expensive to compete with the £500 cassette-based hobbyist systems. It was not appropriate for more professional applications like business work; the one disc stored too little data and, in any case, a second disc is really needed for system security.

The early days were distinguished by solid and good-looking products from the three pioneers of plug-in-and-go personal computers – Processor Technology (which has since folded), Compucolor (which never became a serious contender), and Apple (which for three years never looked back) but the big boys were about to come out and play.

The Commodore: stage-two thinking

Jack Tramiel of **Commodore** is a very different person from most of the young West Coast entrepreneurs and he entered the personal computer business via a rather different route.

He's a lot older than most of the microcrats, for a start, having barely survived all the nastinesses which befell Polish Jews in Europe during the war (including Auschwitz). Liberated by the Americans, he drove a cab in New York for a time and then joined the U.S. Army. While in uniform he supervised the maintenance of the office machines which the army ran in New York; when he left, he joined a typewriter repair firm.

That didn't last long – "they didn't reward me well enough for the work I'd done, so I decided that setting-up my own company was the only solution" – and, oilcan in hand, he went hustling for his own typewriters to repair. That went well, and he also got a hefty contract to supply some new typewriters along with a few (mechanical) adding machines.

That interested him in high technology; he spotted the arrival of electronics, became one of the first distributors for the pioneering Casio Pet-sized elec-

tronic calculators, and subsequently got into manufacturing his own from sub-assemblies.

Things ticked over nicely, though. Tramiel never
liked relying on outside suppliers. Their erratic deliveries caused him to miss one of the key Christmas
markets in the mid-1970s, so he cancelled all the
contracts. Twenty-two suppliers sued him and lost. He
decided vertical integration was the only answer –
"make everything you need, from chips to casings".

He did more and more of that, surviving the crash
in the calculator market (circa 1975) and raising the
cash to buy a smallish West Coast semiconductor
house, Mos Technology, the next year. Mos Technology it was which built the 6502 processor Wozniak
liked so much; it owed someting to the M6800, but
basically represented a third contender in the eight-bit
market alongside the Motorola and Intel families.

Along with Mos Technology came a live wire electronics designer called Chuck Peddle. He wanted to
build a personal computer around the 6502; Tramiel,
who tends to trust his hustler's instinct, gave him a
tight budget and a strict deadline.

Peddle had the prototype Pet ready for the January,
1977 Consumer Electronics Show. At the time no-one
had really worked-out the idea of an off-the-shelf
consumer-orientated plug-in-and-go 'personal' or
'home' computer. Commodore business was still
based on low-cost calculators and cheap digital watches, with a successful oddity in the shape of a Canadian
furniture maker also contributing to its profits.

Certainly it hadn't blown anything on market research; in fact, the only market test Tramiel did was to
invite purchasers to send cash with order.

It worked; Commodore took $2 million in two
months.

Peddle stayed with Commodore for four years as

Director of Development. Apple wooed him away for a time, but that lasted only a month; and to the uncommitted outside, that brief sojourn looked like a master-stroke of industrial espionage.

The often stormy relationship between Peddle and Tramiel foundered at Christmas 1981, though, with a profound disagreement about future Commodore products. Peddle wanted to build an upmarket business microcomputer and Tramiel didn't. Peddle left saying he'd been sacked; Tramiel wished him good riddance, saying he'd quit. Peddle went away to set up his own company amid writs and counter-claims and he produced the good-loking Sirius (an up-market business microcomputer).

Leather Boys and the Sorceror as Apprentice

The other pioneering personal computer was the TRS-80. It appeared late in 1977 and its genesis makes for an interesting commentary on how things were going at the time. The year before, Radio Shack had hired 25-year-old Steve Leininger from National Semiconductor – he'd designed the Nat Semi SC/MP microprocessor development system.

Radio Shack, which was the retail electronics arm of a leather supplier called **Tandy Corp**, wanted him to produce a computer kit; he convinced his masters that "too many people can't solder". Radio Shack eventually agreed to let him do a plug-in-and-go 'home' computer.

When it appeared, the TRS-80 sold for five cents less than $600: the original Pet was $595. The Pet had the like-it-or-leave-it calculator keyboard, a smaller screen, IEEE interfaces, and the 6502; but it was a single package. The TRS-80 was in four pieces (screen, keyboard, cassette, power supply) but it had a real keyboard, the powerful Z-80 processor, and a good 64x16 screen.

There was another, rather belated, entrant of note. **Exidy** was started in 1977 by two middle-aged electronics engineers from the graphics displays specialist Ramtek. Pete Kaufman and Howell Ivy had a good idea; rather than mess around with the limited and specialist technical market in which Ramtek had a strong position, they wanted to use their graphics expertise to build the kind of games you find in amusement arcades. They did reasonably well, having grabbed a place on the bandwagon just at the right time; Exidy quickly reached number three in that business, behind **Bally** and **Atari**.

Ivy and Kaufman had also found Paul Terrell, who had some good ideas for personal computers and some interesting ideas about how personal computers might be sold. Marketing was a strong point with him; he had started one of the first U.S. computer store chains, **The Byte Shop**, before selling it in 1977.

Terrell set up a data products division in Exidy to build the computer, which he designed and Ivy engineered. The Exidy Sorceror appeared for a brief look at the world in April, 1978, at a personal computing show in Long Beach, California. Production models began arriving that August. It was (and still is) a very good piece of packaging; for $895 you have a high-quality Selectric-like keyboard unit containing a Z-80 processor and running with the CP/M operating system. At the back are sockets for printer, TV monitor, and file storage (floppy disc as a rule these days).

The Sorceror is neat inside and out and it is more solid than most of its competition. Its excellent graphics owe a good deal to the arcade-games background but it was perhaps significant that Exidy decided not to base its computer on a games-playing machine. That logical-seeming route produces the kind of watered-down computing in the 'home entertainment centres' from the other arcade-game manufacturers.

Terrell says he designed the Sorceror to take full advantage of the TRS-80 and the Pet, both of which had been widely-available for some months by then. He wanted particularly the graphics capability of the Pet and the expandability of the Tandy machine. The result was a winner with the reviewers – "appears to be the most well-designed computer on the market in its price range" said the PCC *People's Computers;* "stands head and shoulders above the competition", gushed *Creative Computing.*

The penalty was a price tag about 150 percent higher than a Pet or a TRS-80, though, and that is one reason why the Sorceror very quickly found its metier as a small computer system for business rather than a fun machine for the home. Exidy now describes itself as "a volume manufacturer of low-cost very capable desk-top computer systems for commercial, industrial and small business applications".

The Sorceror scored with one technical idea, the plug-in ROM unit it calls the PAC. This provided instant games and a reasonable Basic. Exidy has never really pushed the idea of plug-in software much beyond the starter level, though, and its more sophisticated systems are loaded conventionally from disc into RAM.

In any case, the ROM PAC idea wasn't original. Hewlett-Packard had extra-cost plug-in ROM modules on the 9830 desk-top computer in the early '70s – the 9830 was a minicomputer (with minicomputer prices) for scientific and technical uses. Subsequently the ROM cartridge became the usual way of selling extra games for Atari-style TV toys.

Anyhow, the idea was good. The other impressive

aspect of the Sorceror was the heavily non-technical marketing exemplified by its name. The idea of a computer as a pet is one approach; the idea of the computer as a magician proved to be another.

Real software for real people

The arrival of cleverly-packaged computers was not the only critical aspect of the spread of the micro; the development of genuinely-useful software is as significant.

In a way, the introduction of word processors is much more important even than the widespread adoption of CP/M and Microsoft Basic. The word processor proved to the non-technical that computers could be of value even to them.

Michael Shrayer was a cameraman/producer/director in TV and movies when he became interested in the Altair and helped set up one of the 1975 crop of hobbyist clubs. He wrote an assembler for the Altair and started to make money selling it; then he hit a snag which has always bedevilled programmers – if you want to sell software, you have to provide some documentation so that other people can use it.

"I had a computer; I thought I ought to be able to use it to write a manual." He was correct, but in the absence of any program able to produce and print text, he had to write one himself.

The result he called The Electric Pencil, a name which captures some of the slightly naïve flavour of those times. It appeared in the middle of 1976 and it was the first such program which can be described as effective on micros. Shrayer says he was amazed by the demand for the product, especially as he subsequently lost interest in it.

A number of firms picked up the ball and ran with it. Running faster than most was Seymour Rubenstein, a New Yorker with a cv which read like a catalogue of different ways of making a living from computers. Then, in 1977, he bought an IMSAI, discovered that it was being made by one of his former bosses, and called him for a job. In two weeks he was IMSAI software products manager; in two months he was marketing manager.

In that role he bought CP/M from Gary Kildall, a kind of sponsorship which alone should guarantee him some prominence; but he's the kind of man who likes to be his own boss, and he left IMSAI to set up a software firm. For his products he bought the code for a sort package called SuperSort – and something called WordMaster.

First appearing in 1978, WordMaster developed into WordStar and today that's one of the world's best-selling programs. It is certainly the leading word processing package.

The other characteristic success story in software is VisiCalc. In 1978, Dan Bricklin was doing an MBA (a business degree) at Harvard; during a lecture on budgeting he found himself wondering if there wasn't an easier way to re-calculate the totals when one or more of the variables changed.

Bricklin's first degree was from MIT, so he was familiar with technology; he roughed-out a computer program, called it VisiCalc (for 'visible calculator') and showed it to one of his lecturers. The rebuff didn't distress Bricklin particularly and he contacted a friend who had been doing some programming work for a small software publishing company run by Dan Fylstra. Bob Frankston showed VisiCalc to Fylstra, who wasn't exactly overwhelmed – but he needed more products to sell (his biggest breadwinner was a chess game).

"VisiCalc didn't sound too great", he recalls; but the

alternatives were awful ideas like Calculedger and Electropage. So he took it anyhow, sold approching 500,000 by the time this book went to press, and changed the name of his company from Anodyne Personal Software Inc to the much more explicit VisiCorp.

As with the word processors, the significance of VisiCalc was that it gave instant computer power at a modest price to someone who wasn't a programmer, a hobbyist or an electronics engineer. That kind of universal applicability is what ensures the success of any innovation; you don't have to be an automobile mechanic to use a car, you don't have to play a synthesiser to enjoy *Heaven 17,* you don't have to be an airline pilot to fly.

Back to school
The educational trend in the development of personal computers has also been important. Many of those early hobbyists were equally enthusiastic about the social aspects of computing; while some of the club members were keen to build ever more natty machines, they were eager to spread the word and open the world's eyes.

Naturally this came to the fore in California, in the shape of public-access computing on the one hand and games-playing on the other.

There's a special pedestal reserved for **Wumpus.** Greg Yob produced the game in 1973 and it was a classic – a target/hunter/hazards game which could be played on a screenless terminal. The awful player-eating Wumpus lives in a cave system of 20 rooms connected by passages and its plan looks like a dodecahedron. It's dark, so you don't know where the wumpus is; and some of the rooms have superbats or bottomless pits in them. The messages tell you which room you're in and which rooms you could reach by tunnels.

Wumpus was good because it got away from the simple grid layouts of games like Battleships, and it presaged a whole upsurge of multiple-choice games which eventually lead to sophisticated (and memory-hungry) essays into role-playing games like Adventure.

The other important aspect of Wumpus was that Yob wrote it for the **People's Computer Company** and that bunch of idealistic post-hippies represents a main stream in the delta of the revolution.

The main man was Bob Albrecht, popularly (and self-) styled 'The Dragon'. PCC was set up as a public access facility, mostly for children, and for many years it promoted single-handed the idea of grass-roots computer literacy. It opened shop in Menlo Park, a San Francisco suburb, and filled the place with small computers, terminals and enthusiasts.

Yob also gets into the act via **PILOT**, a classroom language which originated from the Univerrsity of California Medical Centre in 1969. Pilot has never really had the attention or the acclaim it deserved as a pioneering dialogue-based language for CAI on small computers. Yob helped specify the language, ran the Pilot Information Exchange, and wrote several versions of it, including one for the Pet.

Coming soon: the next revolution
Technically it looks as if one of the imminent further developments in microcomputing will be the spread of reasonably-priced and well-supported 16-bit (and subsequently 32-bit) microcomputers. In theory, these will be easier to use and easier to program, because they will be able to run faster and manage bigger, more sophisticated programs. In practice, that kind of

promise is dependent on the availability of good systems software.

A number of 16-bit operating systems are emerging. Leading contenders include Digital Research and its extension of CP/M, **CP/M-86**; Microsoft has **MS-DOS**, the commercially-available version of the operating system it wrote for the IBM Personal Computer.

It looks, though, as if **Unix** could be the really influential one. Even if it is not used directly, variants of it are mushrooming and the principles in its design are being widely-applauded and emulated.

Unix is a general-purpose, multi-user operating system with a clever method of holding files. It is mature and proven; and, like CP/M in the mid-1970s it's in the proper place at the proper time. So there is a good chance that up-market 16-bit micros with multiple users will be adopting it as a standard operating system, just as CP/M became the standard on single-user 8-bit micros.

It became generally available for micros in 1980 from Western Electric, but it dates from 1969 and some work being done by another part of the giant AT&T group. Bell Laboratories, which runs most of the telephone system in the States, had an R&D facility with big General Electric mainframes. On them Bell was using one of the first interactive multi-user operating systems, Multics.

Though it sounds less than revolutionary now, Multics was based on the idea of individual users running individual jobs with their own individual files and several layers of protection preventing people from accessing each other's files. For 'personal' computing in a multi-user environment, this is exactly what's needed.

The problem was that the Bell Laboratories people wanted to run big Multics-based programs on their minicomputers as well – specifically, a man named Ken Thompson had a solar system simulation called Space Travel on the mainframe and he wanted the program to run on a little-used PDP-7 in the laboratory; but the PDP-7 (an early mini) had very limited software and the work proved so tedious that Thompson decided eventually to write a simple operating system for the minicomputer to facilitate the program transfer.

That proved the basis for Unix. The name is supposed to contrast with Multics and many Multics concepts are employed. During the '70s the operating system was developed and became the aficionados' preference for PDP-11 programming. At first Bell Laboratories and its parent didn't seem too interested in promoting it commercially (non-profit users could have it for a peppercorn rent, for instance). Then the new breed of 16-bit micros began to arrive in 1978 and 1979, first the Intel 8086 and then the Zilog Z-8000 and Motorola M68000. They had obvious potential as multi-user computers but they needed a multi-user operating system.

Enquiries began arriving from microcomputer software companies. Western Electric, which had taken over responsibility for Unix early, issued licences for the development of microcomputer versions to the likes of Microsoft (early leader in the micro market for Unix implementations with its Xenix product).

There are several other licensees. There are also a number of Unix lookalikes, operating systems which behave like Unix but which were developed independently – the licence fees Western Electric was originally asking were really high.

Unix was conceived by a user of computers rather than a software specialist or some kind of computer. So it is relatively easy to use, as well as being a powerful and versatile system for multiple users sharing a 16-bit microcomputer. It could become the predominant choice in that area.

The Last Word

The history is still being made, of course; the microcomputer business is changing quickly. For instance, the next edition of this book will surely have to include networking, with special reference to **Xerox** (whose Ethernet system was among the first research projects and subsequently became an able publicist for this style of computing), even though Harry Saal's **Nestar System** probably deserves the accolade of innovation. Nestar's Cluster/One was the first local networking system designed specifically for micros; working versions were delivered in 1981.

True, the original aim was to link just about any micro to any other and, in the event, Cluster/One emerged as a method of linking Apples. Perhaps quick and easy and economical interconnection will be one of the corner-stones of micros in the 1980s.

Meanwhile, the final comment goes to someone who usually has the last word. **Adam Osborne**, a spectacularly impressive self-publicist, is founder and president of Osborne & Associates Inc and Osborne Computer Corp. This expatriate Englishman was influential in the mid-1970s period; a programmer, technical writer and consultant, he decided to write and publish an 'introduction to micros' book. It sold 300,000. He wrote more books, expanded, added software packages for accounting in 1978 (they were some of the earliest ready-to-go business packages for CP/M, in fact), and generally became a well-respected man.

Most recently he has produced the goods in the form of a portable CP/M-based system; $1,800 buys a computer with twin mini-floppies and a screen plus plenty of software (including WordStar, the SuperCalc spreadsheet calculator, and a version of the game Adventure). The designer of the Osborne 1 is Lee Felsenstein who, as it happens, was also responsible for the innovatory Processor Technology Sol.

Osborne's background as a consultant and columnist included the awarding of his annual 'White Elephant' prize for notable achievement in microcomputing. VisiCalc won it in its last year but Osborne's entree into manufacturing rather prohibited him giving it next time round; unkind people suggested he was hoping someone else would nominate his computer for it.

In truth, it might have won. "I saw as early as 1980 that the leading hardware manufacturers were making significant misjudgments. I saw that we must return to the strategies that created the microcomputer industry ... The early losers, exemplified by IMSAI and Processor Technology, were superb innovators but they were lousy businessmen, which is why they failed. Current industry leaders are managed by superb businessmen but they are lousy innovators; therefore, they are vulnerable."

That's an example of his somewhat rhetorical style but it also summarises his conviction that 'I can do it better'. It's this blend of technical competence and bravura marketing which has driven the microcomputer business pell-mell from infancy to near-maturity in less than eight years.

Key Dates in Microcomputing History

When	Who	Why
1971	Intel	First micro
1972	Intel	First 8-bit micro
1975	Altair	First popular personal computer
1975	Digital Research	First common disc-based operating system
1975	MicroSoft	First standardised Basic
1976	Processor Technology	The Sol, the first 'packaged' microcomputer
1976	Michael Shrayer	Electric Pencil, the first acceptable word processor for micros
1977	Apple	Apple II, best-selling microcomputer
1977	Commodore	Pet, best-selling microcomputer
1977	Tandy	TRS-80, best-selling microcomputer
1978	MicroPro	WordMaster, prototype of the best-selling word processing package WordStar
1978	Lifeboat	Arrival of CP/M software publishing
1979	Software Arts	VisiCalc, major success story
1980	Western Electric	Unix, hot contender to be the *de facto* standard operating system for 16-bit micros
1981	Nestar	Viable local networking system designed for micros

7 A PRACTICAL GLOSSARY

There aren't too many businesses which had to invent a jargon word simply to describe their own jargon; but computing did – and you'll find 'buzzword' under 'B'.

This Glossary will help you find your way around the words in the world of the computer. As well as key terms you may encounter, it includes some historical idiosyncracies (like abacus), notes on some of the more interesting people in the game, and references to the top companies and magazines.

To give sufficient information for a definition or a description of anything to be useful, I think it's difficult to avoid being subjective. So I must stress that this is a personal Glossary.

Obviously I do not expect that anything in it is incorrect or even misleading but entries contain comments which reflect my opinions – and in some cases my prejudices. What's more, in the case of suppliers and products mentioned, I have included those which for one reason or another I regard as the more prominent. Such prominence could mean the company is big (like IBM); or it could mean that you're likely to come across it (like Pet); or I think something should be publicised (like Smalltalk).

As is usual with this kind of thing, italics mean that word is defined elsewhere in the glossary.

Abacus

Classic machine for counting – you slide beads along rods. It is still widely-used in the Far East; it's cheap and it's easy to maintain.

There was also a U.K. company called Abacus

Computers; it sold microcomputers, not abacuses (abacii?) but then it did get put right at the front of any alphabetical lists of computer suppliers. There was also a company called Aardvark Computers once; it was right on page one of the telephone directory, too, but that didn't do it much good – it failed noisily a few years ago.

Abend
Interesting alternative to S-bend? No, it's short for Abnormal End. As such it is an entirely unnecessary word among some computer people to signify that a program has ceased to operate because it hit some unrecoverable condition like a power failure.

Abort
One of the many nasty words in the computer lexicon but at least it is graphic; it means 'terminate in the event of a malfunction', perhaps automatically but usually with some human throwing the switch.

Absolute Address
The *address* of a physical memory location, which in practice is a way of describing exactly where in the memory the required location is. The alternative is some indirect form of address, which describes how to find the location rather than precisely where it is.

Absolute code
Synonymous with *object code*, though rarely used. Basically a program in object code is a sequence of instructions which can be read directly by the computer; absolute code is thus represented by a sequence of bit patterns. It is difficult for people to read, of course; it is also what a mnemonic program is translated into before the computer runs it.

In fact, there's a school of thought which gives a more specific definition, whereby absolute code is code which uses absolute (rather than some kind of **indirect**) addressing.

Absolute program
Well, I suppose you might just come across this one. It is just a program written in absolute code.

AC
Alternating current, of course, but sometimes it is also an abbreviation for *accumulator*.

ACC
This might also be encountered as an abbreviation for *accumulator*. It is also the initials of the Amateur Computer Club, a long-established group of hobbyists in Britain.

Access method
A way of getting data between *memory* and *terminals*. IBM has many access methods; most other manufacturers have only one or two. The particular access method is usually a feature of the operating system; if a program is written assuming one particular access method, it won't normally work with a different one. All this is really relevant only to big computers.

Access time
The time taken to reference a particular item in *memory* – to read from or to write to a memory location or a stored record on disc or tape. Not to be confused with *cycle time,* which means the total time taken for a program instruction to reference a memory location, read from or write into it, and then to return to the next instruction in the program.

Accounting machine

Outdated term for a somewhat outdated piece of equipment. It refers to a machine which takes information from a typewriter keyboard, punched cards or paper tape and prints-out lists, tables and totals on paper. These days, in fact, the so-called accounting machine is really a dedicated pre-programmed microcomputer doing very simple jobs at exorbitant prices – but some people still buy them.

Accounts Payable

What the Americans call 'Purchase Ledger'. You might come across the term on a software *package* which hails from the States – and if you're thinking of buying it for your business, be very wary. U.S. accounting procedures differ from ours, and a U.S. package would have to be altered substantially to suit European or U.K. businesses.

Accounts Receivable

Americanism for 'Sales Ledger'. Comments as above.

Accumulator

Also called a *register*. A dedicated storage location within the *processor* containing data on which the computer carries-out an operation. The Intel 8080 CPU chip contains one accumulator, the Motorola 6800 CPU contains two; obviously the more accumulators you have available, the more arithmetic or logical operations may be carried-out in parallel.

Accuracy

It has a very specific meaning in and around the computer business – accuracy refers to the number of *bits* (binary digits) which will define a number.

ACK
Acknowledge. It's a code in communications systems meaning 'I have received your request which will be dealt with as soon as conveniently possible'. The 'request' might be any external event, like the arrival of a message at a terminal.

ACM
Association for Computing Machinery. More or less the U.S. equivalent of the *British Computer Society*.

Acoustic coupler
British Telecom telephone lines are intended for voice transmission signals. The coupler converts pulses of sound from a telephone line into the *digital* signals a computer can understand; and conversely it converts digital signals into the *analogue* pulses which can be sent down a telephone line.

Basically a coupler is the same as a *modem* but it is not plugged directly into the telephone line; instead, it uses an ordinary telephone receiver. If you have a terminal with a coupler attached, and if you know that somewhere there is a computer with a telephone line of its own, you can dial the computer number. You then place the telephone receiver handset into a shaped recess on the coupler and then you can use the terminal in the normal way to send and receive data. It all sounds wonderful, but at the other end your computer normally needs a telephone line of its own (not cheap); and you cannot send or receive any faster than 30 characters per second (usually much slower, in fact). British Telecom isn't all that keen on couplers, either – assuming it learns you're using one – because in theory the digital transmission can affect voice communications on the line.

Acorn Computers

The Cambridge-based company which makes the *Atom* microcomputer and the *BBC Computer*. Acorn co-founder Chris Curry has a technical background which included a stint at Sinclair (he was heavily involved in the design of Sinclair calculators and the ZX-80). He says he developed the Atom when Clive Sinclair wasn't interested in the idea of a £150 computer on to which the ZX buyer could move. It looks as if he was correct; instead, Sinclair developed the £125 computer.

The Atom has a version of the Basic programming language which seems a little idiosyncratic in comparison with the widely-used *Microsoft* implementations of Basic, and that, combined with some deficiencies in Acorn marketing, has meant fewer Atom sales than might have been expected.

Nor has the Acorn *local network* system *Econet* realised its full potential as a very cheap way of linking numbers of Acorns (and BBC Computers). Here the problem was an over-extended development period; Curry has said Acorn lost a nine months' lead on everyone else by being too meticulous. In the early days there were also some complaints about the lack of technical support on Econet.

Acorn is a growing company, growing perhaps too fast in its first year or two but apparently settling-down now. Production and shipment levels are reported running normally, and several interesting developments are in the pipeline. Acorn also has a modification of the basic BBC Computer which involves the clever addition of a second processor, a collection of programming languages, and some business software packages. The result is sold by Torch Computers (a company owned jointly by Acorn and a software supplier, Climar) as the Torch Communicator; prices start at about £2,500.

Acorn is on record as saying total development costs for the Acorn were a mere £20,000, for the BBC machine £70,000. Make of that what you will.

ACR
Audio Cassette Recorder. So an *ACR interface* means that an ordinary cassette unit can be plugged into a computer.

ACT
Applied Computer Techniques. This British computer services group includes the company which has the U.K. franchise for *Sirius*.

Actual address
Same as *absolute* address.

Acronym
Abbreviations of a group of words to from one symbolic word – like Basic, Cobol and Fortran. Or for that matter NALGO and PLUTO (no, not Mickey Mouse's dog – though this provides a much-needed excuse for repeating one of the best jokes from *Soap*. A list of famous homosexuals was adduced in evidence of their contribution to the world; and it included Alexander the Great, Oscar Wilde, and Plato. "Plato??" said Jessica. "Mickey Mouse's *dog* was *gay?*")

ADA
Different sections of the U.S. government have been responsible for many of the characteristic names in computing. Ada is one of its latest tries; it hails from the U.S. Department of Defense, which decided in the early '70s that a single programming language which

could be used on any application would save it a great deal of money.

IBM tried the same thing with *PL/1* a decade earlier, of course, but finished with something which was too clumsy and too demanding of memory. Ada adopts a slightly unusual approach to overcome the inevitable problems of trying to be all things to all men; it's based on you selecting different 'components' of a program from a 'catalogue' and then combining them all to produce a custom-built program. The Ada compiler is thus reasonably big and you need a biggish computer for it but the programs it produces are small and economical.

Ada looks rather like an extended form of *Pascal*, which is one reason why many pundits extol it. The name, by the way, is derived from Augusta Ada Byron, Lady *Lovelace,* on the somewhat tenuous grounds that she, too, was a pioneering programmer – see the entry for *Babbage.*

A/D
Analogue-to-digital. See below; and *analogue.*

Adapter
Pretty obvious, really – it's a device connecting parts which would not otherwise fit together.

ADC
Analogue-to-digital converter – a device for converting *analogue* signals into digital signals – and usually the other way round as well, though sometimes for that there's a separate gismo called (would you believe) a DAC. Basically this is laboratory or process control stuff – typically with analogue signals coming in from some measuring instrument and being converted into digits for processing by a computer.

Add-on
Another obvious one – it describes something which can be attached to your computer to increase its performance or give it more functions.

Adler
More properly Triumph-Adler, and (unlikely though it sounds) a part of the West German Volkswagen group. It sells a *CP/M-based* business microcomputer called the Alphatronic at the Pet/Apple/SuperBrain level.

Address
A way of referencing a memory location containing data or a program instruction – just as your address identifies your house or flat.

Address bus
In practice, this is a physical connection between a processor, the computer memory, and other parts of the system. A dual-bus approach normally separates the memory bus from the I/O bus, which means that two kinds of operation can go on at the same time – for instance, data can be moved between the processor and memory at the same time as data is being moved between the processor and a terminal.

Physically a bus is likely to be a set of wires or a cable connection usually attached to the *backplane*. When you slot a printed circuit *board* into the backplane, the edge connectors on the board make contact with the bus – and if the circuit board holds memory, that effectively plugs some memory into the bus. Similarly, if it holds the controller for some peripheral, slotting-in the board connects that device to the bus.

Address word
One computer *word* which contains only the address

of a memory location.

Addressing

The process of accessing a specific location in memory.

ADDS

Applied Digital Data Systems, a subsidiary of the U.S. computer company NCR which is largely allowed to go its own way. ADDS started by making *VDU* terminals and that still provides its bread and butter but it also has a family of up-market microcomputers under the name Multivision. Those it sells mostly to systems suppliers who add software and re-sell them to you and me.

ADP

Automatic Data Processing. Same as *DP* and *EDP*, which might lead you to wonder why the world needs three similar abbrevations for the same concept. So do I.

Advantage

Neat *CP/M*-based microcomputer with integral screen and floppy discs from *North Star*, priced to aim at the low-end business market – from about £2,300.

Adventure

A great game for playing at the computer, written originally for large machines but now becoming available for micros. It's the classic role-playing game; you take on a character with a number of attributes and use them in searching for the treasure. Various hassles en route will include monsters, pits, wizards and dead-end tunnels.

AFIPS

American Federation of Information Processing Societies – a big deal at the egghead end of computers.

Ahl, David

With *Albrecht*, David Ahl is one of the seminal figures in the popularisation of the microcomputer. His particular contribution was prolonged advocacy of Basic, including his 1973 best-seller *101 Basic Computer Games*.

AI

Artificial intelligence.

ALGOL

A programming language much beloved by some European academics; it stands for Algorithmic Language, it is heavily technical and mathematical and it has been implemented mostly on large computers.

Albrecht, Bob

Bob Albrecht is one of the key figures in the microcomputer revolution. An ardent and articulate propagandist for genuinely 'personal' computing, he set up the pioneering People's Computer Company in California in the early 1970s. This publishes books and magazines (including the excellent *Recreational Computing*) and runs a kind of public-access computer room with the engaging name ComputerTown U.S.A. There is a U.K. version – see the Glossary entry for it.

Algorithm

An algorithm is a set of rules for performing a task or solving a mathematical problem; since one of the definitions in this book for 'program' is 'a collection of rules', there is a clear relationship between programs and algorithms. In practice, a program can usefully be considered as a series of algorithms, if thinking in terms of algorithms is what you like to do.

Someone else defines it graphically as 'a fixed procedure for accomplishing a specific result', citing as an example the algorithm hours per week x hourly rate = weekly salary. This is a simple algorithm for calculating gross pay.

Not that it's particularly important to know this, but the term 'algorithm' derives from the name of a ninth-century Arab mathematician called Al Khwaruznu.

Alpha Micro
Established, keen, California-based manufacturer of up-market, high-performance 16-bit microcomputers for business – prices from about £9,000.

Alphameric
Americanism abbreviation for *alphanumeric*. Just what the world needs, really, an abbeviation for alphanumeric.

Alphanumeric
Combining numbers and letters – and often other symbols like arithmetic signs an puncutation marks.

Alphatronic
The microcomputer from *Adler*.

Altos
Another of the eager California-based manufacturers of up-market, high-performance 16-bit microcomputer systems for business – prices from about £4,000; but it is more likely to sell you a rather more expensive

multiple-user system. Altos features the *OASIS* operating system as well as *CP/M*.

ALU

Arithmetic-Logic Unit. Not often encountered and you probably won't need to know this anyway, but it's that part of the *processor* which performs arithmetic and logical operations.

Amdahl, Gene

Gene Amdahl designed one of the seminal big-computer families of our time, the IBM 360. He then set up his own company to make IBM-compatible computers – they use ordinary IBM software but cost less than the IBM equivalent. Amdahl stepped aside early in 1980 – but Amdahl Corp is doing very well, too. His son, Carl Amdahl, was involved in a similar venture in another company called Magnuson Systems. Bright family.

Analogue

Practically all computer operations are *digital* in nature, which means they refer to distinct states which can be represented, for instance, by particular numbers – like 0s and 1s.

Analogue states change more smoothly and typically have a comparative value – like the position of the hands of a clock or a voltage level.

Charles *Baggage's* difference engine operated in a mechanical analogue mode; there are still analogue computers in use for highly-specialised scientific and military applications, but they don't appear very often even there.

Analysis

See *Systems Analysis*, but basically analysis is the

investigation of a problem and its separation into component parts for further study.

Analytical Engine

Babbage designed two precursors of the modern computer; neither really made it, but his ideas were good. This was his second attempt; it was to do arithmetic calculations, using a kind of crude programming memory in the form of a punched-card control system.

AND

AND is one of several possible *logical* operators. In binary terms, an AND will produce only a 1 where both inputs are 1; if one of the bits tested is not a 1, the result of the AND will be 0.

ANSI

American National Standards Institute. It operates somewhat like the British Standards Institution but rather more aggressively. Among its areas of responsibility lies the specification of some of the high-level programming languages, including Cobol and Fortran.

APL

One of the newer programming languages, and blessed with a small but vociferous band of adherents who trumpet its virtues over all the better-known alternatives; it is quick, efficient, and very well-suited to 'what-if' applications; but ordinary business programs are being written in APL, too. It has another distinction as one of the rare examples of modesty in the computer business – the initials stand for A Programming Language.

The language was designed originally by *Iverson* and Falkoff, then both at IBM, as a notation for communication between mathematicians. Only subsequently (the mid-1960s) did people realise that it could also be treated as a more general programming language.

Apple

The company was founded in a garage by Stephen Wozniak and Steven Jobs in 1977, and its progress since then has been meteoric. When profits increased by only 50 percent during one three-month period during 1982, the New York Stock Exchange was disappointed. Apple is second only to Tandy in the total personal computer market.

That progress is founded on the Apple II, which is a fine computer which happened to be in the right place at the right time. The Apple had a good Basic, a good deal of versatility, colour graphics, and an excellent keyboard; it is sold basically as a box containing the electronics and the keyboard, into which you can plug essentials like a display unit and extras like floppy discs.

The Apple II rapidly became a kind of Volkswagen for the early days of the micro business, selling especially well as an economical general-purpose workhorse of a computer to scientific users and the embryonic business markets. Its position has been maintained by its competitive price, a flood of good-quality software from independent sources (*VisiCalc*, which was first provided on the Apple II, has probably sold more Apples than any other single factor) and a massive investment in marketing – plenty of advertising, a great deal of promotional materials for the *dealers*, and so on.

The Apple II is starting to look a little long in the tooth, though. The Apple III was announced two years before it finally became generally available during 1982 (technical problems, said Apple) but it is not a replacement for the Apple II and it does not appear to be a major step forward for the company. Physically it is an improvement; it has disc drives in the same box as the electronics, with keyboard and the screen as separate components. There is a new *operating system*, SOS, which was apparently the source of most of the delays. Some Apple II software has been modified to run on the III but most of it cannot be transferred.

There are various explanations for the company name, but the founders' interest in fruit and a serendipitous encounter in an Apple-ish Californian town seem to be the main contenders.

Incidentally, this book (and everyone else) talks happily about the Apple II and Apple III computers. In fact, they aren't the Apple II and Apple III – they are the Apple][and Apple ///. Don't ask me why.

Applewriter
A low-cost *word processing* package for the Apple computer.

Appliance computer
Not at all a bad term to use for a computer designed to be sold, taken home in a box, plugged in, and used straight away – just as any other domestic appliance.

Applications
Applications are what a computer does (as opposed to how it does it). For instance, an *operating system* is not applications software, since it does not produce usable end results. A *Star Trek* game or a payroll run qualify as applications.

APT

Automatically Programmed Tools. A collection of proprietary programs for controlling machine tools such as lathes.

Arcade game

The kind of machines you see in amusement arcades and pubs. Typically these days such machines will be programmed microcomputers with a high-quality display and a variety of input devices like buttons and joysticks instead of a keyboard. That's why companies like Bally and Atari, which make money out of arcade games, have found it so easy to expand into home computers.

Architecture

This word is defined vaguely as the way a computer is designed. It refers normally to the design of the internal physical structure of a system, the way its components are inter-related. More accurately the term should be reserved for the *logical* design behind a computer system – and that means there is no *physical* element to the concept.

Arithmetic

Involving addition, subtraction, division or multiplication.

Arithmetical and Logical Unit

See *ALU*.

Arithmetic shift

A *bit* manipulation instruction which moves each bit in the accumulator one position to the left or right. In binary terms this has the effect of doubling or halving the value, depending on whether you shift left or shift right. That is the way binary numbers are; you will really understand this effect only if you understand binary arithmetic.

Array

An array is a set of *variables* which may be arranged within a logical relationship. It may refer to data, or to memory locations, or to components within a processor.

Arrays are used in the Basic programming language, in which case the textbooks usually define an array something like 'a whole set of values designated by a single name'. In effect, a Basic array is a series of memory locations which probably will contain different values. As a block the array is given just one name, usually an alphabetic letter; to reference individual locations within the array, you use a *subscript* – so C(2) indicates the second element in the array named C.

Array processor

A special and rare breed of computer designed for fast execution of array problems which occur in the nether reaches of mathematics.

Artificial intelligence

If you want a really formal definition, try this – the capability for a machine to modify its operation and its actions by reasoning and learning from experience.

I prefer something simpler and perhaps a little more pragmatic – in which case artificial intelligence is a research discipline which is trying to get machines (computers, usually) to do things which would require intelligence if done by people.

Of course, this begs the question of what exactly constitutes intelligence and the whole business of AI necessarily involves day excursions and mystery tours around psychology, philosophy and semantics, as well as the physical sciences. The people at the top of IBM are reported to have stopped AI research at the company in the mid-1960s because of the possibly blasphemous results; it's bad enough having to contemplate the possibility that man might know more than God, let alone building machines which could compete with Him.

Having to cope with this kind of mixture is why definers end up with that 'modifying operation and actions' stuff.

The idea that computers might think had its first serious exposure in an article in a journal called *Mind*. It was written by Alan Turing, a British mathematician, and he's regarded as one of the founding fathers of the subject. There was a conference on artificial intelligence in the States in 1956 which really got things under way.

Artificial intelligence programs have to start from a different viewpoint from most other programs. Instead of moving sensibly through a pre-ordained sequence of instructions, the AI program has to take items of fact and see how they relate to each other and to anything it already has stored in memory. It is all much less rigid and it's more or less how we work, too.

So where has the last 25 years of effort taken us? Well, the Eliza program represents an interesting stab at AI on micros. More significantly, 'thinking' computers are acting as more or less intelligent assistants. Rudimentary systems are emerging for interpreting visual signals – for 'seeing', in other words, and for taking decisions on the view. There are already 'hearing' computers. There are dozens of programs which can make guesstimates – it's called 'heuristic' reasoning, expressed more graphically by some as 'the art of good guessing'.

It's clear that things are rolling. AI-based computers will surely be common by the end of the century, particularly in the form of expert systems which combine the functions of a giant specialist library and someone who'll browse through it to provide the information you want. Or rather, it probably won't be you, because such systems will still have to be so large and so expensive that only the rich and powerful and multi-national and politically-committed will be able to get their hands on them.

The tantalising question, of course, is just how much thinking the computer can do. If it can offer a larger memory than man, if it can make the proper kind of connections between facts and the best kind of guesstimates, if it can 'think' more quickly and ape our senses; if its more or less random thinking is the same as the so-called 'original' thought of people, where does that leave us? What is it about humans which makes them so exceptional?

It might all come down to the question of 'sensibility' – artistic expression, novel and creative thought, the ability to feel emotions. I hope there's something, anyhow.

ASCII

American Standard Code for Information Interchange. This was established by *ANSI* in 1963. It is one of the standard ways of representing alphanumeric characters in *binary code,* where specific binary patterns correspond to particular alphanumerics.

ASR

Automatic Send-Receive. The simplest *terminal* is RO, which means receive-only. That terminal cannot *send* any data because it does not have the wherewithal – it is usually a printer. KSR means Keyboard

Send-Receive; the terminal can receive information and it can also send information because it has a keyboard for input.

An ASR terminal has some capability to store information, usually on paper tape, cassette, or internal memory. This store can be used to receive incoming data without that data necessarily appearing on a screen or printer. More usually, an ASR terminal sends pre-prepared information which is available on paper tape or cassette; the automatic send means that the terminal operator does not have to key-in each data item – he or she can start the paper tape reader or the cassette unit and the input is automatic.

Assembler

The most direct way of programming a computer is by means of zeros and ones; that produces the *absolute* code or *object* code which the computer can understand. People do not do too well with it, however, and it is laborious to write and understand. So a variety of shorthand forms more comprehensible to humans has been developed.

One stage removed from binary coding is assembly code; it uses mnemonics which are decoded (or 'assembled') by a special program (the assembler), into machine-readable code. For example, in the Intel 8080, the instruction 'move the contents of register L into register E' will be keyed in at a terminal as 'MOVE,L'.

After the assembly stage, though, this would be converted to an almost incomprehensible 8-bit binary instruction 01011101.

To summarise, an assembler is a programming language, assembly code is the coding for a program written in that language. Virtually every computer has an assembler of its own, a purpose-designed and very specific programming language which can't be used on any other computer. Assemblers are called *low-level languages* because of this.

Asynchronous

This term is applied normally to terminals. An asynchronous terminal cannot be connected to a *synchronous* connection. More specifically, it is a mode of working which is not dependent on the accepting device or the processor internal timing requirements. For instance, data signals transmitted over a telephone line do not have to be synchronised with a processor's internal machine cycles.

Aficionados abbreviate this term to 'async'.

Atari

Manufacturer of 'arcade' games, especially some of the better ones, which is moving into a new market with an interesting line of microcomputers. Typically the smaller models plug into your TV set and provide only games; the larger ones offer Basic and extra peripherals as well. Excellent graphics, as you might expect.

In 1981, Atari shipped about three million of its video games, which indicates the side on which its bread and butter is falling. It also sold about 100,000 of its 400 and 800 home computers and industry-watchers reckon that total would double for 1982.

'Atari', incidentally, is a Japanese word which means 'warning'. It's used in the game of Go to signify impending defeat, something like 'checkmate' in chess.

Atom

The microcomputer from the British manufacturer *Acorn Computers*. At £150, it competes with the likes of the *Commodore Vic, Sinclair Spectrum* and similar 'home' computers. Based on the *Mos Technology* 6502 processor used by *Commodore, Atari* and *Apple*, it starts with only 2KB RAM and 8K ROM inside its neat keyboard casing and excellent graphics – no colour, though. It can be extended to include colour graphics, 12K each of RAM and ROM, and a *Prestel* connection. There's a fine (if slightly non-standard) version of the *Basic* programming language and a good deal of ready-to-use software is available.

Audio cassette
Normal voice and music cassettes can be used by some micro systems for storing *digital* data. An actual 'data' cassette has much finer tolerances but a microprocessor works relatively slowly and many can read and write data on audio cassettes without being affected by the various electrical interferences to which cheap and relatively simple devices are prone.

Audio response unit
Or voice response. It speaks to you; typically something you do triggers an audible response by generating tones which sound more or less like human speech. Total vocabularies on these things are currently rather limited and they are still expensive – but one day that will change.

Audit trail
Some business computer systems cleverly produce as a by-product of their normal activities a report on which records have been accessed and what inputs made. This audit trail, produced normally on a daily basis, allows you to trace what happened when; it can be helpful in checking breaches of security but its main

use is in deciding why something disastrous happened and how much work has been lost.

Auto restart
There are many automatic functions prefixed as 'auto' in the manufacturers' sales leaflets. This one is an important facility – it means the computer can perform automatically the initialisation functions necessary to resume operation following an equipment or power failure.

Auxiliary storage
Or store, or memory. Storage which isn't the main memory – so it's a generic term for discs, tapes and so on. Not a widely-used term.

Babbage, Charles
Charles Babbage was born in 1791 and effectively invented the *digital* computer. He evolved all the basic concepts of computing, even though not all of them could be put into practice at that time – he used wood and metal but some of his ideas demanded modern electronics. He had help from Lady Lovelace. She was related to Byron and wanted to use Babbage's machines to predict the results of horse races. She also documented his results, which frankly was much more important; and it also wins her the not-unimportant accolade of being more or less the first-ever programmer.

Background
Some computers operate as a background/foreground system (or rather their *operating systems* can). This means less important tasks can be done in the background, more or less at the same time as critical things are happening in the foreground. In fact, the fore-

ground activity gets priority for the computer's attention – but every few milliseconds there's inevitably a temporary hiatus, for instance while you key something in or when a disc is being accessed. That fraction of a second is given to the background task, which will be something you have decided isn't really time-critical – like printing a report. It all happens so fast that you probably won't notice any particular delays caused by low priority, unless the two jobs in question are really big and complex.

Backing memory
Or backing store. Same as *auxiliary* store.

Backplane
The backplane is what circuit boards slot into. It is a piece of the computer chassis, which holds the boards in slots and provides connections for the circuits with other system elements – for example, it may well incorporate *buses*.

Back-up
Cover in the event of a failure – usually there will be 'back-up procedures' in a normal business computer installation, and any sensible user will have 'back-up copies' of all files.

Bally
An American *arcade games* manufacturer which is starting to move into home computers, so far with relatively little effect.

Bar code
Those little vertical black lines you see on most supermarket goods are bar codes – because they are codes comprising bars of different thicknesses. Bar codes are

designed to be read by a 'bar code reader' (would you believe). This is an *optical wand*.

BASF

The West German chemicals giant sells *plug-compatible* equipment to IBM users on the side and it also has a business microcomputer for £6,000-plus.

BASIC

The Beginner's All-purpose Symbolic Instruction Code is popular, easy to learn, easy to use, and available widely on minis and micros. Not the most elegant or space-saving of programming languages, it compensates for this by being one of the easiest to handle. Basic programs are not portable from one machine to another but re-coding for different computers is straightforward and once you have learned it for one machine, it is easy for you to convert to another.

Still, it is worth noting that no two Basics are completely alike. They vary in particular on number-handling and decimal arithmetic, the way they use strings of characters, formatting of output, and file systems.

Nor is Basic entirely the best thing since sliced bread, even in its fullest versions. Its arithmetic capabilities are restricted by the limited built-in functions, limited precision, and slowness of execution. String handling is minimal, making it difficult to manipulate lists of information; and the syntax of the language limits the complexity of the programs which can be written.

What's more, Basic has some defects in the way it encourages you to write programs. Check the entry for *structured programming* for more on this.

Even so, if a mathematical and logical no-no like me can write programs in Basic, surely anyone can.

Batch

One of the ways in which work may be done on a computer is to group together all the information the system will need to do a particular job. It is then loaded on to the computer so that it can be worked on without further intervention. That is batch processing, or working in batch mode, because it involves batching everything required to do the job. The usual contrast is with *interactive* processing, where you have to supply instructions or data while processing is taking place.

Baud

The capacity of a communications line is measured in bauds. The number of bauds tells you the rate at which information will pass down that line. You can often assume that baud is synonymous with bits per second, so that a line with a baud rate of 2,400 will carry that number of bits in a second. That is not always true, though, as it is possible to have bits travelling down a line two or more abreast. There are standard baud rates at which terminals communicate with computers.

Baudot

M Baudot is the man who devised what has become the standard code for representing information in telegraph and Telex communications, just as *ASCII* is one of the standard codes for data communications.

Baudot is a five-bit code, which means different combinations of five bits can be used to represent different characters. ASCII uses eight, which is sufficient to provide unique bit combinations for all the numbers, the upper- and lower-case letters, standard punctuation and arithmetic marks, and so on. Baudot's five bits are sufficient only for the upper-case alphabetic, numbers, and a few symbols.

BCD

Binary Coded Decimal, a way of expressing decimal numbers using bits. Each digit of a decimal number is allocated four bits for its representation. Extended BCD Interchange Code, EBCDIC, is an IBM code which allows you to represent characters, too. (This is not the only way of representing alphanumerics in binary code – compare the Glossary entry for *ASCII*.)

BBC

As an independent purveyor of television and radio programmes, the BBC shouldn't be in the hard commercial world of selling microcomputers. That's probably neither here nor there – it's doing it willy-nilly, and in any case the Corporation doesn't seem to have made much use of its massive potential for self-promotion. Anyway, in 1980 it decided to put together a major 'all about computing' TV series; someone thought it would be a good idea to design and sell a cheap computer with which the viewers could become users.

The original talks were with *Newbury Laboratories* and centred on the then-promising *NewBrain*; but the NewBrain was delayed and eventually Newbury decided it didn't really want to make micros anyhow, so it dropped the project. *Acorn Computers* apparently telephoned the BBC one December morn, having seen mention of the proposed deal in one of the personal computer magazines. "Try us", said Acorn, and the BBC signed for a development of the *Atom* microcomputer – on a Friday the thirteenth (of April, 1981, as it happens).

Bad omens. Everyone loved the specification for the BBC Computer – "easily most the advanced computer available at the price", as one relatively uncommitted observer put it – but nobody could obtain them and by the time the TV series started in February, 1982 there were only a few available to punters, pundits, magazine reviewers and other favoured individuals. The word was that the BBC had 10,000 orders, but that only 300 had been delivered.

The series doesn't rely on the BBC machine and, in fact, it doesn't even mention it much, so you don't *have* to have one to watch it. There's an associated 'teach yourself Basic' postal tuition course from the National Extension College, though, and though that is biased towards the BBC computer there are notes which indicate how the course should be amended to suit other micros. I think it's a reasonably good course, incidentally.

The delivery problems resulted from a few hiccups in design and testing (mostly on one of the special chips being supplied by Ferranti) and many, many hiccups in building the thing. In particular, everyone seemed to have under-estimated both the demand and the manufacturing capacity which would be required to service it. So the Beeb's box was very late in arriving.

Many would say, however, that the wait was worth it. The processor is the *Mos Technology* 6502 micro as used in Acorn's *Atom;* and the casing looks similar, too. It shares the Atom's clever ways with *assembler* language programming, enabling you to put assembler code very easily into Basic programs to speed the operation of your programs. The Basic is excellent and it is designed to encourage *structured programming* – a real plus. Colour, graphics and sound are all provided, there's a connection for Acorn's low-cost *local network system Econet,* and also built-in is a clever method of connecting another and more powerful microprocessor to the basic computer.

All somewhat technical, perhaps, but take my word for it, this is a very full little machine. It's even a good option after the price rise from the original £235 (which wasn't at all bad for a computer like that, with 16K of user memory and a whopping 32KB of ROM holding various pieces of *system software*). The new starting price is £299. Why? Said Acorn: "Since the original price was established we have had to meet very stringent specifications requiring a number of extra components". You might have thought that they'd have decided the price *after* meeting the 'stringent specification' and deciding exactly what components were to be used.

It's still a good buy, especially for schools. The BBC Computer qualifies for the British Government 50 percent grant if a secondary school buys it.

Benchmark

A means of measuring what a computer can do and how fast it can do it – its power, in other words. Normally the benchmark is a program or group of programs whose results are thoroughly known and which can be used to compare the rate at which different computers can run that type of work.

Bi-directional

Usually applied to printers, in which case it's more accurately described as *boustrophedon*. In that case it means successive lines are printed starting from opposite sides of the paper, thus saving the need for a *carriage return* after each line.

Binary

The binary system is a way of representing numbers to the base two – as opposed to the decimal system, to base 10, or the ancient Babylonians' system (base 16). It uses only the symbols 1 or 0, which makes it a useful system for representing numbers in a computer. It can also be used to represent characters, where specific patterns of 0s and 1s can be used for individual characters. Best known of these codes are *ASCII* and *EBCDIC.*

BIOS
The Basic Input-Output System, one of the key element of the *CP/M* operating system.

Bipolar
There are many ways of making *semiconductors* for integrated circuits, and this is one of them. It makes for fast operation but it is expensive and generates a great deal of heat. The best-known type of bi-polar logic is Schottky, named after Mr Schottky.

Bistable
Bistable as a term may be applied to various parts of a computer; it means essentially that what it refers to is capable of assuming either one of two stable states. Now you can forget this word, or you can make jokes about how it sounds like a village in *The Archers.*

Bit
The bit is the basic unit of information storage in a computer. The name comes from *binary digit* and any bit can represent a 0 or a 1. Which it represents depends on the voltage level in that physical location in the computer. A bunch of bits is a *byte.*

Bit density
This is usually the number of bits stored per inch (bpi) on tape or disc.

Bit slice
Well, you might meet this piece of esoterica. A bit-slice

is a relatively new semiconductor component which is effectively a high-speed limited-function microprocessor.

Black Box

Apart from the traditional connotation of a slightly mysterious function-filled piece of equipment, this is the family of business microcomputers from the British company *Rair.* It really is black and a box, built into which are *floppy* or *Winchester disc* drives, with an Intel microprocessor running the *CP/M* or *MP/M* operating systems inside it. Thus it needs a separate *VDU.*

Block

It is often convenient for information to be transferred between components of a computer system – e.g., terminals, disc drives – in regular-sized portions called blocks. When stored on media such as tapes or discs, a physical area of the medium may also be termed a block; it will be separated from other blocks by an inter-block gap.

Not being known for missing opportunities to create new abbreviations, the computer industry calls an inter-block gap an IBG.

Block diagram

Stylised representation of an organisation or activity in which boxes are connected by lines. It shows the principal functional relationships; a programmer might use one to develop the much greater detail of a *flowchart.*

Board

A printed circuit board, or PCB, is sometimes called a printed circuit card – though since the 'card' is a rigid plastic plate, it's really nothing like playing cards or punched cards or clock cards or credit cards, or indeed any other kind of card.

Individual electronic components can be plugged or soldered into the board to make contact with those circuits. At the other end of the circuit is the edge of the board, which is equipped with *connectors*. Those engage with further circuitry in the *backplane*. The processing functions of a computer and its main memory will be held on a small number of PCBs – perhaps only one.

Boolean

Boolean algebra describes a set of logical instructions, which centre on the ability of statements to be true or false – precisely the kind of two-state operation a computer likes. See *AND*, *OR* and *NOT*. The name comes from a Mr Boole, an Irish mathematician (true).

Bootstrap

Before you can get a computer to do anything, you need to *load* a program into it. So you need a way of loading a program before there is a program in the computer which can load programs. While it would be satisfactory if programs loaded themselves by their own bootstraps, a bootstrap is, in fact, a set of resident instructions which are initiated by a special manual switch; they then call in the program which is to be loaded. This facility is often called a bootstrap loader.

BOS

Various manufacturers have used 'BOS' for their *operating systems;* but probably the most relevant here is the Business Operating System which the

British software house *MPSL* has produced for its *MicroCobol* language and the software packages which have been written in it.

Boustrophedon

It means 'like an ox ploughing a field' or some such. It's the accurate way of describing what is popularly but mistakenly called a **'bi-directional'** printer; the printing goes first in one direction, then back again. Just like ploughing, in fact. Silly-looking word, isn't it?

Branch

In most programming languages, one statement in a program is executed after another, except when a statement causes a 'branch' or 'jump' to another part of the program. In Basic, the GOTO statement is used to switch to a particular line number; that's called an unconditional branch (or jump).

A conditional branch means that execution of the program will switch if specific conditions are met. Taking Basic again, there's the IF . . . THEN construction to provide that; see the Glossary entry on *IF* for some more information on this.

The ON . . . GOTO statement provides a kind of conditional branch; well, the program has to choose whether or not to make the branch but it has to determine exactly to where it should branch.

Breakout

One of the early and the best arcade games which was translated on to computers; you have a ball bouncing around the screen which you direct by putting a movable bar in its path so that it rebounds and knocks bricks out of a wall.

British Computer Society

Popularly known as BCS. The premier professional body – it has examinations for its membership qualifications, provides advice to Government when asked, and is very active at the local level with 'special interest groups' on various areas.

British Micro

Newish Watford-based manufacturer of microcomputers, one of the residuals from the demise of *Nascom*. It was formed by John Marshall (Nascom founder) and Manas Heghoyan (who had tried unsuccessfully to buy that company).

BSC

Binary Synchronous Communications is an IBM communications *protocol,* which defines how information is parcelled for transmission along communications lines. You probably do not need to know any more about IBM communications than this just yet.

Bubble

You do not find much bubble memory around commercially but the term occurs very frequently. It uses a form of magnetic technology for mass storage of data. It is one of several promising memory technologies which fit between external devices like discs and *semiconductor* store. All are faster and more reliable than disc storage but are cheaper than semiconductors, but none has realised its early promise – and in the case of bubble memories, two big manufacturers very publicly ceased their bubble development programmes during 1982.

Buffer

A buffer is a halfway house between one part of a

computer and another, where information can be stored temporarily. It is useful because it cushions the impact of the different speeds at which different parts of a computer system can handle data – for example, a printer terminal capable of printing 40 characters a second may accept data from a high-speed communications link at 240 characters per second. So the data has to go somewhere while it is waiting to be printed, and a buffer is one place where it might go. Thus buffered operation allows different parts of the system to work at optimum speed.

Bug

Bugs cause things to go wrong. In particular, bugs are what should not happen when you run a program but invariably do. You have to run it enough times to identify and stamp on all of them, a process known as debugging. I hope I don't have to tell you what a person who engages in debugging is called.

Bureau

A computer bureau is a company which runs other people's work on its computer. It makes money by maximising the use of its system; you might benefit because you know in advance more or less what the work will cost and you don't have the hassles of owning and running the computer.

Burn

Or more likely 'burned-in'. There's a phase in testing electronic components called burn-in, where heat treatment weeds out the duff items. Or programs are 'burned' into *PROM* chips by a special device called a PROM burner – this is the way a PROM is programmed.

Burroughs

One of the big boys in computers, with an upwards-compatible line extending from less than £10,000 to more than £1 million. Burroughs also has its own word processor manufacturer in its fold.

Bus

Information travels from one part of a computer system to another by bus – sometimes called a 'trunk' on larger computers. A bus is a set of connections which enable the hardware components of a system to link or interface.

Buzzwords

The term buzzword is a piece of jargon used to describe the jargon the computer industry generates with such whole-hearted enthusiasm, and which this Glossary is possibly an aid to penetrating.

Byte

If a *bit* is the smallest unit of information stored in a computer, a byte is the smallest unit with any real meaning. It is a collection of bits, normally eight, which together represent a number or a character.

Sharp-eyed readers will note that *ASCII* is an eight-bit code; so one byte usually corresponds to one character, and the terms 'character' and 'byte' frequently are used interchangeably. For example, a *floppy disc* holding 71KB (=71,000 bytes) will store 71,000 characters. Well, it won't really do that, since the usable capacity is always less than the manufacturer says it is – that's because of internal formatting considerations.

There is also an excellent U.S. microcomputing magazine called *Byte*. It's huge. You can buy it in the U.K. now.

C

A programming *language* which was developed originally for the *Unix* operating system. Like any operating system, Unix is a group of programs. The original programming for it was done in *assembler* language; but assemblers are specific to a particular computer family, so in its early days Unix could run only on one manufacturer's machines. Its developers decided to produce a 'universal' version of Unix which would work on several computers; the obvious option would be to use one of the so-called *'high level'* languages but that way the finished program, the operating system, would not be able to operate fast enough.

The answer was to devise an entirely new programming language which has some of the universality of languages like Basic, while echoing the operational efficiency of an assembler. The result was a language modestly called C (there was an earlier version called B, and probably one called A, too). Unix was re-written in C and now runs on several computers; and C is proving attractive for other applications. Since its arrival in 1972 or thereabouts, the development of C and Unix have proceeded in parallel.

Cache

Or cache memory. It's a special kind of fast-access memory used with special *operating system* commands. Accessing information on disc is much slower than accessing information in main memory, just because the cheaper technology used for disc storage storage means you have to accept a lower performance. Some programs need to access disc very quickly – in fact, some programs on some computers reside partly on disc so that relevant sections are pulled into main memory only when they are needed.

The cache memory provides a half-way house – the

operating system tries to predict which portions of the program or data stored on disc will be required next, and it loads them into the cache buffer. Generally it will be correct at least 70 percent of the time, and some cache memory systems have a 'hit rate' (that's what it's called) better than 90 percent.

Obviously if the proper information is in cache disc, the computer doesn't have the bother and the time delay of fetching it from the disc. Cache memory is very quick to access. So everything is speeded.

As a rule it's only large computers which need this level of performance acceleration, and providing a cache memory facility is both complicated and relatively expensive.

CAD
Computer-Aided Design. Generally requires special software to generate graphics shapes and special terminals to display or print them. Some fancy graphics packages are becoming available for microcomputers which have graphics capabilities like this already built-in – the Pet and Apple are notable examples.

CAI
Computer-Aided (or Assisted) Instruction – using computers to teach something, which isn't necessarily using computing to teach computing.

Calculating engine
Early name for early computer-type machines, including some of the designs of Mr *Babbage*.

Canon
Like most of the Japanese consumer electronics companies, Canon has a line of microcomputers, mostly business machines which look like fancy desk-top

calculators. They tend to utilise the relatively unusual *Motorola* 6809 procesor.

Card

There are a number of different cards in and around computers. For a start, there are the uncardlike *circuit* cards – see definitions for *board* and *PCB*.

Punched cards are one of the oldest forms of input medium (Jacquard-loom weavers in the 17th century used a kind of wooden version with holes bored in short planks) and they are now definitely out-moded. They may be long and slim and capable of holding representation of 80 characters, or short and fat and capable of holding up to 96 characters.

Characters are represented by combinations of holes punched in the cards. If your computer uses an eight-level character code, and if you have an 80-column card, the card will be organised as an 80 x 8 matrix – 80 columns vertically, eight rows horizontally. The character code determines which of the eight possible punch positions denotes which particular character. Unlike most other input media, you can rest coffee cups on cards, write addresses on them, and lose or damage single records easily.

Incidentally, 80-column cards were so widespread in the early 1960s that this became a *de facto* standard for record lengths, which is why so many terminals and other things assume that you require lines 80 characters long. The irritating point about cards is that a record is always at least one card long – even if you want only one or two characters on it, you still have to use a whole card. You can forget about this kind of card, anyway.

There are two other types of card but they're vanishing, too. One is the ledger card, which often has a magnetic stripe down an ordinary ledger card –

machine-readable information is encoded magnetically on the stripe as well as the human-readable information printed on the card.

The other special occurrence is a small magnetic card used in word processing; again an IBM invention, these hold about five to 18,000 characters – about one reasonable-length letter. They, too, have been largely superseded.

Card frame

Or card cage. A skeletal chassis with slots for printed circuit *boards* (which are also called cards).

Cardbox

One of the early offerings from *Caxton*, this is a clever little program which provides you with a kind of electronic card-index filing system (if you have a computer with *CP/M* on it).

Carriage return

The 'carriage' in question was originally that portion of a printer mechanism which holds the print element, the part which causes a character to appear on the paper. So a 'carriage return' takes the print element to the start of a new line.

You can cause this to happen by including a 'carriage return' command in a program, or you can do it yourself on a keyboard by pressing the key labelled 'return' or 'carriage return' (or sometimes 'enter').

You get the key on the keyboard of a display terminal, too, and, of course, a program which outputs to a VDU can include a carriage return command. Obviously you wont't be moving any print element, since your screen won't have one. Instead the command moves the *cursor* and takes you to the start of the next line.

Cartridge

There are three kinds of cartridge you might encounter. One is the tape cartridge, patented and apparently made only by 3M – these are usually called 'data cartridges'. They are rather like a cassette, but are more robust and more expensive.

Disc cartridges generally hold from 2,5 to 12 megabytes. As removable storage media go, they are the next stage from *floppy discs* and cost considerably more.

Now there are also ROM cartridges – see *ROM* and *firmware*. These are plug-in modules which provide whole programs (like TI's maths tutor or Atari's games) or helpful programming aids or other operating system tools (like the *Programmers' Toolkit* for the Pet).

Cassette

Philips has set the standard for both audio and data cassettes. Micros will work satisfactorily on audio cassettes – although if you need to keep data very clean and tidy you will probably have to pay more and buy a special high-quality version called a 'data cassette'. Typically cassettes store about 300KB.

Cathode Ray Tube

See CRT.

Caxton

A British software publishing venture. Caxton seeks programs (either commissioning them or inviting submissions); it checks them, fills the gaps, and generally spruces them up; it writes some worthwhile instruction manuals; and it sells the resulting package through dealers. So far, its products have been excellent.

C Basic

There are different versions of the *Basic* programming language and several of them have been designed for the *CP/M* operating system; two predominate, C Basic and M Basic.

C Basic (usually in a form called C Basic 2) is number two in the popularity stakes. It is from the progenitor of CP/M, *Digital Research.* It's cheaper to buy than the other contender, *M Basic;* and since a large number of ready-to-use programs require CBasic there are good reasons for having it on your CP/M system. CBasic is a compiled variant of Basic rather than an *interpreter.* So you must first write a program and then run it against a special program called a *compiler* before you can use your program. If any faults are revealed you have to amend the original and go through the process again.

It's all more time-consuming than using an interpreter like MBasic, which enables you to check and correct the program as you go, but, as with any compiled program, the resulting code will, in theory, run faster than an equivalent program written in MBasic; what's more, compiled code doesn't need as much memory and so programs can be larger. In practice, that comment about faster execution of the code hasn't always been borne out in *benchmark* tests.

CCD

Charge-coupled device. A memory technology in solid-state electronics, akin to *bubble memories* in that it will fit between *discs* and *semiconductor* memories in terms of both price and performance. CCDs are also a little like bubble memories in that neither has realised its early promise. CCDs first appeared in the early 1970s and they are still both expensive and rare.

CCITT

Comité Consultatif Internationale de Telegraphie et Telephonie. An international committee which effectively sets international communications usage standards, though it usually calls them 'recommendations'. In practice, it is these CCITT recommendations which have determined exactly how terminals connect to and communicate with computers – among other things.

You might see a mention of a CCITT recommendation called V24. This covers the specification for an *interface* and is effectively the same as *RS232*.

CDC

Control Data Corp. Another of the big names in big computers, though unlike most of its fellows CDC concentrates on large computers. It also runs a worldwide bureau division, operates the training organisation Control Data Institute on a similar scale, and is a top manufacturer of OEM peripherals.

CEEFAX

The BBC *teletext* service.

Central processor

See *CPU*.

Centronics

A major manufacturer of printers. It makes some low-end models of interest to the microcomputer user; and because Centronics printers are now so widespread, the *interface* Centronics uses has become something of a *de facto* standard for *parallel* interfaces.

Chain printer

A type of *line printer* – and you don't need to know

..h more than that, except that as with most line
..ters it has a solid character font. So it prints solid
..aracters rather than the dots of a *dot matrix*
..inter.

Chaining

A clever programming technique. You split a job into
separate *programs* and they run in sequence, so that
each segment uses the output of the previous one.
Chaining is used to run very large programs which
would otherwise exceed the storage capacity available.
Not all computers (or rather, not all *operating systems*)
allow this.

Channel

Or communications channel, or I/O channel; often
synonymous with terms like data path, link, circuit and
line. A channel is just an electronic path along which
signals can be carried, typically between a *peripheral*
and the *CPU*. Not exactly a very important concept to
have to grasp, except that the capacity of a channel –
that is, the speed at which information can be transmitted along it – may be a significant constraint on the
system. There again, it may not.

The word 'channel' is also a very specific term used
by IBM – which probably originated its use in the
computer context, as it happens. In IBM parlance it
means a full-blown input-output control unit, not just
the data path – the IBM I/O channel would usually run
one or more control units, for instance for disc or VDU
subsystems.

Character

A letter or numeric digit. Included here for the sake of
completeness, although you probably knew what a
character was anyway. Didn't you?

Character generator

This circuitry, which usually is a separate *ROM* within the computer, decodes data and translates it in dots of light on a display screen.

Character set

A collection of letters, numerics, and symbols such as punctuation marks.

Chassis

The computer chassis is the box which contains the processor and main memory. It incorporates various elements, like the *backplane,* so it is an integral part of the computer system rather than a receptacle.

Checksum

A clever programming technique used to make sure that the contents of a word read from memory or backing store are the same as those originally put there. Forget this term.

Chip

A chip is a piece of silicon, normally about a quarter of an inch square and thick, holding the components which make up all or part of a microcomputer – one micro may be split across several chips. It is effectively the medium which holds the message. Anyone who uses the phrases 'chips with everything' or 'when the chips are down' or 'chips that pass in the night' automatically gets a special prize which consists of an on-line boxing glove loaded with a horseshoe for ritual self-effacement.

Circuit

Only a little more specific than *channel.* A circuit is the complete electrical path between two points.

Clear
To erase the contents of a storage location.

Clock
The rate at which a computer performs operations is controlled internally by a clock. That is an electronic circuit or group of electronic components which generate a set of control signals. Each set of control signals will initiate an action on the part of the central processing unit (CPU).

CMI
Computer-Managed Instruction. More or less the same as *CAI.*

CMOS
One of three types of MOS (metal-oxide silicon) semiconductor technology, the other two being *PMOS* and *NMOS.* It beats the other two for low power consumption, which makes it satisfactory for some electronic applications – especially those requiring portability and/or high reliability; but NMOS is able to operate faster and gets the vote over others.

Co-axial cable
Like TV aerial cable – it has one wire within and insulated from another. It's widely-used to connect peripheral devices like disc drives or terminals to computers, or computers to other computers; *fibre optics* is an up-and-coming alternative.

COBOL
The COmmon Business Orientated Language is one of the best-known (and best-standardised) high-level programming languages. It was designed for commercial applications, so its mathematical abilities are limited –

some of us can sympathise with this. Because it has been designed to make program-writing easy in a commercial context, it can occupy a good deal of room in the computer; this makes it more popular on larger systems rather than micros. Having said that, there are a number of microcomputer versions of Cobol – and as it happens the version which is probably the best of them is British (shout "Hurrah!" and see the entry for *Micro Focus*).

Cobol dates from the late 1950s, with the U.S. Navy for some reason doing much of the pioneering work. Its major boost followed a few years later when the U.S. government decreed that any computer bought for Federal use must offer the language – well, it's one way of ensuring success.

CODASYL

The U.S. organisation responsible for the design of Cobol. It also has a detailed specification for a database manager, a particularly complex piece of *system software*. Codasyl consists of representatives from government bodies and suppliers of computer systems and services, and promotes standardisation. Its outpourings are detailed and esoteric, which means that Cobol and Codasyl-compatible database systems are complex and verbose.

It stands for Committee on Data Systems Languages.

Code

This can be a noun or a verb. As a noun, a code in computer terms means the same as in other contexts; it is a means of representing one thing by something else. Sometimes a code is used for secrecy; in a computer a code is used for efficiency. Some programmers are confused by this.

The most common codes in computing, used to represent numbers and letters, are *ASCII* and *EBC-DIC*.

The term is more often used to refer to program statements, which if you look at it literally, constitute a representation of one thing (your ideas about what you want the computer to do) in terms of another (a bunch of cryptic acronyms and numbers). Program code is simply the statements in a program.

As a verb, to 'code a program' is to write a program in terms of programming language instructions.

Coding form

Or coding sheet. A pre-printed form for programmers to use. Some programming languages are rigid about laying-down the format you have to follow in programs, so coding forms can be very useful. Other languages are much freer in format.

Column

Printers are sometimes described in terms of 'columns' – for example, 'an 80-column printer'. This is just a historical irrelevance; it means 80 characters per line but if you fill several lines with print you will indeed have vertical columns of characters.

COM

Nobody seems able to agree whether this stands for Computer-Output Microfilm or Computer Output on Microfilm or Computer Output Microfilmer. Anyway, you get the idea – instead of producing printed paper the computer produces microfilm or microfiche. The advantages in terms of space-saving and cheaper distribution of the end-result are obvious. It's expensive to do; you need a special film developer, for a start, and all end-user recipients have to have microfilm viewers.

COM is satisfactory for some high-volume use
though.

COMAL

A programming *language* for computer-assisted learning. It hails from Denmark and has achieved a good
deal of success, particularly in Europe. In its homeland
it is reported to be the language which more than 95
percent of schools use for teaching the basics of
programming. Its enthusiasts say it has all the simplicity of *Basic* and inculcates all the good habits of *Pascal*
(including a bias towards *structured programming*).

Comal was implemented first on a Danish
microcomputer from a company called Regnecen-
tralen but it also runs on *Commodore* computers and
has been taken-up by Commodore – which means it
will be spruced-up, extended with more facilities and
functions, and generally promoted on a wide scale.

Comart

An established and substantial British microcomputer
distributor (notably for the fine computers made by
North Star) and now a manufacturer in its own right,
too – see the entry for the *Communicator.*

Comb printer

A type of *line printer,* though unlike most of the other
examples of that genre it uses *dot matrix* printing
rather than solid, fully-formed characters.

Command

An instruction to the computer, usually given by you
from a keyboard, which initiates or terminates something. Classic examples are commands to RUN a
program or PRINT some results.

Comment

Usually refers to part of a program put there by the programmer to indicate to other programmers what is going on in that particular piece of code. So it identifies or explains one or more steps in a routine or program but it has no effect on the execution of the program.

Commodore

Once a repairer of electric typewriters; subsequent business ventures included metal office furniture.

Recent product developments have added versions of the basic Pet which dropped that name and added features to appeal to business users. Commodore is unusual among the microcomputer makers in owning its semiconductor company and microprocessor supplier – *Mos Technology,* which makes the 6502 microprocessor, is its subsidiary.

Commodore's main strength is definitely selling computers outside the States – in fact, the company has probably out-sold *Tandy* and *Apple* put together in the non-U.S. markets, while those two have each sold something around twice as many computers as Commodore in the States.

In the mid-1970s Commodore went through a difficult period when the bottom fell out of the market for calculators and digital watches. By accident or design, it acquired the microprocessor manufacturer *Mos Technology,* a move which introduced a man named Chuck *Peddle* to the fold. He designed the *Pet* and Commodore made a mint.

Common carrier

You might come across this term – it's what Americans call those companies authorised to provide communications services to the general public. So British Telecom would be one; so would a private venture supplying such services.

Communications

This one is a real jungle of techniques and terminology. As a blanket term, it can refer to computer systems where one part is linked to another to allow transmission of information over a communications line, which is normally an ordinary telephone line. Things become very complicated when there are numbers of system components sending data to each other, and a whole sub-culture has developed in the computer industry which concerns itself with exactly how you organise those components and the information flowing between them.

So let us remain with the simple end; communications are what happens when two system components communicate, and they communicate by sending data to each other.

Communicator

As a trade name, it's the microcomputer made by the British *Comart* group. It uses *CP/M* and the *S-100* bus; it is sold as a box with floppy disc drives, so you add a VDU; prices from about £2,600; used mostly in business.

Compatible

Means one computer can handle something designed for another – typically that is programs and data but it may be *peripherals*.

Compiler

The language in which instructions for the computer are written – in the form of a *program*, normally – is not one which the computer can use directly. It needs to be changed into a form which the computer can recognise. One way of doing this is to use a compiler.

A compiler is a specialised program which translates the *source* program into code which the computer can execute. It does so much faster than the other method of translating the instructions, which involves using an *interpreter*. The interpreter has the great virtue, however, of enabling the user to change portions of a program and test the change immediately, which makes it very useful for program development.

You can also interrupt an interpreter in full spate to obtain some intermediate results, say, and then let it continue. A compiler would not like you to do that.

What goes into a compiler is *source code;* what comes out is *object code.*

Compuserve

A public-access information service in the States (and spreading to Europe, too). It works something like Prestel in the U.K., except that you need a small computer and a telephone rather than a specially-adapted TV set. Compuserve charges a subscription and you also pay a 'connect time' charge while you're using the information it contains, and there's a great deal of it available.

Compustar

An extension of the *SuperBrain* from *Intertec* which enables up to eight users to share one disc unit. It's basically a multi-user business microcomputer system.

Compute!

A good U.S. personal computing magazine dedicated

to microcomputers which utilise the *Mos Technology* 6502 micro, including the *Pet, Vic, Apple, Atari* and others.

Computer

Ah-ha, the $64,000 definition. To me a computer is really a fast rule-following idiot with the ability to remember things. It operates at electronic speeds, it can recall and then follow the rules you give it in the form of programs, and it does so with pathetic single-mindedness.

Alternatively try this one for size – a computer is a clever collection of components which enables you to put in information, store it, modify it, and get it out again. That is a very arbitrary definition and one which would fit a programmable calculator, too. A programmable calculator can be distinguished from a computer by its name – the distinction is a marketing one.

Computer and Video Games

One of the few British magazines the title of which describes its contents with reasonable accuracy. It's part of the EMAP publishing empire; see chapter 8 for more examples.

Computer Retailers' Association

Trade association of U.K. microcomputer vendors which covers most of the big names (but by no means all of the possibilities). It was noted in its early days for stormy meetings but now it is solidly established.

ComputerTown

A more or less informal network of 'computer literacy centres', the U.K. version of which is called ComputerTown U.K.! (and it must have the exclamation mark). CTUK! is promoted and publicised particularly on a regular page in *Personal Computer World* magazine.

What's a computer literacy centre, daddy? Well, there aren't many hard and fast rules; to quote *PCW* on its function, though, "members of the public are given free access to microcomputers, courtesy of those willing to volunteer their time and equipment". Many of them are associated with or exensions of or run by local computer clubs; and venues for a ComputerTown might be anywhere – a library, a school, church hall, a firm's premises after hours, and so on.

The idea is good and, thankfully the activity is entirely non-commercial (*PCW* isn't involved, either). If you want to locate your nearest one, or if you want some guidelines on setting-up your own, write to CTUK! at 7 Collins Drive, Eastcote, Middlesex HA4 9EL – and don't forget to enclose a stamped addressed envelope.

Computing Services Association
A trade association of the principal computer services companies in the U.K. It includes bureaux, consultancies, recruitment companies, and software houses.

Computing Today International
One of the longer-established personal computing magagines in Britain, it has a background in electronics publishing which is reflected in its slightly technical bias.

Comshare
This U.S.-based but internationally-active computer services company recently announced a *spreadsheet* calculator package called *Plannercalc* at the extraordinarily low price of £39. It is Comshare's first dabble

with the microcomputer business. It has an excellent reputation for its other financial planning software but they are all big-computer packages.

Concentrator

A device, usually based on a mini or microcomputer, which takes as input the data being transmitted down a number of local telephone lines and sends it on via a single long-distance telephone line. Time-sharing *bureaux* with numerous geographically-dispersed customers use them a good deal; the customer pays only for the call to the concentrator, even if the eventual destination of the data is miles away. So the concentrator enables you to make more efficient and less costly use of the lines.

Configuration

Loosely-used term to mean the collection of things which make up a computer system and the way they are arranged. Usually this means the hardware elements but software could be included. So could any options – 'configuring a system' normally means specifying and supplying particular options.

Connect time

The amount of time a terminal is in communication with a computer. Usually used only in reference to *on-line* access to a *bureau*.

Console

What you do to mournful micros. Also the control point of a computer system from the human operator's point of view. It is probably a keyboard and printer or VDU, for inputting messages to the system and getting back a response.

Sometimes the term is used for the front panel of a

mini or a micro, the switches and/or pushbuttons which initiate system operations. Some minis have a programmer's panel or programmer's console, which include switches to set the contents of particular memory locations.

Constant
As opposed to a *variable,* it's a numeric quantity or some alphanumeric data which doesn't change with time – or during the running of a program. Your company name used in report headings could probably be treated as a constant, for example.

Consultants
Defined classically as someone who borrows your watch to tell you the time – and then charges you for the service. Anyone can set up as a consultant, and as a result the impressive-sounding term covers a whole mass of different types of service and different levels of ability. At one end are the genuine independent consultants who make money only by selling advice; much more common are 'consultants' whose advice proves to be that you should use them to write programs on a computer they happen to be able to supply. Several microcomputer dealers who sell whole computer systems also like to describe themselves as 'consultants'. Hmm.

Real consultants are expensive. If you intend to use one (and in general I'd recommend that you do if you are to spend more than £10,000) for Heaven's sake ask for and check three or four references. Anyone can set themselves up as a consultant if they can convince you that they know more than you do.

Content-addressing
A method of referencing information in the main by

looking for the information rather than looking at the computer memory address where it is supposed to be. Conventionally, you have to ask the computer to tell you what is in a particular address. You need the very special, very expensive, and very unproven 'content-addressable memories' to do it. The idea sounds fine, in principle.

Continuous stationery
The type of stationery for computer printers which consists of a long strip of paper with holes down the sides (to engage in the sprockets of a *tractor feed)* and perforated horizontally at regular intervals so that it can be folded concertina-style.

Control character
A special one-character code which stops, starts or changes some process.

Controller
The device (usually on one or more *PCBs)* which runs a peripheral such as a VDU, printer or disc drive.

Conversational
This describes a mode of operation in which the computer can react after each input from the user – just as in a two-way conversation between people, in fact.

CORAL
CORAL, usually CORAL 66, is a language developed for real-time applications by the Royal Radar Establishment at Malvern. It is a trifle esoteric for the average user. Still, the hills there are pleasant and you can drink the water.

Core

Or core memory, or core store. There used to be plenty of it about, which is why old-style computer people often use 'core' as a synonym for *'memory'*.

Memory used to consist of little iron rings called ferrite core which could be magnetised or not to record a 0 or a 1; and on some systems it still does; but core takes up plenty of room.

It has the great virtue of not losing the information it held if you turned-off the power; the modern alternative, semiconductor memory, is volatile, which means its contents are lost when you switch-off. There are ways, though, of overcoming that disadvantage.

CPS

Characters per second.

CP

Abbreviation for card punch.

CP/M

An *operating system* which has been adopted in one form or another on numerous microcomputers – often with name-changes to disguise the origins. It was developed originally by Digital Research Inc in 1976 and is now a mature and widely-available system. The point about this is that it is the operating system which broadly determines whether a particular software *package* will run on your computer – and if you have CP/M, there are dozens of off-the-shelf packages available to you.

CPU

The central processing unit of the computer used to be easy to define, since it was the black box into which everything else on a computer system was hooked. It was big, and performed all the calculation and control functions in the system. A popular analogy was with the human brain and that was about as useful as most analogies.

It is more difficult today to identify the CPU as a unit in its own right. It is still the part of the computer system which carries-out the arithmetic and logical processes to which data is subjected, and it exercises final control over the physical components of the computer system.

CR
Abbreviation for (punched) card reader.

CRA
Computer Retailers' Association.

Cray
Seymour Cray is one of the world's top men in designing really big computers. Having done the biggest Control Data could build, he left to set up his own company to make even bigger and faster machines. He modestly calls it Cray Research and it did produce the world's mightiest machine, although *Control Data Corp* recently built a bigger and better computer. One is used for Britain's weather forecasting, which is a subject which either needs the biggest-ever computer or a cup-full of tea-leaves; the Meteorological Office reckons its Control Data Cyber 205 is "about seven times faster than any other existing machine". The Cyber 205 hits about 400 million arithmetical operations per second; the Cray 1 struggles to do more than 80 million or so per second. Still, as a measure of comparison you might well have one of the ageing IBM 370/168s which were so popular in the early and

mid-1970s; the Cray 1 has computing power equivalent to about 15 370/168s.

So what do you get for your money (about $15 million)? The basic Cray 1 consists of the CPU, power supply, cooling equipment (freon), one or more minicomputers which act as front-end consoles for maintenance and job entry, and two or more disc units.

The CPU cabinet is round, 4.5ft., in diameter by 6.5ft. high. It consists of 24 'chassis' organised as upright wedges radiating from the central pillar and standing on a 9ft. diameter base (which is upholstered in tasteful vinyl). It weighs 25 tons and it occupies 70 sq.ft. of floor-space.

Inside, there are 1,662 plug-in modules of 113 types – enough circuitry to equate to 2.5 million transistors – and it's all *hard-wired,* so there's a vast amount of spaghetti-like wiring there. The memory holds up to four million 64-bit words in *bipolar* chips, equivalent to 32 million bytes.

Funnily enough, there isn't much available in the way of software; you get no more than a fairly simple *operating system* plus an *assembler* and *Fortran* for programming.

Cray's next machine, the Cray 2, looks like a 26in. high oil drum because it's round (38in. diameter). It will have four processors instead of one and will run between six and 12 times faster than the Cray 1.

Won't it get warm in the average office or living room? Well, yes it will, but Seymour Cray is nothing if not thoughtful; the Cray 2 will be complete with a tank of inert cooling fluid, the same stuff used for transfusions. You place the drum into the fluid and leave it there and, presto, no over-heating problems.

The Cray 2 should cost between $10 and $20 million and might well be ready in 1985.

Meanwhile, if you want to do some old-style *number-crunching*, the Cray 1 is for you. That means medium- to long-range weather forecasting, encapsulating nuclear fission, creating 3D images of the human heart, and suchlike. Other good applications of which we've heard are geophysical research, seismic analysis and aircraft design.

Another use is in finding new prime numbers. A Cray employee, David Slowinski, and a computer scientist in the States, Harry Nelson, jointly used a Cray to find a prime number 13,395 digits long. That easily beats the previous record holder (a prime which is only 6,987 digits long).

Incidentally, if you want a standard of comparison, a billion billion is a large number but it's only 19 digits long. A number of 13,395 digits is estimated to be bigger than the total number of atoms in the universe.

Creative Computing
Excellent U.S. personal computing magazine.

Cromemco
One of the leading U.S. independents in the market for disc-based microcomputers and one of the first to espouse the *S-100* standard. Most of its 40,000 or so users are in scientific and engineering applications, with a sprinkling in the business world as well.

Funny name, isn't it? It seems the two founders lived in something called Crothers Memorial Hall when they were students in Stanford, and the place was sometimes abbreviated to Cro Mem.

Cromix
Cromemco version of the *Unix* operating system.

Cross-assembler

A cross-assembler (or cross-compiler) is used on one computer to produce *object-code* programs which will run on another. Generally this means you use the facilities of a big, fast and fancy computer to write programs for a skinny, skimpy micro; so you don't have to buy for the micro all those things needed for program development, like special software and expensive extra hardware.

CRT

A cathode ray tube, or CRT, is used to provide the visual display in most types of visual display unit – though it's not the only option, it is the best available at a reasonable price. It is the same kind of cathode ray tube as in a television screen, which is why a TV set can sometimes be utilised as the display monitor of a terminal. The term is sometimes used sloppily as a synonym for *VDU*.

Current loop

There are two widely-adopted electrical *interfaces* for connecting terminals to computers; this is one, the 20mA current loop method. See *serial*.

Cursor

Someone who gives a cry of rage at finding the gerbils have made a nest out of their *Star Trek* source listings. Also a means of indicating that position on a VDU screen where the next character will appear, either by typing-in the character or the computer sending it to the screen. The cursor might be a square of light, a blinking underline, or an illuminated hollow square.

Cursor was also the name of the first magazine to be published as a cassette (rather than as paper) for microcomputers; each 'article' was a program. Some of the programs just displayed information like news and views; others would be games and routines you could use in your own programs. A neat idea.

CUTS
Computers Users Tape System – one of the standard cassette tape *interfaces*. At up to 120cps it is much faster than the *Kansas City* interface from which it derives.

Cycle time
The time taken to access and read from a location in memory – not to be confused with *access time*. Cycle time is a good indication of the performance of a mini or micro system; there tend to be too many other considerations for it to be as useful a measure on a *mainframe*.

Cycle time is a function of memory, the processor and their connections, rather than of the processor alone.

DAI
Data Applications International, a company which has a £600-plus microcomputer, the specification of which includes excellent colour graphics.

Daisywheel
There's no point in spending money on word processing if you can't print something neat and readable at the end of it. The best-quality print is from IBM-type 'golf-ball' typewriters, but they were too slow to be adopted for most word processors. *Matrix printers* weren't good enough; *line printers* were too expensive.

So a number of types of letter-quality printers have been developed to fill the gap and the early honours have been taken by the daisywheel or *petal* printers. These use a removable print element in the shape of a disc, with characters on the end of stalks radiating from a central hub – so they look a little like a flower.

These printers represent a good compromise between cost, speed, and print quality. They can be attached to almost any computer, too.

Data

This is what it's all about; everyone knows data is what the computer 'does' or 'uses' or 'has'. Data is information which is processed, stored or produced by a computer. There are two wrinkles, though. In fact 'data' is a plural noun – one piece of data is a 'datum'; but you don't find many people following the strict grammatical rule. The language moves on and so data is generally singular. In any case, it is more helpful to think of data as a composite rather than a collection of individual items.

The other interesting point is the distinction between data and *information*. Data is the abstract and uncoloured subject on which the blind, rule-following computer performs its programmed operations; information is data which has been given some meaning, the kind of data humans can use.

Databank

Ill-defined word, usually encountered in popular parlance to mean a *database* containing information about people.

Database

Sometimes two words but not in our style. It is a large file of data organised so that all users draw on a common pool of consistent up-to-date informtion.

A database usually needs large backing memories and a filing system developed with all potential users and applications in mind. The emphasis is on the shared pool. In a non-database environment – which is the norm, of course – each user generally has to set up separate files for each application. The database approach means that if the programmer knows the information is already there, it is no trouble at all to get at it – in theory.

Database management system

A DBMS is a software system for designing, setting-up and subsequently managing a database. In practice, it smoothes the interface between a programmer and the data, providing the kind of facilities to allow the user to specify which data a program requires. Database managers are complicated and are usually expensive pieces of software; even so, some have been developed for micros.

Data capture

Getting the information at the instant a transaction occurs – for instance, a till recording information as customers check out in a supermarket point-of-sale system.

Data collection

Obvious, really: bringing data to a central point.

Data dictionary

Or data directory. A complex but usually useful software system which describes the forms and characteristics of data within the computer and also defines the relationship between data. A data dictionary usually applies to big systems, especially those using databases, where the exact nature of data items can be difficult to find. The programmer has to know the agreed name for a field in a particular record, its size and the type of data it can contain, and with which other data and programs it can inter-relate.

The data dictionary ought to be a necessary precursor to installing a database system, since it avoids duplication of the names used by programmers for files, records, and data items. The data dictionary thus guarantees uniformity, and so is very wonderful.

In fact, the data dictionary idea can be extended into a really sophisticated system design tool. This is because if you define data in sufficient detail you'll find that you start implying the way whole programs should be put together. Take my word for it.

Data entry

Getting data into the system; *validation* often takes place at this stage.

Data General

The world's second largest manufacturer of *minicomputers*. Although it occasionally squabbles with *Hewlett-Packard* about which of them makes more money from minis, Data General is definitely ahead of everyone except *Digital Equipment* in terms of total sales. The company product line runs from very large (the Eclipse family) to very small (the microNOVA line and the Enterprise business computer); the bottom end includes two systems which are based on its own 16-bit microcomputer.

Data preparation

Pre-processing of 'raw' data before a *batch* data entry input. Typically, it means card punching or keying on to magnetic tape or disc. Subsequent data entry from input devices like a card reader or disc drive is much faster than any other direct data entry method, like input from a VDU. Those by-pass the need for data prep, though, and if you have to key-in some information once, it might as well be at a VDU rather than a card punch keyboard.

Datapoint
Independent Texas-based minicomputer vendor with products and aspirations for the *electronic office* market.

Data processing
Recording and handling information – not necessarily by electronic means, though of course that's usually assumed. For no good reason the term 'data processing' often refers to the use of computers in commercial appplications as distinct from scientific or engineering applications.

Data set
Or dataset. American alternative to *modem*. IBM also uses the term to mean *'file'*.

Data transmission/communications
Sending and receiving of data via telecommunications network.

Datastar
A data entry package for the *Wordstar* word processing program. It permits you to set up 'forms' on your display screen to simplify the entry of some kinds of information. Like Wordstar, it is from *Micropro*.

Dataview
A modest British success story, Dataview is best-known as the distributor of the excellent *Wordcraft*

word processing program which runs on *Commodore* computers. Dataview is also a Commodore dealer and it has several other packages to sell, too.

DBMS
Database management system.

DDP
Distributed Data Processing.

Deadly embrace
Beautifully graphic term, alternatively defined by the much less lurid expression 'deadlock'. It describes a situation in relatively complex computer systems; two or more programs demand resources – like access to a particular disc file – in such a way that neither can proceed because each is waiting for the other to release resources it holds.

Dealer
A company which will sell a computer (or any product, in fact) to you and me. Most micros and most of the other computer-type items you can buy are retailed by dealers, who are supplied by *distributors*.

Debug
Remove errors from a system. A canny debugging operator is a good programmer. You can have plenty of jokes with this word.

Decay time
Time during which an electronic impulse fades. It usually applies to characters on a CRT screen, which have to be 'refreshed' before the decay becomes noticeable.

Decimal notation
System of writing numbers where successive 'digit' positions are presented by successive powers of radix 10. It's what we use in day-to-day living.

Deck
Frequently-used alternative to *drive* when referring to magnetic tape. Alternatively a pack of punched cards.

Decoder
A device which converts numbers from one number system to another – binary to decimal, for example.

Decollate
To separate the parts of a multi-part forms set and remove the carbon paper.

Dedicated
Some part of a computer system (or all of it, perhaps) which is devoted to some particular job. A word processor could, in fact, be a dedicated microcomputer, since the system is given over to just one type of work.

Degradation
The computer business is full of scope for anyone lusting for *double entendres*. This one relates to a lower level of service in the event of a computer breakdown. Graceful degradation is the ability to ensure that failure of certain parts of equipment does not result in complete breakdown but allows limited operation.

Diablo
With Qume, the top manufacturer of *daisywheel* print-

ers – a *Xerox Corp* subsidiary.

Diagnostic
Routine or program designed to detect faults. Minis often have them built-in on ROM chips. For micro systems, diagnostics are generally little software programs which have to be loaded and run.

Difference Engine
The first of Babbage's prototype computers.

Dictionary
See *spelling checker*.

Digital
As opposed to analogue, a system or device using discrete signals to represent data numerically. Most digital representation in computing is based on the *binary* system.

Digitising pad or tablet
Neat input device which allows information in the form of hand-drawn lines to be entered into the computer.

Digital plotter
See *plotter*.

Digital Equipment
The top specialist manufacturer of minicomputers and the kind of company into which you wish you'd put a few bob 20 years age when shares were 10 a penny. Today the company sells big computers and peripherals as well as a whole range of minis and micros.

Digital Microsystems

Californian manufacturer with two U.K. distributors for its *CP/M*-based business microcomputers. They start at around £3,500, but can expand substantially; unusually, Digital Microsystems has a genuine *local network* system called HiNet which allows for considerable enlargement at minimal disruption.

Digital Research

The U.S. company responsible for *CP/M*.

DIP

Dual In-line Package. An arrangement of integrated circuits, the familiar black slab with gold legs running down its long sides.

Direct access

Ability to extract required data immediately from memory, regardless of its location. As opposed to sequential or *serial* access; so you can't have direct-access magnetic tape systems.

Direct address

Or absolute address, machine address, specific address; a standard, permanent identification of location in main memory.

Disc

A disc is usually plastic or metal, coated with a material on which data can be recorded on tracks. The tracks are concentric rather than the spiral of an LP. Read-/write heads can position themselves quickly over the required data without having to get through all the preceding storage area; that's why disc storage is described as *direct access* or random access (though it is not necessarily random).

Discs are fixed or removable. Fixed discs have permanently-inserted read/write heads, so they are very fast at reading or writing data. Obviously the disc can't be used to back-up the system via a *dump,* or for file storage; but it can be used as an extension of main memory. Fixed discs used to be expensive and rare on smaller systems – but that's changing.

Removable or exchangeable discs can be used for back-up and you can keep files on them for use as and when required. Access is slower than on fixed disc but much faster than tape. In the removable category you get:

Floppy discs. Everybody's favourite because you get cheap and reasonable fast direct access. Small and large size, single- and double-density; plenty of variety there.

Cartridge discs. The next step up. Usually 5 to 20 megabytes stored in what look like a large plastic plate, two inches thick and inserted into the front of the drive – some go into the top. Faster than floppies, of course.

Disc packs. For the big boys only; usually 20MB up (as far as 300MB). A stack of discs, normally six or 11 for protection in a plastic hood, is the cheapest way to store plenty of data.

There has been a very sudden boom, however, in the last year or two in a newish type of non-removable disc. The so-called *Winchester* disc gets its name from an IBM code-word for the original development project, which was reported to store 30MB on a removable disc and 30MB on the non-removable disc. In the Wild West there was a Winchester 30/30 rifle (or was it a carbine?) and the story goes that this is where the name originated.

Anyway, a Winchester is a hermetically-sealed, dust-free, high-reliability disc with relatively simple manufacturing and maintenance constraints. Winchester-type discs are now becoming available for small systems with capacities from about 3MB to more than 60MB – replacing floppies on the one hand and cartridge discs on the other.

Diskette

Or floppy disc or flexible disc, both of which are very explicit descriptions. A standard 5¼in. mini-floppy gives *direct-access* storage for about 80KB; at the other end of things, a double-sided, double-density 8in. diskette stores one megabyte – and Burroughs has announced a floppy disc which holds 3MB.

Distributed processing

Or distributed data processing, or DDP. It refers to the use of smallish computers at various locations within a big organisation; they may be tied to a central computer, or they may communicate among themselves to share the workload. This de-centralised approach allows much of the local work to be done locally, but other theoretical attractions include much greater up-time (when one system fails everyone else can continue) and probably cash savings (you can have a much smaller mainframe in the middle – or none at all).

There is also a way of putting distributed processing into a single computer system to achieve similar results on a local basis. Ponderous terms like 'distributed architecture' are usually bandied about in this case. See the notes on *multi-processing*.

Distributor

Most of the microcomputers and related products sold in the U.K. are manufactured by one company, which arranges for distributors to buy in bulk from it. The distributors, in turn, use local *dealers* who sell to the end-user (you and me).

DMA

Direct Memory Access is a technique for high-speed transfer of data directly between a peripheral and the computer memory, by-passing the need for repeating a service routine for each word of data being moved. This greatly speeds the transfer process. With DMA, an I/O device takes control of the microprocessor for one or more memory cycles to write to or read from memory. The order of executing program steps remains unchanged.

DOS

Generic abbreviation for an *operating system* most of which resides on disc rather than permanently in memory (which would be too small to hold all of a fair-sized operating system) or on tape (it is slow to find the required portion and read it into memory to be executed). Operating systems have names; most disc operating systems are simply called DOS by the manufacturer.

Dot matrix

This technique for printing or displaying builds-up characters as a pattern of dots with a 'matrix' which comprises a rectangle of possible dot positions. See *matrix printer*, too.

Double density

A way of doubling the amount of storage on a *disc drive* by doubling the number of *bits* which can be encoded in the same area of the disc surface. This adds to the price, of course; you'll need special drives and special discs and you will pay a premium on the standard prices for both. The price increase is nowhere near so great as using additional single-density disc drives to obtain the extra capacity.

An alternative is to use a *double-sided* disc drive. In fact, most micros are being shipped with one or the other; you will encounter single-sided, single-density disc drives less and less frequently. The price difference is not so great, and doubled capacity is very attractive.

Discs which have double-sided *and* double-density recording are also common but there have been reliability problems with some drives in the past; using both methods of increasing storage capacity means that the price rise starts to be a deterrent. When you have boosted the storage per disc to one million characters or more, you might as well start looking to the greater reliability of a small *Winchester* disc – the price contrast won't be too great and the storage space will be even greater.

Double-sided
Some *floppy discs* can store data on both sides. This usually needs a special premium-price disc and it definitely needs a special disc drive which will cost more than a standard single-sided drive. See also the notes under *double-density*.

Down time
Or down-time, or downtime. It's a period during which the computer is inoperative, usually because of a fault but perhaps for routine maintenance.

DPM
Data Processing Manager, the person who runs all the computer activities in a reasonably big company.

Dr Dobbs Magazine

The very best magazine for anyone who considers themselves a computer freak. It's American.

Dragon Data

A subsidary of the Mettoy toys and games company, this British microcomputer manufacturer first appeared in 1982. Its Dragon 32 is a £200 home computer aimed at "the family man with teenage children" (no kidding, that's what the press release says). The computer was designed by a firm of specialist technical consultants, which is an unusual way to do it, and is being built in Wales, hence the name. The Dragon 32 is built around the little-used *Motorola* 6809 micro; features include a good *extended Basic* with sound, colour and graphics. The price also includes 32K memory, which can't be bad.

Drive

The electro-mechanical device on which a tape or disc is loaded and run.

Drum

Old type of *backing storage* – it's simply a magnetically-coated rotating drum.

Drum printer

A type of *line printer* which has now largely been displaced by newer technology. It used a metal drum on which the characters were embossed.

Dual-port memory

Some computers can have memory boards in them with two access connections – which means a second computer can be plugged into the same memory (and therefore the same programs and files).

Dual-processor

Putting two *CPUs* into one system sounds like a really clever way of doubling the speed and throughput, rather like having two steam engines to tow a train up a steep incline.

In practice, it's not so easy. Some dual-processor systems have a second CPU simply as a *stand-by,* so it can instantly take over if the first one fails – electricity supply would be one instance where the system could not afford to stop working.

More likely there will be two (or more) processors because the system designer has cleverly split-off some of the functions. One processor decodes program instructions and tells the other(s) what to do: subsidiary processors might look after disc accesses, they might be devoted to some types of high-speed arithmetic work, or they may run that end of a complicated communications link. All processors can operate in parallel, so the big advantage is in reducing the chances of the bottlenecks which sometimes occur in a single CPU.

Dump

Transfer the contents of main memory on to backing storage, typically to give you a security copy.

Duplex

System which permits transmission in both directions simultaneously.

Dynabyte

Now one of the best-established of the microcomputer makers which flowered in the Californian microcomputer boom of the mid-1970s. Its computers are sold mostly to business users by distributors, typically with prices in the range £2,500 to £12,000 or so. The specification reads like the classic West Coast micro-*Zilog* Z-80 processor, *CP/M* and *MP/M* operating systems, *S-100* bus. Dynabyte products also have a good reputation for solidity and reliability.

Dynamic RAM
See *RAM*.

EAN
An uncharacteristically short acronym, EAN stands for European Article Number. Designed to simplify classification of consumer items, it appears typically as the *bar code* – the row of little black lines on your tins of rhubarb (or whatever).

EAROM
Electrically-Alterable Read-Only Memory. It is effectively a synonym for *EPROM* and you can probably forget it.

EBCDIC
Extended Binary Coded Decimal Interchange Code. One of the two principal character codes, the other being *ASCII*. EBCDIC is another helpful IBM contribution to standardisation.

The EBCDIC code allows for many more control characters and special graphics symbols, including the highly-useful 'hook', 'fork' and 'chair', than does ASCII.

Most micros usually stay with ASCII. We won't be dogmatic about it because some systems might have to communicate with an IBM mainframe, though you might still be able to use ASCII code.

These character codes become important when you're attaching terminals. That is why ASCII is so popular – plugging-in terminals is simplified when you can be certain that the list and the peripheral will assign the same meanings to the same bit patterns. Connecting an IBM terminal which generates EBCDIC code is almost impossible on an ASCII-orientated system.

ECL

Emitter-Coupled Logic, a type of *logic* circuit used in the fastest computers. Also known as MECL – Monolithic ECL. Now forget it.

ECMA

It may sound like a skin complaint but it stands for the European Computer Manufacturers' Association. Although it specifies Europe, included in the membership are branches of the large American corporations. The clans gather and establish standards which subsequently are rendered obsolete.

The best such joke was ECMA agonising over a standard for 80-column punched cards; when the infighting had produced a result, IBM announced the totally different 96-column card and very quickly followed with the floppy disc, which effectively outmoded cards altogether. Well, perhaps that's a matter of opinion; let us say the floppy disc contributed to the use of a new type of computing which has meant the decline of the 80-column card.

Edit

As a verb, it means to re-arrange data. In practice, an edit is an instruction or group of instructions (or a button) causing data to be inserted, deleted, or re-located. Editing is, of course, a vital feature of word processing equipment – it is about the only feature on some.

An *editor* in this case is not an individual with ever-poised red pen but a program for editing data.

EDP
Electronic Data Processing is what the Americans call DP or plain old data processing. They're correct, of course – *electronic* data processing is not the only way to process data.

EDS
Exchangeable Disc Store. This is basically ICL terminology but it is a neat abbreviation to cover removable discs – cartridge discs and disc packs. ICL normally puts a figure after the abbreviation, denoting the capacity of the disc drive. So an EDS 5 is a 5-megabyte unit, probably a cartridge disc at that capacity; EDS 30 is a 30MB drive and probably a pack.

EDSAC
The Electronic Delay Storage Automatic Computer was the first of the computers as we know and love them. It was constructed in the mathematics department of Cambridge University and its first real task was to calculate a table of prime numbers in 1949. EDSAC's other main claim to fame is that it shows you what happens when you don't try to force your acronyms to make words like BUCKET, BITWIDDLE, and FAME.

Educational Computing
Magazine devoted to the use of computers in schools and colleges, concentrating on microcomputers.

EFTS
Electronic Funds Transfer System. Generic name for any inter-bank communication system which uses computers rather than Securicor-type vans to transfer money between them.

Elapsed time

This usually means the time taken to carry-out a particular job – it might be called 'clock time' by some people. Processing time ('run time' or 'mill time') is very different. You can be on the computer for several hours but the processor will have been active for a few seconds.

Elapsed time is defined formally as the time between entering the data and initial instructions and extracting the required final information.

Electronic brain

Paranoid, ill-informed and totally unnecessary description. Computers are fast idiots; they do what they are told. In many years' time, the technology may have advanced to the stage where machines can originate thought and reason themselves into new ways of behaviour. But that's a long way ahead.

Electronic composer

A typewriter-style machine which simplifies type-setting and upsets printing unions. Alternatively, a micro which can turn out *I wanna hold your hand* in the style of Stockhausen.

Electronic office

All-purpose *buzzword* of the 1980s, used at the drop of a hat by all computer vendors, all conference speakers, and shortly all journalists. They may call it 'the Office of the Future' or 'the Automated Office' but basically they all mean the same thing – a system using one or more computers which provides an integrated approach to business communications, operating more efficiently and more economically than present techniques with little or no use of paper.

In practice, the key concepts are making better use

of management time, improving the availability and dissemination of relevant facts throughout an organisation, and speeding communication both inside a company and outside with other firms.

All grand ideas, of course, and we now have the technology to do something about them. Or rather, some computer companies have the technology – we get it only if we pay for it.

The electronic office will mean a revision of existing office procedures and job roles but broadly the functions it should include are:
- data processing
- word processing
- electronic mail.

The DP and WP functions utilise the same records; in a small company they would all be stored on disc, though at present-day prices a large organisation with large files might need some kind of automated microfilm system. The electronic mail component is a kind of super-Telex which would handle voice, data and *facsimile* transmissions internally and externally – and at your end there would be a kind of electronic mailbox for you to check to see if there's anything waiting for you.

There's more to it than that, of course, but even from this outline you can see that offices will have to change. Managers will do much more of the work with which secretaries now become bored; the filing clerk's job will have to change radically; the typing pool may well disappear.

Frankly, business can't afford *not* to automate the office. The anti-Luddite argument is that, overall, the increased efficiency will guarantee employment levels because of increased business for the automated companies; whether you adhere to that view depends on which side of the fence you've fallen.

Electrosensitive printer

Some types of *dot matrix printer* build a character on paper by using electricity to create the pattern of dots. This they do usually by using a paper with a special coating which disappears when an electric charge is applied to it; most of these printers take a silvery paper and when a dot-sized bit of the coating is removed a black underside is exposed. All this sounds complicated and clumsy but, in fact, electrosensitive printers are compact and very fast. They're almost silent, too.

The paper is the problem. It is satisfactory for till rolls and such like; it might just about be acceptable for your program listings but it doesn't look good for long texts and it is much more expensive than ordinary paper.

Electrostatic printer

Electrostatic printers are non-impact, so you don't get copies, but they are also quiet and fast because they don't involve many moving parts. You need special paper with a di-electric coating, though. To cut short a longish story, the technique involves charging the paper in a dot pattern – characters and shapes are built in a matrix, as with impact matrix printers – and then passing the paper through a toner solution which causes black particles to adhere to the charged dots. Hey presto – black dots on white paper.

Electrostatic devices are usually fairly expensive and are promoted as printer/plotters, with resolutions of 400 or more dots per inch; output speeds for text can be more than 2,000 lines per minute.

Empty medium

Hold on to your hats, it's joke time again. Empty medium contrasts with virgin medium and neither has

anything to do with redundant nubile spiritualists.
Virgin medium is completely untouched, like a coil of
paper tape. Empty medium is ready-to-record data –
paper tape punched with feed holes, perhaps. You'll
never hear either term but the first person to work them
both into the same sentence during a normal conversation receives the *Good Computing Guide* award for
effluence beyond the call of duty.

Emulation
In this procedure one computer duplicates the instruction set of another. In practice, it usually involves
using a large computer to develop programs for a
smaller one. The full facilities and speed of the bigger
system make for easier program development; and
because it is emulating the smaller machine, the programs which result can be transferred to the target
system and run happily.

Enable
Essentially, to 'enable' a function is to switch it on. In
literal terms, it is defined as setting the processor to
accept interrupt signals.

End-user
Obviously it's the person who finally uses a computer
system. This may not be the person who bought it – if
your company buys a computer and you have on your
desk a terminal attached to it, you're an end-user.

Enquiry
As the word suggests, an enquiry is an operation which
accesses a record or some other item in storage without
altering the contents – that is called an update. There
is an important distinction to be made between enquiries and updates, because the amount of processor

effort required for an update is considerable, while an enquiry takes very little.

In a fairly simple multiple-terminal system, several terminals can be making enquiries on files and one can be updating. If you want more than one simultaneously-updating terminal, you will require a much more complicated operating system and generally a more complex computer.

EOB

End of Block, usually a special code defined by a computer to indicate the end of a segment of data being transmitted over a communications link.

EOF

End of File, a special code which is defined to indicate ... you guessed it.

EOM

End of Message. Another of those control codes for transmissions.

EOT

End of text, an ASCII control code. Or end of transmission.

EPROM

Erasable Programmable Read-Only Memory. ROM is read-only memory supplied as ready-programmed. PROM is read-only memory supplied empty and programmed by you, if you have the special tools. EPROM is PROM which can be erased and re-programmed.

The sharp-witted will spot that EPROM sounds a little like RAM, which is random-access memory (or read/write memory). RAM is the 'user' memory in a system; you can load programs into it and read from it at will.

The difference between EPROM and RAM is that with EPROM you need a special erasing device which utilises ultra-violet light – with RAM the new programming over-writes the old, as a rule. With EPROM you need a special re-programming device, the same 'PROM burner' required for non-erasable PROM.

Epson

This brand name belongs to a Japanese firm, Shinshu Seiki, which in turn is part of the Seiko group (other Seiko interests, incidentally, include the printer manufacturer *Seikosha*).

Shinshu Seiki was originally a supplier of watch parts, but in 1978 it launched the Epson MX family of low-cost *dot matrix printers* and now watch parts represent about eight percent of its turnover. Epson was among the first to see the potential for compact, well-designed low-cost printers and now it is the leading supplier of such printers for the microcomputer business, with a market share estimated at fully 40 percent. Bulk-buying customers among the personal computer manufacturers (who re-sell Epson printers under their brand names) include IBM and Commodore.

Epson MX printers are relatively inexpensive, quiet, reliable, and generally they exhibit a neat and thoughtful design. I use one and I can vouch for that list of epithets.

Toward the end of 1982 the company also announced its first microcomputer, another attractive piece of design. Called the QC-20, it is a fairly conventional *CP/M*-based computer with a U.S. price tag of around $4,000.

There is also a hand-held micro, the HC-20 (or

HX-20, depending on which version of the brochure you have). This sells for between $500 and $1,000 and weighs just under 4 lb., yet still manages to incorporate a 'real' typewriter-like keyboard rather than the calculator-style keys of its principal competitors. Inside is a full Basic, a built-in printer and four-line display, and dictation-type mini-cassettes. It looks like one to watch.

Erasable memory

Memory of storage facilities which can be written, erased, re-written *ad infinitum*. Magnetic core, tape, and disc files are all erasable memory. You'll never hear this term but we thought it ought to be included.

ERCC

Error-checking and correcting memories are becoming more common on bigger minis; mainframes have had ERCC memories for some time. Each word stored is checksummed very time it is used – you remember *checksums,* don't you? – and the system makes sure that no unexpected alteration of its contents has occurred.

ERCC typically can detect and correct any and all single-bit errors; other errors are usually detected and logged, which helps at least. ERCC involves adding six bits to a 16-bit word; that's for the checksum and checking; it can slow things a bit, which is why ERCC is limited normally to fast machines. See *parity,* too.

Error correction

As systems become more complex, it is important that errors are detected without stopping or re-running the whole thing. Facilities are being developed to effect local correction of errors without interrupting the major activities of the system, hence error correction.

Error message
A code or message displayed on a computer printer or CRT to indicate that an error has been encountered in a program or in the hardware. You should have a handbook which tells you what you can do about the error, though typically error messages are terse codes which you look up to find they mean 'unspecified error condition'.

ETB
End of transmitted block (ASCII again).

ETK
End of transmission – another ASCII control code.

Euromicro
European association of academically-inclined people in the microcomputer game.

Evans, Christopher
The late Dr Chris Evans was one of the better things about the British computer business. An original and entertaining thinker, he was a great advocate of improving the relationship between people and computers – would that there were more like him working in DP. His book *The Mighty Micro* is recommended, though its enthusiasm is occasionally slightly naïve.

Execuplan
A *spreadsheet* package aimed particularly at users of *Vector Graphic* computers.

Execution time

Not only the cold, grey hour of dawn but also the time required for the computer to carry-out an instruction, or a sequence of instructions. It varies, of course, depending on the machine and the operation. It is generally expressed in terms of *clock* cycles. Also known as Instruction Time. Or Instruction Execution (or Execute) Time.

Executive

Either the grey-suited individual concealing *Bits 'n' Tums* inside his *Financial Times* as he boards the 7.57 from Woking or, wait for it, the basic system software which runs a computer, The term 'executive' is used often as a synonym for *'operating system',* which means that nobody really has a clear definition. Ours is as follows: the executive is that software which resides in main memory and provides control functions for the computer system.

In general, those functions would include handling interrupts (defined later), reading inputs from and despatching outputs to the control console, giving each component part of the computer circuitry a slice of the processor's attention, and so on.

Executive is not a term encountered frequently in the micro world. You are much more likely to encounter 'monitor', which so far as we can see means exactly the same (though usually implemented in ROM) or 'operating system' which , in practice, will incorporate many more system functions than something called an executive.

Exerciser

A 'prototyping' or 'development' system for a micro is a set-up which allows the user to write and debug programs, so usually it includes some kind of I/O device and local storage medium. Those programs, once they are working, can then be loaded into a micro configuration which probably does not need to have all those peripherals. The key point is that many applications for microprocessors are in systems which have no requirement for man-machine interaction, but to produce the software which drives those systems you need such facilities.

An exerciser is the very simplest form of development system. Usually it consists only of a small display screen and a hexadecimal keyboard.

Exit
To leave one program or one mode of operation to move to another.

EXORciser
The Motorola development package for the M6800 microprocessor; it minimises the time needed to develop M6800 systems.

Extended Basic
Basic was designed as a fairly simple language for beginners and accordingly it is not so rich in facilities as some of the more complicated programming languages.

Many people have been beavering away at Basics to maximise the potential of the language on their own computers, so most of the Basic implementations you'll meet have been somewhat enhanced by comparison with the original specifications.

There is no universally-agreed official definition yet for Basic, so there is no officially-agreed definition of what an extended Basic includes. Typically, though, a beefed-up Basic will allow you to do clever output formatting and pleasant things with files (what is called

Record I/O, for instance – look for the provision of commands like GET and PUT).

There will also be extensions to the existing facilities, like a greater range of line numbering, a greater range of permitted numbers, a greater range of permitted variable names and types of variable.

Above all, though, the basic Basic is generaly not good enough to handle commercial applications even with difficulty. It can become very difficult to do an invoice calculation and then to print an invoice. The extensions to Basic generally are provided to simplify commercial programming.

That is a kind of superset of Basic. There are also subsets of Basic which provide some if not all facilities of the language in very small systems – Tiny Basic is the best-known example.

Extender board

Or *chassis*. Computers are a collection of printed circuit boards which slot into a chassis. The processor normally is one or two boards and so takes one or two slots. Depending on the supplier, one memory board occupying one slot can store from 4KB to 64KB or more; the controllers for disc, cassette and other peripherals are all implemented as circuit boards and take more slot positions.

Obviously you reach a limit to the number of PCB slots but some manufacturers will sell an extender or expansion board or chassis or cage. This is generally a separate chassis with more PCB slots and it plugs into the power supplies and data buses of the main chassis.

External storage

Same as *backing store*. Speaks for itself, really; any type of memory which can be stored away from the computer, like discs and tapes. Internal memory is core or semiconductor storage.

Exxon

U.S. multi-national, best-known for Esso petrol but also very active in the microcomputer/word processing/electronic office fields. It has a subsidiary called Exxon Enterprises which buys small but potentially-important companies; the clutch includes Zilog for micros, Periphonics for voice I/O systems, Vydec for word processors, Qyx for electronic typewriters, and Qwix for facsimile transmission. Exxon Enterprises isn't doing too well at the present, as it happens.

Facilities Management

A kind of extension of the *bureau* idea, where someone else houses and runs your computer for you. So you don't have the trouble of staffing it, programming it, and generally operating it – you just pay for it.

Failsoft

Failsoft is essentially the same as graceful *degradation* but provides less scope for double-entendres. A system is 'failsoft' if it switches itself off in the event of breakdown, so that no important data is lost. Failsoft usually implies that things can be re-started from the point at which the system broke down. Some machines fail softer than others.

Fairchild

The Fairchild Instrument Co is one of the big fish in the micro sea, though like many large corporations it has not exactly siezed the opportunities open to it in the microprocessor game – and that is one reason why Fairchild has long had a perfectly respectable line of microcomputers (deriving from the F8) without setting the world on fire.

Fairchild's other significance lies in its proximity to Silicon Valley. As a result, its alumni have spawned most of the top micro and mini companies in the area.

Fault
You will not believe this but a fault is what happens (or doesn't happen) when something doesn't work. In practice, the term usually refers to a *physical* malfunction, which means a hardware defect like a short circuit, a duff piece of soldering, or a broken wire. By contrast a *bug* is usually a fault specifically in software.

FDX
Conventional abbreviation for *full duplex*.

Feasibility study
An initial examination of the pros and cons of a particular project. Typically it's the acquisition of a computer, and typically the would-be acquirer will skimp on the feasibility study.

Feed
What happens to the sea-lions at 1430 hrs. Or how cards and paper get into the computer. A card feed is the mechanical device which (wait for it) feeds cards into a card reader. A paper feed is the mechanism whereby paper is fed into a printer.

A **front-feed** is a particular device which allows you to stack a pile of single sheets on a printer, dropping a sheet at a time automatically into the printer.

Feedback

The easiest way to get feedback is to try giving an obstreperous infant liver and spinach broth for its din-dins. Ho-ho. The word also has two less frivolous meanings. Feedback is what occurs when an output impulse is picked up and fed back into the circuit as input. It happens with any electrical transmission device – frequently between electric guitars and amplifiers. A big hand, please, for Jim Hendrix and Pete Townsend who pioneered its deliberate use in that department.

A second, more abstract meaning of feedback is the getting of information from one operation which can be used either to alter that first operation or to initiate another.

Ferranti

Historically significant in Britain. Ferranti's present interest is in military and process control systems with its minis and one of the earliest 16-bit micros.

Fetch

What happens when a computer processes one *object code* instruction is a multi-stage process – for instance, fetch, decode, execute. The fetch part means going to a specified memory address and reading the instruction stored there.

FF

Conventional abbreviation for *form feed*.

Fibre optics

Very promising alternative to *co-axial cable* for sending information between portions of a computer system – and it can also be used to transmit voice or data over long distances, so it's likely to replace ordinary

telephone wire, too. Another major benefit is its
capacity. Basically the fibre-optic cable is a bundle of
continuous glass rods, very thin and very flexible; the
transmission is done by light pulses passing down
them. It's all very clever and it has many advantages
over cabling, which uses electric pulses.

Field

A file consists of records, a record consists of fields.
It is easy enough to produce a logical definition of a
field – something like 'an area where data of a given
type will be found for processing or storage as a single
entity'. In practice, the definition is likely to be practical and obvious. For instance, membership records
might comprise fields for name, address lines, membership number, and membership fees paid. Or you
might set up the system at a greater level of detail, plus
one field for surname, two for first names, one each for
house number, street town, county, postcode, country
... and so on.

FIFO

... I smell the blood of a jargon-monger. This whimsi-
cal term stands for 'first in – first out', a method of
storing items of data so that the first one entered is the
first one retrieved. The average use of the term is for
a FIFO buffer, which is typically a sequential list of
things queueing for processor attention – instructions
to be executed, perhaps, or events in the outside
world.

File

An attempt to organise related information; or a collection of records. In practice, a file in computer terms is
the essential input for a processing program. Some
systems require you to set up your programs as individ-

ual files; you read the (program) file into memory, and that file contains all the instructions you need. Data files contain all the data a particular program needs; a subscription program might use one file of subscriber records, another with subscription rates.

Filing system

All but the smallest general-purpose computers have system software which includes at least some method of organising files. The filing system lays down the rules about how you store and retrieve files. In particular, it tells you how to relate the organisation and structure of a file to the patterns of access, but for an exposition of this see *indexed sequential.*

Fill

A *field* may be larger than the information you put into it. An address field, for instance, may be set up to cater for large addresses with up to seven lines of 35 characters apiece; so a short address won't take up all the space available. Some systems and some applications require at least some data in the unfilled area – so you have to 'fill' it, usually with meaningless space characters or zeros. This may also be called padding or packing.

Firmware

Is it a corset? No. Is it a toupee adhesive? No. Is it a hardwired program? Yes. Firmware is essential software fixed in the computer in read-only memory *(ROM).* For example, the operating instructions may be held in ROM – as they are in the Pet; or a computer which controls traffic lights may have its program permanently resident in the same way.

Because it is in ROM, firmware executes very quickly – getting instructions from ROM is much faster than from ordinary read-write memory. Since it is difficult or impossible to alter the contents of ROM, firmware has to be correct before it is committed to ROM.

The same attributes make it more secure than a conventionally-stored program, since it can't easily be corrupted by a programmer accidentally over-writing it, for example, or by internal electrical hiccups. Firmware therefore tends to be used where an application requires maximum freedom from problems – like air traffic control, nuclear power stations, and the like.

On a more modest level, we are starting to see plug-in firmware becoming available for the more widely-used micros. These are ROM modules which you put into the specified place on the printed circuit board of the computer; the firmware generally provides for more system software.

Fixed disc
A type of *disc drive* with which the discs cannot be removed. The most popular example now is the *Winchester* disc.

Flag
This is what a person does towards the end of a day of glossary-writing. For a computer, a flag is a sequence of bits which signals the beginning and the end of a piece of data, or indicates something about it.

Typically, a flag is an indicator attached to a data field; it is likely to be a single bit position. For example, it you have a record to be printed you might set a flag to '1'. Your print program would then hunt around the files looking for all records with the flag set.

Flexible disc
Same as *floppy disc*.

Flexidrive
ICL name for a floppy disc drive.

Flip-flop
Woollies used to do good ones and if you can afford
them surf shops tend to have great flip-flops. The rest
of us will have to make do with something along the
lines of a bi-stable electrical component – which could
be a toggle switch, or it could be a logic *gate*. Forget
it.

Floating point
Sometimes called scientific notation. It's a method of
holding very large numbers in limited amounts of
storage. The number is stored in the form of argument
and exponent – don't worry if that doesn't mean much
to you, it's just a way of taking-up less space in
memory. In practice, a number would be stored as the
significant digits in the number and a power of 10. For
instance, 9,999 might be stored as 9.999E3 – which is
the same as 9.999×10^3.

If all this means nothing to you, just think of floating
point as a nifty way of handling numbers – so if you
want to use numbers a great deal, make sure your
computer has a floating point facility.

Floating point gives you maximum accuracy. You
might also look on floating point as a clever way of
manipulating numbers so that no matter how big or
small the number is, it always takes up the same
amount of storage space.

Frankly, most micros do not have the ability to
handle floating point, and unless you're a scientist or
a numbers nut you probably don't need it.

Floating point extends a computer's calculation abilities and simplifies the programming of complicated arithmetic operations.

The opposite of floating point is, would you believe, fixed point, which means ordinary, familiar decimal numbers with a point in the same position all the time – after the whole number, before the fraction – remember?

Floppy disc

Floppy discs are, as the name implies, a flexible storage medium, rather like the plastic 45rpm records given away as promotions. Each disc is in a protective envelope – the read/write head passes through a slit in the cover. We discuss disc storage in depth under our *disc* entry.

Floppies are in a range of sizes from 5$\frac{1}{4}$in. mini-floppies to double-sided, double-density, full-size floppies. A normal mini-diskette holds between 50 and 90KB; a typical double-sided, double-density minifloppy holds about 280KB – and some can store 1MB. Average 8in. floppies go from a minimum of 250-315KB to a maximum of around 1.4MB (though Burroughs has one which will store 3MB).

The most recent development, courtesy of *Sony,* is at the other end of the size scale, a 3.25in. disc. Such is the pace of technology that this midget disc holds more data than the original 8in. discs: when used in the Sony micro, this disc stores about 280KB but other versions of it can store more than 320KB.

Access time for floppies is reasonably fast; they are not expensive; they are easy to handle and to store. Rumour has it that the hole in the middle bends, too.

Flowchart

A flowchart is a graphic representation of a system or a program. As a concept it is brilliant. It is an explicit and easily-understood description of what is happening – or what ought to happen, since flowcharts are usually produced after you have done some thinking but before you write any program code.

It is difficult to over-estimate the importance of drawing a flowchart. Everyone should learn flowcharting before they learn a programming language. This is my view, so be warned that many people disagree – and it's true that some of the newer programming languages may not need the flowchart approach.

Flowcharts use a number of conventional symbols. The important ones are 'process' boxes and 'decision' lozenges.

Flowriter

A *daisywheel* printer based on the *Ricoh* unit.

Foreground

Where the foreplay takes place? No, it's just a way of indicating what's happening in the computer when two (or more) tasks, programs, jobs, or whatever are competing for resources. It applies only to *multi-programming* systems and denotes the program with the highest priority.

The converse is *background,* naturally enough, and what happens is typically something like this. Your printer program is happily trundling away, printing. Then in comes something from you on the VDU. The computer knows that the VDU doesn't want to wait for the printer program to complete, not in view of the fact that it's printing the whole London telephone directory and has reached only AAA Car Hire; so it suspends the print job automatically, gives its full resources to this piece of VDU activity, and returns to the printing when the VDU interaction is finished. Servicing the VDU is the foreground job, the printing is going on in the background.

Format

The logical organisation of programs or data. In practice, this formatting will cover all kinds of preambles, postambles, check digits, stop and start indicators, beginning and end marks, and so on.

Format-80

One of the best (and at £300 or so, one of the most expensive) *word processing* programs available for the Apple II.

FORTRAN

FORmula TRANslator. It's another IBM invention (c. 1957) though it's travelled a long way since then; it is still the single most widely-used scientific programming language. It's not much good for anything else (though a company called General Automation has a business version called Commercial Fortran). Basic owes some of its parentage to Fortran.

FPP

Floating point package – a software or *firmware* facility which handles *floating point* arithmetic for you.

Front-end

All-purpose *buzzword* meaning 'at the front', though often used as a verb, meaning 'to put on to or at the front'.

It's not all so silly as it sounds, though. A front-end processor is a separate mini or micro which does something to input (pre-processes it, in fact) to help optimise the work of the main processor. This might be unscrambling a coded message of some kind, figuring what files will have to be accessed, and so on.

Full duplex

This describes a simultaneous but independent two-way transmission of data. It is distinguished from *simplex* (one-way transmission only) and *half-duplex* (two-way transmission, but alternatively rather than simultaneously).

Function

In practical terms, a function is essentially a *sub-routine* – either literally (a bunch of program statements) or figuratively (a set of operations and events which can be repeated as required when they are called on).

The classic functions are the four basic arithmetic operations. In a pocket caluculator, for instance, pressing the ADD key initiates a (quick) set of programmed operations which produces the desired result for the data presented to it.

Function key

Obviously, a key which calls-up a *function*. Your keyboard may not have any (there are two other types of key on it, alphanumeric and control). You can activate functions in other ways, though, typically by a code key sequence like pressing CONTROL and another key at the same time. On the other hand your keyboard may have a row of keys with no labels, perhaps, or cryptic messages like 'PFO'. In that case you'll have a manual which shows you how to set up functions (typically as conventional program codes) and assign them to particular function keys. Subsequently you can call-up the function with a single keystroke.

Nearly all keyboards will have some function keys, in any case – like NEWLINE, CR, RETURN, LF, ENTER. They're just not very complicated functions.

Functional specification

This is a description of *what* a program does (or more likely what it's supposed to do). It's not usually a description of *how* the program does it.

If you've commissioned someone to write some software for your computer, before any programming is done you should be able to look over this document to ensure that you're getting what you want. It may be too technical for you, in which case demand to see a slimmed-down version called an 'outline' specification.

Games

You don't really need a definition of a game, do you? It is, however, worth spending a few words on the subject, because it is far from trivial. On the one hand, games represent an excellent use of computers; they involve rules and alternative decision paths, both of which are highly appropriate to the computer. So games make good use of the computer.

They also make good use of you, not least because you can plumb your potential and exercise your mind in a situation where you are calling the shots. If you don't like the game or if you don't want to play, that is up to you; if you win, it's you who did it; if you lose, it doesn't matter; and if you don't like losing, that's your business, too.

There are more serious games, too, of course – 'serious' in this context referring to social repercussions. You might be playing in a team – the family which plays together stays together? – and there isn't really much difference between *Adventure* and the kind of what-if business planning programs widely available.

Gas-discharge display

Also called a plasma display. This is an alternative to the TV-type cathode ray tube as a way of displaying man-machine communication.

The CRT works by firing electrons at a phosphor-coated surface, which lights-up at the point where the electrons hit. The gas discharge display consists of many tiny gas-filled cells, the gas in which lights up when a small electrical current is passed through it. The character which results depends exactly on which cells in the matrix are illuminated, of course, since the illumination produces a pattern of dots just as the glowing dots build up a character on a CRT screen.

There are good and bad points to gas-discharge displays. In particular, you do not have to fit in an electron gun; so this kind of display can be very flat, and that means a VDU using it doesn't occupy so much space on the table as one with a CRT screen. Also the electrical stimulation can be constant, so you don't have the flickering which sometimes occurs with a CRT; the phosphor glow starts to fade when the electron gun has moved on to illuminate the next dot, and the flickering is caused when the electron beam re-stimulates the point.

The cells have to be reasonably large, and the dots can't be defined as clearly as the small CRT dots. So you don't have many characters on the screen and they certainly do not resemble 'joined-up' writing in the way CRT characters sometimes do.

The killer is that gas-discharge displays are more

expensive than CRTs on a cost-per-character basis. If you have many characters to display, CRTs give you the most legible solution; and LEDs are cheaper if you want to display only a few. So you probably won't see many gas-discharge displays around for some time.

Gate

A single *logic* function. Formerly, electronic systems used electromagnetic relays which opened and closed electrical paths in different directions; that's where the term originated, for the way a path was routed is analogous to a gate opening or remaining closed. A gate is thus a point at which a logic decision has to be made.

General Ledger

Americanism for 'Nominal Ledger'. See comments under *Accounts Payable*.

General-purpose computer

Largely meaningless phrase, useful only to distinguish a system from a *dedicated* computer.

Gigo

Acronym for 'garbage in, garbage out'. The sense is obvious; if you use duff input you can't expect elegant output. It's not much used these days, but oldsters of the computer business go into paroxysms of knowing chuckles whenever they meet the term.

The concept is really old. An anecdote in one of the books by *Babbage* had the computer's great-grandad reflecting on a Lord and an M.P. both of whom asked: "If you put into the machine wrong figures, will the right answers come out?" Not being given to sarcasm, the worthy Mr B commented: "I am not able rightly to apprehend the confusion of ideas that could provoke such a question".

Glitch

Graphic description for an unwanted burst of electrical *noise*. Not that it's particularly important, but a small glitch is called a 'snivitz'. Do you really believe that?

Global (variable)

Variables are in two varieties – local and global. Local ones can be accessed only from a particular segment of a program; global variables are available for reference from anywhere in the program.

Golf-ball

The resemblance gave the name to the type element on IBM typewriters and this genre of electric typewriter. It's properly called a 'typesphere', in fact. The key points so far as the personal computer user is concerned are two; the typesphere rather than the paper moves, and the printing produced is of excellent quality. A moving type element involves much less mechanical effort than an ordinary type-bar typewriter, so it is reliable enough and fast enough to be used by a computer. If you want to do word processing – like write form letters to your bank managers, lovers, or wine suppliers – the print impression cannot be bettered.

On the other hand, the design of the golf-ball-type mechanism is such that you'll never achieve much faster than about 15 characters per second. If you use it for long jobs, it is likely to fall apart; wondrous though it is, the typesphere printer is still delicate by comparison with other printer mechanisms, notably the *matrix* printer.

GOTO

A programming instruction, sometimes called an explicit jump instruction – see *Jump.* Encountering a GOTO in a program switches the instruction execution sequence to the specified line – the GOTO command usually occurs with a label or line number, as in GOTO NEWCODE or GOTO 1100; that indicates the instruction to be executed next.

All this technical stuff is here because there's an interesting argument in the nether regions of programming about the best methods to use in producing software. GOTO is frowned on by most of these people because jumps make the sequence of logic more difficult to check – and, Lord knows, the more checking a program receives the better. The emphasis these days is more on what is called 'in-line' code, which means a more sequential logic flow with the order of instruction execution much clearer. In practice, this means GOTO is Bad, the *IF-THEN-ELSE* construction is Good. There is a Glossary entry for it: see *structured programming,* too.

Graph

Properly defined as a figure with nodes (which is a point where actual or imaginary lines cross) and edges.

Graph plotter

See *graphics* and *plotter.*

Graphics

Any output which is not alphanumeric; more specifically, the term refers to pictorial symbols and representations built from them.

There's much to be said for using graphics as much as you can, largely on the 'picture being worth a thousand words' principle. That applies as much to the design of a screenful of information (try arranging information as organised blocks of copy to make it more meaningful) as it does to creating charts and pictures (Lunar Lander games gain from the inclusion of a lunar module about to hit the surface; seeing a string of changing figures labelled 'height' simply isn't the same).

Many personal computers have graphics built in. For others there are several option boards which provide graphics, especially if you have a micro using the *S-100* bus.

Hard-copy output in graph form can be done by some printers – it looks a bit jerky if you're doing curves, though, because the printhead cannot move in fine enough increments. A graph *plotter* can do those really small movements and they tend to use ink-filled pens to draw a continuous line – the printers tend to do it as a string of dots. Plotters aren't cheap, however, though there is at least one U.S. plotter below the $1,000 mark. Can't you do without graphical hard-copy?

Grosch, Herb

Herb Grosch is one of the grand old men of the computer business. An active and engaging pundit, he operates in the more rarified regions of computer technology; he is best-known for 'Grosch's Law', the highly-contentious proposition that big computers are best – for each increase in cost, you get a disproportionately favourable increase in the computer power available. In fact, the Law says that computer power increases as the square of the cost. Thanks to the advance of the micro, this proposition is now extremely debatable. Grosch is no fool, though, and has argued consistently that the Law applies even to micros; it could well be that two microcomputers linked together, say, by a *local network,* provide an increase in overall capacity out of proportion to the cost.

Half-duplex

Refers to a communications link in which data may travel in both directions along the connected line, but not at the same time. See *full duplex* for an equally interesting definition using slightly different words.

You'll probably encounter the full- or half-duplex question only as a user of a computer *terminal,* and generally you don't have much say in the matter – your terminal will probably have a switch marked FULL/-HALF or FDX/HDX and if it isn't set appropriately you won't be able to talk to the computer.

Hall Effect

A type of solid-state electrical switch used on some keyboards.

Halt

An instruction or internally-generated condition which switches the computer out of the 'run' mode in which it was executing a program. The computer doesn't lose its place, though – it HALTs, remembering which line of the program is due to be executed next. HALT is used usually in program development; you can set the computer cleverly to detect mistakes, for instance, and cause it to suspend operation temporarily to allow you to do something about it. The HALT state frequently gives the user the chance to set and re-set internal conditions from the keyboard, so that when you re-start the program it continues executing but with slightly altered conditions.

Handler

A device (or peripheral) handler is alternatively called a *driver;* it's a piece of a program (usually a portion of the *operating system,* in fact) which communicates with and generally controls one of your system's peripherals. The handler for the keyboard, for instance, will detect what you mean when you depress a particular key; and it will pass that information to the central processor for some action.

Handshake

What you get from writing too many Glossary definitions too quickly. Alternatively, it's a term which refers to communication between two parts of a system, typically a terminal and the central processor. It means that the receiving end is confirming that it has, in fact, received something. It's a pleasantly graphic term, isn't it? Still, it is a bit heavy; you can now forget it.

Hard copy

Hard copy is computer output on paper, printing or graphics. You may hear the term 'hard-copy printer'; that is tautology, since all printers, of course, produce hard copy. It is called 'hard' to indicate a degree of tangibility; 'soft copy' is what appears on a VDU screen.

Hard-sectored

Data is stored on disc in *tracks,* concentric rings around the spindle. So if you know which track a piece of data is on, you have to get the read/head on to that track and read around it until you reach the data; you don't have to read the whole disc looking for it.

Sectoring speeds the process even more. Discs are also organised into *sectors,* which are wedges rather like slices of cake. So each track is split effectively into a number of sectors; and if you can identify the location of data by track *and* sector, the read/write head can be directed to the start of the sector on the particular track and it doesn't have to read round the whole track looking for the data.

Tracks are fixed on the disc by the factory. On some disc systems this applies to sectors, too; the start of a sector can be defined by a hole punched in the disc surface. That's hard-sectoring.

By contrast, soft-sectoring means that the start of a sector is defined by a program – usually the operating system.

Harding, A.J.

A.J. Harding is the country's principal purveyor of ready-made programs for the Tandy TRS-80. His trading names include Molimerx, which he says means 'wonderful software' in Latin. Hmm. Still, his programs are good and he knows a great deal about the TRS-80.

Hardware

Hardware is the physical side of computing, the equipment and physical components. *Software* is the paperwork, the programs, even the idea involved in programming. The third element is *data,* operated on by software within hardware.

We've said this before but the dividing line starts to blur if you do not make a distinction between programs and media. So here's your starter for ten – is a programmed read-only memory software or hardware? The PROM is an IC chip, so it's hardware. In practice, it might be more useful to think of it as software. Some people have tried to call hardware-implementation programs 'middleware'.

The semantics are not really worth bothering about too much, so long as you know what *you* mean when you use the terms.

Hardware multiply/divide
Firmware routines execute more quickly than software, so some computers speed things by providing a special firmware option for multiplication and division.

Hard-wired
Not a very necessary or a very specific term, used merely to indicate some facility being provided in hardware rather than software.

Hash
Pre-digested version of dead Argentine cows, much beloved by Boy Scouts. It's also a sign – the hash mark – which Americans use a good deal as shorthand for 'number' (just as we use 'No.'). That connection means that the hash mark appears frequently on U.S.-derived keyboards and internal computer codes; the hash is printable, of course, and the code relating to the hash frequently has an inescapably important internal meaning.

Haywood Electronics
A British microcomputer manufacturer which probably merits more attention than it receives. Its computer features three of the near-standard elements of micros today – *Zilog* Z-80 processor, *CP/M* and *MP/M* operating systems, *S-100* bus. Prices from about £2,400.

HDLC
High-level Data Link Control. In sophisticated com-

puter networks, many different computers talk to each other and use each other's facilities. A communications *protocol* is a format to which inter-system messages must conform if all participants in the network are to understand them. HDLC is an example of a protocol. It is utilised by several computer manufacturers as their standard protocol.

HDX
Abbreviation for *half-duplex*.

Head
Or read/write head – that part of a disc or tape unit which reads or writes information from or to the surface of the media. Tape heads touch the tape; so do floppy disc heads. Other disc heads usually 'fly' above the surface of the disc – see below.

Head crash
Bad news. It's what happens when the read/write head in a disc drive hits the surface of the disc. Disc drive technology is such that a minute particle of dust might cause the head to bump on to the disc; at the very least you are likely to get duff data from the event, and the impact might damage the surface permanently.

Header
Also heading, leader, or preamble. The header is some control information preceding a message or a record, for instance in transmissions between computers or in tape files. The kind of information it gives might include source and/or destination codes, priority, message type, and so on.

Heath
Now called Zenith Data Systems, so far as its com-

puter activities go. The company is an established manufacturer of electronic equipment in kit form for the hobbyist; it has now added microcomputers and terminals, ready-built – as well as kits.

Hertz

Hertz is a measure of frequency and means 'cycles per second'. Electricity supply has frequency. Things which run from the electricity supply have to reflect its frequency, its Hertz rate; and in Europe the supply is at 50 Hertz, while in the States it is 60.

This is important, because it means that something designed to run off a U.S. power supply probably won't work here. Converting from 60 to 50 Hertz isn't too difficult, but this is one reason why you can't run an unmodified U.S. microcomputer in Britain.

Heuristic

Means that you rely on trial and error for your result, learning by experience. It sounds trivial, but it isn't. There is a methodology called heuristic programming and it is a trifle esoteric. The classic textbook on the subject is Slagle's 1974 opus *Artificial Intelligence – the heuristic programming approach.* Slagle describes 'a heuristic' as 'a rule of thumb, strategy method, or trick used to improve the efficiency of a system which tries to discover the solutions of complex problems'.

Hewlett-Packard

HP has a running battle with Data General for No. 2 spot in the minicomputer business – Digital Equipment is unassailably top dog, of course. DG ships more minis than HP, but HP minis are worth more, so HP may make more money.

In fact, they are in different (albeit related) markets.

The bulk of HP mini sales tend to be commercial systems accoutered with terminals, database managers, high-level languages and the like. DG does such systems but most of its shipments are of cheaper and less full-specified minis.

HP makes its own micros, using SOS – silicon-on-sapphire – technology rather than the MOS – metal-oxide-silicon – which everyone else has. HP micros are embedded in HP products, notably a line printer and the HP small business system. You can't buy HP micros like you can the LSI-11 or microNOVA.

You can, however, buy a number of personal computers from HP. One group is the HP-80 family, neatly-packaged desk-top computers with a compact integral display (some models have a small *thermal* printer built-in as well). They are aimed principally at scientific users; prices from £1,500.

The HP business microcomputer is the *CP/M*-based £3,400-plus HP-125. This uses the *Zilog* Z-80 processor (two of them, in fact) rather than one HP micro chip.

There are other important strings to the HP bow, of course. It is one of the leading manufacturers of programmable calculators and its product lines in this area extend up to the cost and complexity of its minis. HP is also big in instrumentation for hospitals and laboratories.

Hex

Abbreviation of hexadecimal. Since we shall not repeat it, read carefully. Hex is a number system to the base 16, just as decimal is to the base 10, binary to the base 2, and octal to the base 8.

Hex uses numbers 0 to 9 and letters A (for 10) to F (for 15). In this way a *byte* can be represented as only two digits, one for the first four bits and one for the second four. Hex is thus a succinct way of relating numbers to internal computer operations.

A practical example: the decimal number 183 can be represented in binary as 10110111 (which is a precise equivalent to what's going on inside, but it is somewhat clumsy). In hex it is B7 – B because the first four binary digits represent '11', if you like, and 7 because that's the hex notation for 0111 (which is also 7 in decimal).

High-level language
Optimistic name for a group of programming languages which try hard to be independent of any computer. A 'low-level language' is one specific to a particular computer. The lowness of the level refers to how closely the programming language matches the computer's internal machine code; a high-level language needs a good deal of translation and conversion before it can be expressed in machine code. A high-level language tends to use single powerful commands which initiate many machine code operations.

Machine-independence is something of a chimera, of course. Languages like Cobol, Fortran, APL and Basic are largely machine-independent, but the programmer who knows Basic on one computer will have to learn some new wrinkles before writing (or running) a program on another.

Highway
Alternative name for *bus.*

Histogram
A type of graph involving solid rectangles shooting up from a common base-line – as used in General Election reporting on TV.

Hitachi

This electrical and electronics giant vies with Fujitsu for the leadership of the Japanese computer industry. It hasn't had much to do with smallish computers but recently announced a business micro.

HLL

Abbrevation for *high-level language*.

Hobby computer

A computer not used for profit, though many companies with conventional computers would find it difficult to identify any profit from them. Computing as a hobby implies that you get your buzz from computing, rather than from applying the results of computing.

As it happens, this is true of most professional programmers – and so it's both their strength (they really *like* the job) and their weakness (they get very blinkered about it).

Hobbyist

One who practises a hobby, of course. It's an ugly word, but try and produce a better alternative. Anyhow, it's one of those words which if you repeat it for long enough takes on a life of its own.

Hollerith, Herman

The man who effectively specified the punched *card* as we know and detest it; at the time (1889) it was a great idea, though. Herman H was involved in statistical analysis of the U.S. census and immigrant information and evolved the idea of putting all the information on to cards with holes punched in appropriate places to denote specific information.

He then unveiled a machine called a tabulator which

detected whether or not a hole or a series of holes
occurs in particular positions; if that was the case it
added one to a counter. In fact, this proved to be the
only possible way to do the census economically.

So if you had a series of columns on a card which
denote respectively age groups, sex and marital status,
you could detect which of the alternatives in each
column a particular card represented, and you could
also sort particular combinations of age, sex and
marital status.

Hollerith died rich and the particular code used by
him, called the Hollerith code, is still the standard for
punched cards.

Home computer

You will not believe this, but a home computer is a
computer which can be used in the home. It sounds like
a silly name, but there is a useful distinction to be made
between home computers and office computers. An
office computer presupposes hard-copy output, for
instance, and it tends to be bulkier and more robust
than something you can load into the boot of your car
or move around from room to room. 'Home computer'
isn't exactly a technical definition, though.

Honeywell

One of the big American companies in mainframe
computers. Honeywell also has a process control
division which, among many other things, makes intelligent thermostats for domestic central heating.

In the early 1970s Honeywell had the chance to
become a major force in the mini business but it chose
to concentrate instead on its big computers. With the
Level 6 mini line launched in the late 1970s, it is once
again looking strong at the small end of things.

Honeywell doesn't seem very interested in micros

and really small computer systems. It is well into the use of micros for process control, though.

Housekeeping

This is a good analogous term. Housekeeping in a computer system covers all those internal activities which don't relate to solving problems or executing user programs but which contribute to the system's general capability for solving problems and executing programs. It's a little like dusting and sweeping-up at home; these operations don't have much specifically to do with what your house is for but they contribute to the 'operation' of the home.

There probably isn't an exact definition of what constitutes a housekeeping routine but we would include such activities as checking files for unused space and compacting everything if possible. For instance, you may have a name and address file with space for you to list 50 friends. If you have only two friends at the moment, you might as well reduce the file size and give yourself some more space on the disc or cassette. You can also forget that football fixtures program you've been writing.

HPIB

Hewlett-Packard Interface Bus. Essentially a plug-and-socket connection defining one way in which peripherals (typically laboratory instruments, in this case) communicate with a computer.

The HPIB was adopted more or less wholesale when the independent American Institution of Electrical and Electronic Engineers produced its own standard interface. That one is known as IEEE-488. Among other places, it's used by the *Pet;* the standard peripheral connector at the back of Pet is an IEEE-488 interface. Many people were irritated by this, because many

standard peripherals (especially printers) have an
RS232 interface but not IEEE-488. See *IEEE*.

Hybrid

There are three uses of this adjective or noun you
might meet, and all are rare. A *hybrid computer*
combines analogue and digital processing and is used
only in esoteric technical applications. A *hybrid circuit*
is an IC package which incorporates separate chips
inside.

A *hybrid disc* is a unit with a fixed disc and a
removable cartridge disc. The two are usually the same
capacity – 2.5 or 5 megabytes seems to be the norm –
and the idea is that new data or programs can be taken
to the computer on the cartridge and loaded into
memory and/or the fixed disc. The fast-access fixed
disc is then used for most of the processing work and
at the end of the day the cartridge takes a back-up copy
for security purposes. This set-up is sometimes called
a FEDS (fixed-plus-exchangeable disc store).

Not many people use hybrid computers, not many
need to know about hybrid circuits, and not many
would recognise the term 'hybrid disc'.

Hz

Abbreviation for *Hertz*.

IBG

Inter-block gap. See *block*.

IBM

International Business Machines Corp can astound
people with the amount of money it makes but it also
means that IBM can pay for some of the best R&D in
the computers and telecomms business.

It dates from 1911, when it was the much less

exciting Computing-Tabulating-Recording Corp and
its interests lay principally in punched card machines
deriving from *Hollerith* and his ideas. Big dates in its
history include 1914, which was when a brilliant ex-
NCR salesman, Thomas J. Watson, became president;
1935, when IBM produced the first commercially-suc-
cessful electric typewriter; 1958, with the first real
IBM computer; 1959, with the arrival of a pioneering
smallish business computer, the 1401; 1964, when it
launched the stunningly successful 360; and 1970,
when the 360 was updated to become the 370.

IBM is big enough to set *de facto* standards. It was
responsible for Fortran, PL/1, and APL among languages; it invented the golf-ball typewriter and many
of the basic functions in word processing. One of the
standard communications protocols, binary synchronous, is from IBM. In big computers, IBM is king.

IBM makes its own microprocessors by the ton and
builds them into many of its products, including the
Series/1 line of minicomputers, various devices like
printers and disc controllers, several of its special
terminal systems for banks and department stores, and
its low-end business computers.

It looks as if IBM will have a say in smaller computers now, too. The company's so-called 'Personal
Computer' is a microcomputer for very rich persons,
at the moment; it's a high-powered 16-bit micro (which
uses an Intel CPU rather than one from IBM) aimed at
business uses but also selling well to the better-heeled
hobby user.

The IBM Personal Computer is a reasonable
machine in its own right. It has some fine software; it
also incorporates some excellent principles of ergonomics, notably for its keyboard and the quality of
its display. The most important aspect of the Personal
Computer launch is simply that the IBM seal of ap-

proval will persuade more people (especially in business) to trust and to buy small computers; and it will also further encourage investors to put money into new microcomputer developments.

IC
Integrated circuit.

ICL
International Computers Ltd.

Idle time
The time when a computer is switched on and ready to go but is doing nothing; typically it is waiting for something else to happen.

IDPM
Institute of Data Processing Management, a British organisation of DP managers and others more or less concerned with the way computers are used in organisations.

IEE
Institution of Electrical Engineers, which has a micro group among its members and a home near London's Savoy Hotel.

IEEE
Institute of Electronic and Electrical Engineers. A U.S. body whose significant activities include the propagation of standards – like IEEE-488, which is the same as *HPIB*.

Like other interface standards (and there are several others) IEEE-488 defines what the wires in a particular plug-and-socket connection mean. In the mid-70s Commodore caused some eyebrow-raising when it produced a computer using the IEEE-488 layout for its standard interface. The Pet was an 'appliance' computer apparently aimed at a target market of enthusiastic hobbyists; IEEE-488 was a laborotory technicians' standard. Commodore has stayed with it, though, and IEEE is provided on the Vic, too, as the method of attaching standard Commodore devices like printers, disc drives, and a *modem*.

IEEE-488 is referred to by some people (notably Tektronix, which espoused it from the start) as GPIB – General Purpose Interface Bus. Anyway you cut it, it's basically the same interface specification as one Hewlett-Packard developed in the early 1970s and proposed to the IEEE for wholesale adoption. The HP version is still in use as the HPIB, Hewlett-Packard Interface Bus; it's almost the same as IEEE-488 but, as with all standards, some latitude is allowed in interpretation of the specification. That means you cannot assume automatically that all HPIB-compatible devices will plug straight into a Pet.

Anyhow, the aim of Hewlett-Packard was to design an interface which would be suitable for attaching laboratory instruments to computer controllers – not exactly the same kind of environment you would demand for the discs and cassettes and printers and such like that you might want to plug on to a general-purpose microcomputer.

As it happens, there is an alternative standard developed for precisely that kind of requirement in the form of *RS232C*. This isn't necessarily any better from a technical point of view than the IEEE/HP standard but it is widely-used by minis, mainframes and other micros. So there are a many off-the-shelf products, like printers, VDUs and other I/O devices, which use the RS232C connection as standard. That means there's a wide range of devices which plug straight into most other minis and micros.

It's clear that the choice of IEEE reflects the background of the Pet designers (fairly traditional electronic engineering, really; even they were applying their skills to exciting new gadgets like calculators and digital watches). It also mirrors the ready-made market which Commodore designers saw in providing themselves and people like them with a low-cost alternative to Hewlett-Packard equipment which has never been cheap, particularly when it has to be used on the relatively simple applications like data logging. Instrument control often doesn't need very sophisticated configurations; you can frequently manage with an 8K cassette Pet. So the Pet as a sub–$500 controller looks very attractive to engineers and technicians.

An unkind commentator might also argue that by forcing Pet users on to the IEEE standard Commodore effectively reduced the number of instantly-available add-on products and thus it removed most of the potential competition for its discs and printers. It's true that there are now at least 3,000 commercially-available IEEE-compatible devices which can attach more or less instantly; but almost all of them are laboratory instruments.

IF

A conditional statement in Basic and other languages. You always need a THEN (IF some condition is satisfied THEN something) and some versions of the language allow you an ELSE as well. See *GOTO*, too.

IF-THEN-ELSE

An extremely useful bunch of programming statements used in most high-level languages. If something is the case, then the program does whatever you've specified, otherwise it goes off to some other specified statement. IF you don't have Poulenc's *Stabat Mater,* THEN go out and buy it; ELSE try his *Concerto in G for organ, strings and timpani.*

IIL
Isoplanar Injection Logic, also wittily referred to by some as I²L. It's a way of making expensive high-performance *integrated circuits.*

Image scan
A generic term for devices which work on shapes – typically *input* devices which accept handwriting.

Immediate
An *address* mode in which the memory address to be referenced is contained explicitly in the instruction. This is why it is also called explicit addressing.

Impact printer
A printer with a mechanism which hits something to create a character. Typically a metal type-element bangs against an ink-coated ribbon on to paper. Examples are typewriters, teletypes, daisywheel printers, and most conventional matrix and line printers, though these days some high-speed line printers use non-impact techniques, like xerography and lasers.

Imsai
Pioneering U.S. microcomputer company which ceased to function in 1979.

Inclusive OR
A logical operation in which the result is 'true' if one

at least of the input values is true, and 'false' if the input values are all false. See *logic* and *truth table*.

Increment
Literally, to augment or increase – that's all. Sometimes it means 'add 1'. It also used freely for several internal operations but it still means to add something – usually to a particular *register* or memory location.

Index
There are a number of occasions in computing where you will find an index. Wherever it is used, the term means that something indirect is happening. That is analogous to a book index – to find a reference to 'aardvark' you could read every word in the book or you could go to that summary of key words at the back and be directed to the correct page number. The direct mode takes you straight to your aardvark without intervening stages; the index mode puts in an extra step or two but simplifies things.

Index hole
Read the piece about *hard-sectoring* in the Glossary. Hard-sectoring means that your floppy disc has a hole punched into it to indicate to the drive where the data starts. That hole is called the index hole.

Indexed addressing
A computer instruction which references an address can do so directly, which means that the memory location is stated in the instruction specifically – like 'store the contents of this variable in memory location starting at number 3,517'. The problem with that is two-fold; the way the computer handles instructions may not allow sufficient bits to contain large addresses

– which is why eight-bit micros typically cannot access more than 64KB of memory. In any case, direct addressing can be a little unsubtle – you have to know almost everything about the address before you can reference it.

Indirect addressing is the alternative, and indexing is one form of it – the computer calculates the desired address by adding the contents of an index register to what is called a 'displacement' value in the instruction. A special location, the index register, is set up; it points to a particular memory location and the displacement value in the instruction is added to that to produce the address you want.

The contents of the index register are usually called the base address, and obviously by modifying them – and/or setting-up more than one index register – you can set this to point to alternative memory locations.

To put it another way, it is not unlike sending a letter to 'The Brown House Next to the Pub on Noel Road'. Indirect addressing means that the memory location to which a particular instruction refers will not be included in that instruction. The computer will have to work it out by reference to other memory locations.

Indirect addressing thus means that the instruction references a memory location which contains the address of data rather than the data itself.

Indexed sequential

There are three widely-used ways of getting at data stored as records and files in a computer system. 'Sequential' mode means that your program starts at the first record and reads through the lot until it hits the one it is seeking. 'Direct access' or random mode means that you can get straight to the record you want without having to read anything else first, but the way you reference a particular record has to include a key from which the location of the record on backing store can be calculated.

Ordinary sequential access is simple and well-suited to cheap storage media like cassette, but it is slow. Random access is fast but it is complicated and if you have too many records the algorithmic calculation can be a bit silly.

The wonder solution fitting between them is indexed sequential access. Records are stored sequentially in some kind of logical order, just as with plain sequential mode, but the records can be accessed selectively, so that unwanted records can be skipped past quickly.

The point is that you use the filing system to set-up indices which point to the records, just as a book index points to the terms referenced. So your program goes to an index, looks for the location of the data it wants, and then goes directly to that location.

Indexed sequential file access is generally slower than random (or 'direct') mode and more complicated than sequential mode but it provides a reasonably fast way of reaching large amounts of data, and so it is practically a prerequisite in commercial systems, where a great deal of file accessing on many files is taking place.

Information

The straight definition says that information is any electrical signal or bit pattern with 'defined meaning'. The emphasis is on the word *meaning,* of course; the distinction between data and information is that data has no inherent meaning, while information is meaningful data.

As an example, take the number sequence 170179. This is data, but it is just a bunch of numbers. It becomes *information* when someone tells you it refers to 17 January, 1979.

Inhibit
To prevent something happening.

Initialise
To re-set a system to its starting condition – typically to set various parts of a program to starting values so that the program will behave in the same way each time it is repeated.

You also have to initialise newly-bought discs, which means to ensure that there are no sneaky bugs and flaws in them which will prevent them working satisfactorily on your computer. Most tapes and some discs are pre-initialised these days, though.

Ink-jet
An alternative to *daisywheel* printers as a printing technique which produces letter-quality output good enough for word processing. A.B. Dick, now a GEC subsidiary, invented ink-jet printing and still holds the patent; IBM is one of very few companies with a working ink-jet printer to sell, though it seems to have lost some enthusiasm for the idea. Other activists are a bunch of small independents in the States; and Siemens on this side of the water, which is pushing the technique as hard as anyone. The Japanese are also reported to be coming up strongly.

The technology involves charging particles of ink electrically and squirting them through an invisible electrostatic 'mask' which screens out all but the ink droplets which will make up the shape of one character.

It sounds complicated, messy and bulky; well, it is

complex – but it's compact, and the early problems of reliability and mess appear to have been overcome.

Siemens appears to have helped the price of ink-jet printing to fall to a reasonable level but its ink-jet mechanism looks more like dot-matrix than typewriter-style printing. For letter-quality ink-jet output, the technique is still reasonably expensive and that alone prevents such printers competing with daisywheels, even when the print quality is as good or better.

Input/output
What happens when a computer communicates with the outside world – the transfer of data between a *processor* and *periphals.*

Two means of I/O are available – programmed and automatic. For programmed I/O, all information is passed, as a result of executing programmed instructions. For control, information is passed to a controller for a particular device, like the screen, keyboard, or cassette unit.

That information will specify the mode of operation, the memory area involved in the transfer, and the amount of data to be passed. Once the transfer operation begins, it needs no further intervention by the program; completion of a data transfer often causes the device controller to signal that the device is available for another transfer.

Fast devices, such as discs, usually require automatic block I/O. Slower devices can operate under either regime. Since hardware controllers for block I/O are relatively expensive, the control information for automatic transfers can be put into special memory locations associated with one or more data channels, or it may reside in the device controllers.

Inquiry

Or, more often, *en*quiry. Either way it means accessing information stored by the computer. In practice, the term applies particularly to *ad hoc* inquiries, which means getting information as and when required. Typically this will involve some keying-in at a VDU; the alternative is premeditated, formally-structured, prewritten reporting functions.

Inquiry is a helpful concept because it allows your system to look interactive. File inquiries do not alter anything, unlike file updates, so you can have a *batch* computer system – with all alterations and amendments done in batch mode – with interactive inquiries without it being a 'true' on-line system.

Truth tends to reside in the eye of the beholder. In our view, however, an on-line system is one in which a file update is entered and processed immediately. That's also called *transaction processing*.

Instruction

Tells the computer what to do, so it's an apposite term. More explicitly, an instruction is a single program step; a program is composed of a number of instructions.

One instruction may not correspond to a single basic computer operation and indeed it probably will not. This is because a high-level language instruction by its very nature is executed or implemented by several internal operations. On the other hand, a low-level language like an *assembler* will have instructions which correspond closely to computer operations. The operations available on a particular computer are called collectively the 'instruction set' or 'instruction repertoire'.

Integer

A whole number. Well, there's nothing wrong with

short definitions, is there?

Integrated circuit

An electronic circuit formed on a single chip of semiconductor material. Frankly we do not intend to become involved in a heavy discussion on electronics, so you cannot expect a definition of a circuit or a discussion of the properties of semiconductor materials. The chip in question is usually fabricated chemically from silicon (clever version of rock) and the resultant IC is characterised generally by very small size, very low cost, very little heat dissipation, and comparatively simple electrical requirements. Computer manufacturers buy ICs in bulk; there are only a few manufacturers and they deal in extremely large production volumes.

It is an interesting sidelight on the economics of IC manufacture that something more than 80 percent of normal production comprises unserviceable chips, which are thrown away because it is not worth repairing them.

The big semiconductor houses include Intel, Fairchild, Motorola, Texas Instruments and IBM. Apart from IBM, all make ICs for other manufacturers as standard catalogue products; they will include memory and CPU chips. They also become their own customers; all of them assemble computers and all will shop from each other for standard components, if necessary.

Intel

Intel is a contraction of INTegrated ELectronics. It started only in 1969, produced the world's first microcomputer, and now is one of the market leaders in semiconductor components.

Intel founders used to work for Fairchild. The

pioneering Intel 4004 (circa 1971) was the first micro, a four-bit device. Intel also had the world's first eight-bit micro. Apart from micros and microcomputer components, Intel's other main product line is semiconductor memories and in 1981 it shipped 200 billion bits' worth of memory.

On the micro side, Intel has about 175 products. The principal ones are the 16-bit 8086; the trusty 8080A, current version of the eight-bit processor-only chip, and the faster 8085; and the 8048 family, which gives you memory on the processor chip.

Interesting goodies in Intel's future include the takeover of a Texas software house, MRI. This has a well-known *database manager* called System 2000 which runs on big IBM computers. Intel apparently bought MRI because it intends to develop a micro-based box containing the database manager; that would plug into the IBM mainframe and allow the user to operate a database system without all the overheads of a software database manager.

Intellec

Brand name for the Intel line of development systems. They comprise appropriate hardware and software to allow you to develop programs which will run on the relevant Intel micro. Like all development systems, the Intellec line is intended for people who build micros into other systems, which means that in operation use of the processor will be invisible and unalterable, probably with a program stored irretrievably in read-only memory.

A development process employing a system like one of the Intellec line is used to get the operational aspects of that system to perfection before it becomes buried inaccessibly inside a weighing machine, a pocket calculator, or whatever.

Intelligence

Applied to computers or any mechanised or automated object, it normally means programmability – the ability to perform alternative courses of action on the basis of an internally-stored and theoretically-alterable set of rules.

Intellvision

The video games system from *Mattel*. It has marvellous graphics, good colour and excellent controls. A keyboard and a plug-in ROM *cartridge* for the *Basic* language have been promised for some time to turn the thing into a real home computer.

Interface

A word much-loved by the jargon writers, an interface is the boundary between two systems – and within that it can be practically anything from an airy concept to a piece of very solid hardware.

On the one hand it is possible, and even sometimes helpful, to think of the man-machine interface as residing somewhere in the brain of the human who perceives what is happening and who decides to interact with the machines.

On the other hand, it is generally more useful to think of an interface as a plug, a socket, or a cable; or all three.

The interface between a cassette player and a microcomputer is the connection between them, the connection which passes information or data from one to the other.

Programs can have interfaces, too, which is where the 'logical' bit occurs; they aren't solid, physical interfaces, but those parts of a program which can pass information or data to other programs; and so on.

The crucial aspect of interfaces is that they should

be well-defined, wherever or whatever they are, so that both sides of the connection should know what to expect, and so that information can be passed satisfactorily from one to the other.

Take the CCITT V24 standard, also known as the EIA *RS232C* specification. This is a well-accepted standard for connecting things physically; mostly it defines which wires go to which pins in a plug-and-socket connection, and effectively that defines the shape of the plug.

It is widely-used and most terminals and printers offer a V24 connection; even so, there is plenty of room for variety and many terminals require you to juggle the wires somewhat before the plug is satisfactorily into the socket.

Interleave
This has two alternative connotations, neither of which applies only to microcomputers. It can refer to memory, in which case it means dividing memory into two parts with separate data paths to the processor; this can sometimes speed throughput.

Alternatively, interleaving refers to some clever juggling with the execution of programs which definitely speeds throughput; parts of one program can be inserted into another so that the two can be executed more or less simultaneously. The system does this automatically.

Internal storage
Same as *memory*.

International Business Machines
See *IBM*.

International Computers Ltd

The British answer to IBM was something of a shotgun marriage in the late 1960s, tacking together some of the more active indigenous computer makers of the time; and a curious mixture they were, too. The Government of the day provided paternity, midwifery and intensive care in an attempt to get at least a little warmth from the white heat of the technological revolution.

Inevitably the strains of the mix showed from the start, notably with a proliferation of different managements doing similar things on their separate and virtually incompatible lines of product development. Empires were established, boundaries were guarded jealously, and the whole edifice was under-pinned by a policy of 'preferential tendering', which meant that ICL automatically got just about any British public-sector business available.

Those product programmes emphasised large computers to the almost total exclusion of any interest at all in small systems, largely because the empire-builders were from that kind of background. So the minicomputer revolution of the early 1970s and then the micro boom towards the end of the decade largely passed ICL by on the other side (though ICL made a nod towards the less-than- £50,000 world by buying the minicomputer side of Singer, basically an odd but strangely likable machine called the System Ten which ICL proceeded to leave to its own devices).

It couldn't last for ever. The company suddenly registered a loss and its shares, which once were flying high, at more than 350 pence – plummeted to 25 pence. The pressure resulted from high interest rates, EEC policies about protectionist favours for national companies, a sudden awareness that ICL was missing-out on many of the key technological developments of the day (micros, word processing) and a dawning appreciation that the company was top-heavy with management and with people generally. Thrusting young new-broom executives were drafted-in at the top with the promise of a free hand to make improvements.

And lo! Things are picking up. A degree of what business likes to call 'rationalisation' has made ICL a much tighter, better-organised firm. Instead of the 'not invented here' syndrome, which meant using only in-house development and spending 10 years on R&D for every single product, ICL is now prepared to buy things like everyone else, from bits and pieces to put into its existing products to more or less complete systems to re-sell with ICL software and an ICL badge on the front.

That has been exhibited enthusiastically in the ICL deal with a Japanese firm to sell its big IBM-compatible computers. *Japanese?* It would never have been heard of previously but the Japanese make excellent computers of this size and they do so at a good price. And *IBM-compatible?* That, too, wouldn't have been contemplated previously but it's a good, strong market.

The other new product of some significance was bought from a British microcomputer company. It is the Black Box from *Rair,* a smallish system for business and scientific use; for the first time it gives ICL a competitive product in a burgeoning market.

Confusingly, ICL calls it the ICL Personal Computer (meaning 'one computer per user', rather than a friendly machine for the a average person) but it makes an interesting contrast to the IBM Personal Computer.

All in all, it looks as if ICL is going places again. Management is making some good moves, anyhow, and I wish I'd bought more of those 25 pence shares.

Interpreter

Software which translates a program in a high-level language into machine code – the binary instructions which correspond directly to computer operations.

A *compiler* also does this but with a compiler you have to put your program through it (compiling) to obtain what is called an *object-code* program in machine code. You then run the object code.

With an interpreter, each statement in the high-level language program is translated and executed immediately. This means you can add or delete instructions and see the effect immediately, so it speeds the process of getting a program into its final state.

Interpreters might take-up some memory, since they have to be waiting to translate; and interpreted programs are certainly slower when it comes to run-time, because a program already in machine code is inevitably much more efficient.

Because interpreter languages do not require the compile process they are generally preferred for personal computers – they are simple and humane to use. Apart from Basic, you will find APL frequently in interpreter form.

You won't find many interpreters, however, for Cobol or Fortran. Those well-developed languages are very rich in user facilities and powerful commands; an in-memory interpreter capable of translating each possible statement as it is input would be gigantic. It would occupy too much memory and the translation would be burdensomely slow.

Interrupt

What happens when something causes the temporary suspension of activities inside the computer. Usually control is passed to an 'interrupt handler' or 'interrupt service routine' which is part of the operating system.

That decides what caused the interrupt, what is going on and what should happen. When the interrupt has been handled, the original processor status is restored – all the relevant parameters having been stored as part of the interrupt handling – and the previously-executing program may be allowed to continue from the point at which it was interrupted.

The interrupt signal is typically from an I/O device, like the keyboard demanding the processor's attention when you type something.

Interrupt handling can be a very powerful tool for doing many useful things in fairly complex applications. Looking after interrupts on a personal computer tends to be totally transparent to the user, for whom this information will be of academic interest only. If you are prepared to grub around in the innards of the operating system you might find the interrupt vectors, which are the memory locations at which the interrupt handlers start.

So you might be able to force your own interrupts, even if the manual does not exactly tell you how. You might set-up 'traps' related to a real-time clock, for example, to take snapshots of the system status during execution.

The other buzzphrase you might encounter on the interrupt front is 'interrupt priority'. It establishes a hierarchy of importance for attention-getting signals and allows the operating system to decide which to look at first. On a personal computer the number and variety of interrupts you might have are comparatively limited, so the operating system decides which interrupting device should be handled first.

More complicated systems use *microcoded* or *hardwired* priority systems, either pre-set – so that some types of interrupt always receive top priority – or alterable in some applications (in which case the relative importance of peripherals will vary from program to program).

I/O
Conventional abbreviation for *input/output*. An I/O port is a plug-and-socket connection for a *peripheral* device.

IS
Conventional abbreviation for *indexed sequential*.

Iverson, Ken
A genial man who was largely responsible for the programming language *APL.* Almost his whole family now work on APL for a Canadian computer services company, I P Sharp Associates.

Jacquard
Joseph Marie Jacquard rather capitalised on the unsung ideas of a man called Falcon when, at the end of the 18th century, he devised a loom controlled by wooden punched cards – and the Jacquard loom made it into the history books (at least the history books concerned with knitting and computers) while Falcon remains in the ornithology section. *Babbage* adopted and adapted the card idea.

More up-to-date, there is a U.S.-owned company named Jacquard which makes small business computers and word processors. It was acquired recently by a group called Applied Technology Ventures, though, so the name 'Jacquard' might soon disappear.

JCL
Job Control Language.

Job

Loosely (and frequently) used for any data processing activity. More specifically, it's one or more programs and related data which solve a particular problem.

Job Control Language

A collection of commands provided with big computers which enables the *operator* (or more likely a specially-trained programmer) to set up the system for a particular processing run.

Joystick

A normally vertical lever which can be tilted in any direction. When provided on a computer system, it usually moves the cursor around the screen.

Jump

A program instruction which switches processing to some other part of the program – so it results in a change of sequence. The next instruction to be executed is the one at the address specified by the jump. Typically, a jump is conditional; branching will occur only if the specified condition occurs. Otherwise, sequential execution will process.

See *GOTO,* too.

K

Symbol for 1,024 – but then it also means 'kilo', the prefix for 1,000. Basically, when referring to storage capacity K means 1,024 (that happens to be a binary number, too); so 'a 4K chip' is a memory module containing 4,096 bits. It is loosely used to mean '1,000', though.

Mind you, things aren't necessarily so simple. Computer people use 'K' without saying what it's one thousand of. There's a deal of difference between 4Kb

(4,096 bits), 4KB (4,096 bytes – or 32,768 bits) and 4KW (4,096 words – which if they're 16 bits in length means 65,536 bits).

Kb
Kilobits – and 4Kb is 4,096 bits.

KB
Kilobytes – so 1KB is 1,024 *bytes,* more or less equivalent to 1,000 characters in most small computers.

KW
Kilowords, which aren't necessarily the same as *kilobytes.* 32KW means 32,000 words (literally 32,768, in fact) but if the computer in question has a 16-bit word, 32KW equates to 64KW.

Kansas City
One of the standard formats for cassette tapes attached to computers. It is relatively slow (data moves to and from tape at only 30 characters per second) because the designers wanted to avoid over-straining the capabilities of cheap audio cassette decks.

Kemeny, John
With Tom *Kurtz* he invented Basic.

Key
A retrieval code contained within a record – for example, surnames are the key field for entries in a telephone directory; employee number is typically the key in personnel records.

Key in
To use a keyboard.

Keyboard

Input device normally containing alphanumeric keys in typewriter-style layout plus some *control* keys. A separate numerics-only keypad is a useful extra on the keyboard if you usually have a great deal of numeric data to include, for instance in business computing.

The keyboard usually shares an *I/O port* with the printer device or VDU with which it comes.

Keypunch

Device for punching holes in *cards*.

Keystroke

Happens each time a key on a keyboard is depressed. A count or estimate of keystrokes is often used to determine how long a function will take, or to price *data entry* services.

Key-to-disc

A *data entry* technique. Data is keyed on to disc at a small computer, where it is checked for accuracy; it is then transmitted or taken to a larger computer for *batch* processing.

Keyword

Characteristic word in a file used to retrieve its contents by meaning.

Kilobaud

One thousand bits per second. Also the name of a successful and amiably idiosyncratic U.S. microcomputing magazine.

KIM

A single-board microcomputer which was made by *MOS Technology*.

Kludge
Temporary patch or trick to correct an error or fault. Lovely word, isn't it?

KSR
Keyboard Send/Receive – a terminal with a keyboard and a printer or screen. Compare *ASR*.

Kurtz, Thomas
Thomas Kurtz invented Basic with John Kemeny at Dartmouth College, Massachusetts, in the early 1970s.

Label
Like the literal definition, it's a descriptive identifier. Typically a label is a group of characters used to identify a file, a message, or a record; very specifically the term also denotes an instruction in a program.

Some programming languages allow you to reference a label rather than an absolute address or a particular line number; so instead of a branch instruction like GOTO 40, where 40 is a line number, you might be allowed to say GOTO SUB-ROUTINE 'B'.

Language
This one's tricky; Wittgenstein and Chomsky had great difficulty in finding a universal definition, so how can I hope to compete? Still, it is obvious that the essential element is communication; and in computing, a programming language is a code – or a defined set of symbols or a notation or a systematic means of communication – whereby humans can communicate with computers.

The analogy with human languages is very good. There is no point in using Swahili to a Pathan if the

Indian doesn't know the language. Speaking in Swahili to someone who knows that language is a good method to impart information. In fact, the only simple way for two people to pass information is by agreeing, probably implicitly, on what a set of written squiggles or spoken grunts means.

So it is with computers. Basic and Cobol and the rest are alternative ways of expressing information; if you and the computer both 'know' one of them you can write a program which will run on that computer.

With a definition like this, it should be said that languages are in several varieties. Very broadly, there are three – machine code, assemblers and high-level languages. All are being defined as we go, but briefly *machine code* relates directly to how the computer processes instructions; so normally it consists of a binary code, a string of 0s and 1s, which will be meaningless to anyone who doesn't know this is a code the computer can understand.

Assembler is one step up, coding the binary instructions into more or less meaningful alphanumeric symbols. But it's still related directly to the way a particular computer operates.

High-level languages are distanced one step further from the insides of the processor; the instructions usually bear some resemblance to English but, more important, the high-level language can, in theory, run on more than one computer, In practice, for each computer there's a different translator which converts the high-level language into machine code.

Latency

It is just possible you might meet this word. It refers to a delay or a waiting state in the middle of some operation. You might encounter it among the fine print of a floppy disc manual – it's the delay while the

read/write head is moving, plus the time the disc takes
to rotate to the required data position. In other words,
nothing happens during latency, but something is about
to happen.

LCD

Liquid crystal display. Some crystals are liquid and
some liquid crystals light-up if you tickle them with a
burst of electricity. LCDs are used in pocket calculators and digital watches, normally as an alternative
to LED displays. The technology probably isn't a
serious contender when a great deal of information has
to be displayed quickly; you can't beat the *CRT*
(cathode ray tube) for that; but stand by for really large
LCD screens from various sources.

Leased line

If you want to link your computer to another some
distance away, there are realistically two ways of doing
it – a cheap way and an expensive way. The cheap way
is via the ordinary dialled telephone system. You'll
need a *modem* or an *acoustic coupler* but you'll pay
only the normal dial rates.

   You will be competing with crossed lines and other
interference, though, so if you know where the recipient of your transmission is, and if you need a high-quality transmission signal and if you have the extra
money, you might lease your own private telephone
line to do the job. You will still need modems – more
of that later.

LED

Light-emitting diode. Most digital read-outs on laboratory instruments, calculators and watches use LED
displays. A diode is a simple electron tube which lights
when you pass electricity through it, so where you

need a simple display LED displays are the natural choice.

LEO
Lyons Electronic Office, an optimistically impressive name for an early business computer – probably the very first business computer, in fact. The teashop company was amazingly far-sighted for the times (early 1950s); everyone else thought computers were for counting heads or calculating shell trajectories.

Leibniz, Goffried Wilhelm von
Gottfried Wilhelm von Leibniz was one of those 17th-century polymaths you usually see wearing an unlikely curly wig and looking coolly benign. Leibniz was reported to be a cheery soul who dabbled with law, logic, religion, politics, diplomacy, philosophy, history, librarianship, inventions and mathematics. He has a place here because, around 1694, he invented a mechanically unreliable and economically unmarketable calculator. *Pascal* had already built one to add and subtract; the Leibniz version could multiply and divide, too. Since it didn't work he moved to other things, notably letter-writing – there are at least 15,000 of his letters around – and philosophy.

Library
A collection of *subroutines* to insert in programs or data files.

Life
One of the classic microcomputer games, a kind of 'patience' expounded originally by John Conway of Cambridge University in 1970. It's a cell automaton; you set up a couple of 'cells', and thereafter they reproduce automatically or die, according to some

simple rules. The result can be fascinating and, if nothing else, it illustrates the fact that at the very roots of life you find the same principles which apply throughout science.

Lifeboat Associates
Pioneering software publisher, started in a basement in New York in 1977 and now a $10 million company which commissions products and writes some of its own, as well as inviting submissions from outside. At present Lifeboat is supporting something around 100 packages which run on computers from at least 50 manufacturers.

Light pen
A photo-electric device which can detect the presence of light at a particular point on a CRT display screen. It looks like a pen but it's connected by cable to a controller. You point it at the place on the screen you want to reference; the controller detects where you are. Depending on the programming, the computer could then modify the display or perhaps accept something as input data.

Incidentally, if you want to try building your own, obtain the February, 1978 issue of *Byte* magazine – an article there tells you how to do it for $4.

Line
It's a connection, usually a cable, between one part of the system and another – like screen and keyboard – or one computer and another. See *line speed*.

Line feed
The command which moves the paper in a printer up by one line; on a display screen the effect is to move the cursor on to the next line.

Line number

Some programming languages – notably Fortran and Basic – require you to assign a particular line number at the start of each instruction line in a program. The program is then executed in numerical sequence – unless you have inserted a *JUMP* command.

Line speed

This is about the only time you'll use the word 'line' in the communications context. Line speed is the data rate, which means the maximum rate at which data can reliably be sent down a line.

Linear programming

Some programming techniques are mathematical; they utilise equations, follow mathematical logic, and essentially calculate things. Linear programming is a branch of this esoterica, much used in 'what if' problems – like routeing vehicles to optimise fuel consumption, economic planning to balance all the variables, and so on.

Line printer

A line printer is a printer which prints one line at a time. It contrasts with a *serial* printer, which prints one character at a time. Line printers are generally faster and more complicated, so they tend to be more expensive.

There are three basic printer technologies in use, and they correspond more or less to the output load. Smaller systems will use a *matrix printer,* with characters formed by dots in a matrix; most of these are serial printers but some print a line at a time.

More output will justify the extra cost of *chain, train, drum* or *belt printers;* these all have fully-formed characters to give a solid impression on the paper and they print one line at a time. The fastest is 3,000 lpm, the bottom figure is around 300; many people buy 600 lpm printers, bigger users will go for 1,200 to 1,500 lpm.

Really big users will buy one of the newer laser-based or electrostatic *page printers*. They print a page at a time and there's little or no variation if the page is full or blank. A reasonable average throughput in lines per minute would be in the range 16,000 to 30,000.

LISP
Programming language which belongs to the intellectually-refined reaches of programming – essentially it's specially designed for *list processing*, which makes it somewhat esoteric. Lisp is used typically by scientists and academics on largish computers. Lisp is considered to be one of the pioneering computer languages for developing *artificial intelligence*.

List processing
List processing is processing data in the form of lists – that's all.

LLL
Occasionally-found abbreviation for *low-level language*.

Load
To transfer something from memory to backing store, or vice versa. You load a program from cassette or disc into the memory when you read it in.

Two other loads are of some importance. One is the obvious physical action of placing a cassette or floppy disc or paper in the appropriate device. The other usage refers to internal operations of moving around data – your programming language may well allow you to load specific locations with specified data, especially if it's an assembler.

Loader

A program designed specifically to assist in loading other programs from backing store. Compare *bootstrap*.

Local (variable)

A variable with restricted access – see *global*.

Local area networks

Or just 'local network'. This is one of the most popular terms in computing at the moment and as it happens it's one which lends itself to bafflingly abstruse definitions. In practical terms, though, the word 'network' implies an arrangement where several users can plug their own individual computers into some kind of connecting link. That means they can exchange information, use the same common files, and share peripherals like discs and printers which might be too expensive for a single user.

You can do that if you have several users attached to a single computer, of course, but the network solution means no significant hiccups in performance (a single computer operates more slowly if everyone wants to do something at the same time); and if one computer breaks down, it shouldn't stop everyone else's work.

Ethernet and *Econet* are two examples of a local network, the 'local' implying that there's a geographical restriction – local networks are generally confined to a single building. Technical restrictions start to apply if you want to spread the network much further afield, particularly if you want to utilise the telephone system (which is a network of a non-local nature, of course). Ordinary telephone lines can't carry data at anything like the speed of a simple cable running around your building.

That connection, incidentally, is likely to be one of *co-axial, twisted pair* or *fibre optic* cable.

Location
Loosely, it's a synonym for *address.* More precisely, it means the same as *absolute address,* a particular storage area in memory.

Log
A record of what the computer's been doing, either written by hand or produced automatically by the system.

Log on
Or log in. A set of procedures whereby a terminal user gains access to a computer – it usually involves giving a password. At the end of the session you have to log off (or out) to tell the system your terminal is no longer in use.

Logic
Computers are fast idiot rule-followers because they are electronic and logical. In rarefied terms, logic is the formal and systematised inter-connection of discrete components. The emphasis is on the inter-connection – logic relates things together – and on the formal portion – logic doesn't necessarily have any relationship to physical matters like a hardware organisation.

In practice, and in microcomputers, logic means the circuitry which performs logical functions, and since much micro circuitry does this, the term 'logic' is applied loosely to any of its circuitry.

You might meet the phrase 'hard-wired logic'; these are logic circuits for specific purposes, formed by interconnecting ICs in a non-alterable, non-programmable form. Usually this involves solder or printed circuit boards.

Logical operators

See *truth table*. Logic functions are shown usually in a truth table, which indicates exactly what will happen (as 'output' from the logical operation) according to alternative 'input' conditions. The principal logical operators are AND, OR and NOT; others you might see are NAND, NOR, EXCLUSIVE and INCLUSIVE OR.

Logo

A programming language developed originally by MIT. According to its inventor, a genuine genius called Seymour Papert, "Logo is the name of a philosohpy of education" as well as merely a computer language; that's because it was intended to facilitate 'discovery learning' for children – rather than following instructions presented by the computer, the child *teaches* the computer.

Logo includes several concepts which make it akin to *artificial intelligence* languages. It also features English-language commands, the ability for users to define their own procedures and commands to add to the language, and many graphics commands. It's great.

It's also the standard language for controlling a *turtle*. So its commands include simple, obvious statements like FORWARD and RIGHT 30 (which means turn 30 degrees to the right), REPEAT and SET-SPEED. It doesn't have to be a turtle drawing lines which is moved; you can run through the same program on a graphics display screen.

At last count, Logo was available for the *Apple* II and *Texas Instruments* TI 99/4 micros.

Loop

The ability within a program to return to a statement which has already been executed and do it again. So a loop is a group of instructions in a program which may be executed more than once before the program continues. The loop includes one instruction which increments some kind of counter and another which checks the counter to see if it's reached a specified exit number. All this is the same as *iterate*.

This isn't explained too easily in a Glossary entry but take it from me, it's a useful and indeed powerful little facility.

Low-level language

A programming *language* which is very close to *machine code;* usually the term is synonymous with *assembler.*

LSI

Large-scale integration. *See integration.* All micros use LSI, a loosely-defined term meaning electronic circuitry with a large number of logical operations per component.

The name is also used by a company called Computer Automation for one of its minicomputer families; and *Digital Equipment Corp* employs it as a prefix for its microcomputer boards, as in LSI-11 and LSI-11/23.

LSI Computers

British manufacturer of *CP/M*-based microcomputers

for business use.

Lucas Logic
The Lucas electrical group set up to run *Nascom* when it bought the ailing microcomputer maker.

Machine
Another all-purpose jargon word for processor, computer or system.

Machine code
A programming language which identifies and alters the contents of memory locations by instructions encoded in a form which relates directly to the internal operation of a computer – the binary notation, which makes machine code programs an arcade of 0s and 1s.

The binary code the computer uses is the lowest possible level of programming. All other computer languages have to be translated into machine code before programs written in them can be executed. Machine code is sometimes called machine language.

Macro
Or macro instruction, or macroinstruction. One macro equals several instructions; it's a kind of shorthand by which the computer recognises the macro and generates several operating instructions for it.

All this is relevant more to big computers, since micro-sized machines don't really need macros much. Or at least, the term isn't used much – the concept might be, though.

Instead of writing the same sequence of instructions every time they are needed in a program, you give the patch of code lines a name.

Magic Wand

A *word processor* package for *CP/M* systems, second only in popularity to *Wordstar;* it offers extra facilities without costing any more.

Magnetic tape

A long strip of plastic, usually mylar or acetate, which is coated with a magnetisable oxide material.

Those spools you see whizzing round are normally 2,400ft. long and the tape is 0.5in. wide; some mainframe manufacturers opt for different widths. The length is not critical, so some tapes are 1,200ft. long, others top 3,600ft. More familiar to the personal computer world are cassettes, typically ¼in. wide and easier to handle. They don't store so much information and data cannot be read from or written to them as quickly.

Data is stored on tape by magnetising an invisible row of spots across the tape. Depending on which possible spot positions you magnetise, the computer is able to pick up and translate a line of spots as a particular character.

Magnetic tape is cheap and well-understood these days, not least because all manufacturers are used to making tape for audio recording. The tape is much the same, and ordinary audio cassettes can be used on personal computers. On the big reels, the data tape has to be made to a much finer specification to guarantee maximum discrimination and maximum strength, because these spools are pulled around somewhat enthusiastically by the tape drive.

The only real disadvantages are transfer speed and the serial access. With disc you have random access to information; you don't have to read everything on the disc to see that it's the information you seek. With tape you have to move the read/write head over the tape –

or the tape past the head – until you find the place you want.

That reduces speed, of course, and some applications become impossible – like interactive queries on files – because they would take too long.

Another problem can arise. How do you add information in the middle of a sequential stretch of records on tape? You can add it to the end but that way it is out of sequence. What you have to do is read the entire tape file into memory, insert your amendments – easy enough in the fast random-access world of semiconductor RAM – and then write it out to tape again as a new Master File.

Discs are fast enough to permit a degree of automation of this process in the disc operating system. Because they operate on non-sequential lines, the physical location on disc of the amendment is not necessarily relevant – it can somehow be linked or keyed to the correct reference. That capacity varies from one operating system to another.

The problems with tape become heavy only when speed of access is the main criterion. So for the starter personal computer system, cassettes are a good, cheap, easy way of providing back-up storage; that is called archiving – taking a copy regularly of your data just to forestall any disastrous disc crashes.

Mail-merge

A really useful *word processing* facility; it's the ability to create many individualised letters by merging the text of a standard letter with a file of variable information like names, addresses, and so on. The standard letter contains marker points of some kind at which the variable information is inserted automatically.

Mainframe
Basically a big computer.

Map
A memory map is a diagram of memory showing which particular routines take up which particular memory locations.

There are other kinds of map in computing but this one is most important. It allows what's called 'memory-mapped I/O' which means you can address an I/O device by an address in memory. At that address the processor will find the start of a code routine which handles data transfers to and from the device. The technique is often easier and neater than addressing an I/O channel or port.

Map
Microprocessor Applications Project, a Government-funded scheme to publicise the subject of micros. If you run a business, or if you have computer microprocessor-related services to sell, there are many ways you can benefit from different portions of MAP, including money and information.

It includes MAPCON, the Microprocessor Awareness Project Consultancy, a Government scheme to fund the development of many small consultancies. It tries to promote the spread of micros in industry by contributing some of the cost of consultants' feasibility evaluations.

MARS
A *spreadsheet* calculator program for microcomputers with the *CP/M* operating system.

Mask
There are two available definitions, neither of which is

particularly relevant here. In the semiconductor chip manufacturing process, a mask is used to define the areas of the chip. In processing, a mask is part of a logical operation; it's a pre-set pattern of bits you can compare to another bit pattern.

Master
The word is used freely as a prefix to mean either 'control' or 'most up-to-date'. A master file is the most accurate, most current version; a master/slave system is one in which a particular system component (the slave) cannot function without control signals from another (the master).

Mattel
The U.S. company responsible for the *Intellvision* video game 'computer' (it also makes Barbie dolls).

Matrix
Same as *array*. Mathematicians won't need this definition and non-mathematicians won't understand it – but here goes. A matrix is a rectangular arrangement of numbers in rows and columns, organised in such a way that certain specific mathematical operations can be applied to them.

A matrix really is a bunch of numbers on which you can perform matrix arithmetic. Most Basic include Matrix statements; and if the manual for yours is not clear enough about what they are and why you'd use them, try David Lien's *Basic Handbook*.

Matrix printer
A matrix is a grid of rows and columns. Well, translate that into a rectangular array of needles – say 63 of them, seven rows of nine. If you push a needle forward so that it thumps against a typewriter ribbon and bangs

it on to white paper, you'll have a dot printed. By firing forward the proper combination of needles you'll have a dot pattern which resembles an alphanumeric character.

The needles move backwards and forwards in 'barrels' rather like those of a gun; but this impact printing is not the only use for matrix techniques. Put a heating element in the barrel and use heat-sensitive paper and you have thermal printing, which causes a kind of scorched dot on the paper. The other popular matrix print method is electrostatic; firing a minute electrical charge at special paper changes the nature of its coating so that a dot is created there.

MBASIC

There are two versions of the *Basic* programming language widely-available on microcomputers, this one and the version called *CBasic*. Their pros and cons are discussed at length under the entry for CBasic. Briefly, MBasic is an *interpreter* (which means it is quicker and simpler to write programs) while CBasic is a *compiler* (and compiled programs generally operate faster and occupy less memory to do an equivalent job).

MBasic hails from a company called Microsoft, which has provided variants of it for almost every major micro maker; often it is provided at no extra cost when you buy a small computer. It's sometimes called Basic-80.

Medium

Apart from the usual meaning of 'in the middle', the term is usually employed in computing (along with its plural, 'media') for the material on which data and programs are stored. So examples are tape, disc, punched cards, paper tape, and so on.

Mega
Ugly prefix meaning million. A megabit (abbreviated Mb) is one million bits.

Memorite
The *word processor* available with computers from *Vector Graphic*. Though more expensive than some other *CP/M* word processors, it is easy to use and includes some good built-in facilities like a spelling checker.

Memory-mapped
Memory mapping is a technique available with some computers whereby each possible screen location – each possible dot of light on the screen – can be addressed and turned on or off separately. That's done by setting aside an area of memory which is equivalent to the dot posititions of the screen, so that you (and the computer) always know exactly what's on the screen at any time.

The alternative is to read on to the screen all the items of information you need there, irrespective of where they are located in the computer memory. In fact, that is probably simpler for computer designers to implement but there are several very clever consequences of doing it the other way.

One is that you can move the cursor around the screen to re-read something which is already there; so editing a program line is simple, because you can move back through a listing and change the offending character without having to re-type the whole line.

The other effect is greatly-simplified high-resolution graphics; when you can tell each point on the screen to switch on or off, you can control very precisely what's happening.

Memory

We use 'memory' to mean internal storage for data and programs. Other people call it 'store' if they're British: or 'core store' if they're British and outdated; or 'immediate access store', which is accurate but clumsy.

We don't use the term 'memory' to refer to discs and tapes, although some use the term to mean all possible media for storing things in a computer. What they call 'main memory' is probably a strictly accurate description.

A fair definition used to be the storage space which can be addressed directly by a processor but the newish up-market 'virtual memory' operating systems enable the processor to visualise all internal and external storage as one continuous block, so that's not really accurate any more.

Rather than take idealistically pure definitions, let's opt for one or two pragmatic statements. Memory is RAM, ROM and derived abbreviations; or memory comprises printed circuit boards containing semiconductor chips or lattices of ferrite cores; or memory is what is sold in KB.

Menu

A list of options presented to a user.

MICR

Magnetic Ink Character Recognition. Those funny-shaped numbers on cheques are printed with this special ink, which a special MICR reader can detect. The banks are the only people to use them.

Micro

Unwitty but workable and chatty abbreviation for microprocessor or microcomputer.

Micro Focus

Small, independent and successful British software-writing company which has a competitive version of Cobol called CIS-Cobol. It has had a good deal of success with it.

Micro-C

The computer retailing arm of the Currys group. "Computers explained by human beings", says its motto, somewhat ingenuously. The company sells mostly to business users.

MicroCOBOL

A slimmed-down version of standard Cobol for microcomputers; it was developed in Britain. It is from a software house called Microcomputer Products Software Ltd, or MPSL for short (or sometimes MPS).

Microcode

How the instruction set of a particular computer is implemented. Microcode statements convert the machine instructions into electronic activity.

Normally you don't see microcode at all. It's there – typically implemented in *firmware* – and as it happens it's what you're using when you use the instruction set but you don't have to know anything about it.

Some of the classier and more expensive micros, however, allow you to write your own microcode to create new instructions on your computer. If you have applications which frequently involve complicated references to an I/O channel you might create a new machine instruction or two to simplify that referencing. For this user-microcoding, the vendor will give you a little software development package which includes a kind of assembler.

Microcomputer

Really it's a small computer. Look at the glossary reference to 'C' and check what we wrote there on *computer* – a computer is more than just a processor, it's a functioning whole with I/O and some storage capability as well. So microcomputer includes a microprocessor but it involves sufficient extra equipment to be usable – like some memory, a cassette deck or disc drives, a VDU or a keyboard and screen, and a printer.

MicroFinesse

A good *spreadsheet* calculator and financial planning package for the Apple II microcomputer.

Microinstruction

One statement of *microcode*.

MicroModeller

Possibly the most sophisticated *spreadsheet* calculator package available on micros, a fact which is reflected in its complexity and its price. Versions are available for *Apple* and *CP/M* computers. It's better described as a financial modelling package, which implies much more capability for doing future projections.

Micropro

An American software supplier, probably the top vendor of ready-made word processing programs for micros. Its Wordstar package claims more than 5,000 installations, which is a good deal for microcomputer software. Wordstar runs on micros with the *CP/M* operation system and it is probably the world's best-selling word processing program.

Microprocessor
One of the $64,000 definitions. What exactly is a micro? Simple, it's a small central processor – a programmable, electronic, logic-driven, rule-following idiot.

Microprogram
A bunch of microinstructions.

Microsecond
One-millionth of a second, usually abbreviated as M (M being one of those Greek symbols mathematicians use which typewriter manufacturers include on typewriters). Incidentally, you might see 'Mμ' used; it's a witty shorthand for microprocessor.

Micro Scope
A newspaper published every two weeks for the computer trade, it first appeared in the Autumn of 1982. It was set up by a company called Bunch Books which had just made its bank manager very happy by selling *Personal Computer World* to VNU.

Microsoft
Impressive, independent and small U.S. software-writing company which is best-known for producing versions of *Basic* for many microcomputers. It has also done other languages for micros, including *Fortran* and *Cobol;* and it produced one of the *operating systems* on the IBM Personal Computer.

Microwriter
A novel word processor, devised by an unusual man, Cy Endfield, who became bored with writing film scripts on an ordinary typewriter with a QWERTY keyboard. So he devised a kind of single-handed

keyboard which uses only six keys, different combinations of which can represent characters. The unit has a built-in strip display so that you can check what you're keying, and there is also a memory of 8KB (roughly equivalent to four A4 pages).

The thing is designed for 'information originators' rather than typists. One effect is that there's rarely any typing skill to unlearn; and though you have to acquire a whole new code for the alphabet, the key positions aren't too difficult to learn.

The basic Microwriter sells for around £560. As such, it's not really a word processor; the editing is fairly limited, and you have no way of storing and recalling text other than the internal memory; but you can plug it into a computer to obtain more document storage capacity and additional editing functions.

In theory, this thing could be revolutionary and in practice it will at least carve itself a neat little niche.

Millisecond
One-thousandth of a second, abbreviated as 'ms'.

Mimi
The microcomputer from *British Micro*. Properly titled the Mimi 801, it was first shown in prototype form late in 1980 (under the name Gemini 801) and the volume of enquiries apparently persuaded the designers to re-work the thing before its re-launch nine months later.

It has two built-in *floppy disc* drives, the *CP/M* operating system, and a range of attractive facilities, including very good graphics. The price of about £1,200 excludes a monitor or a printer but, even so, that's attractive, too.

Mini

A *minicomputer*.

Minicomputer

A small computer. Nobody really has a better definition so here's a pragmatic one. A minicomputer –
colloquially a mini – is a small computer which is not
a micro and which is made and sold by a company
interested in volume production and low overheads. A
mini is sold as a system component, usually in quantities bigger than one and without the noisy support,
software, customer service people, pamphlets,
manuals and prices of the mainframe computer
vendors.

The mini makers want volume sales and high turnover; their profit margin per machine is small, so they
want to sell plenty. Micro maunfacturers take the same
line.

By contrast, the mainframe makers sell comparatively few high-cost systems; they make their high
profits per sale by all the extra services, products and
general support provided with the computer.

MITS

The personal computer business really got under way
late in 1974 with an unlikely parent. MITS was Micro
Instrumentation and Telemetry Systems, a small company in the southern United States which began in 1969
making electronic control systems for model rockets
but moved to $199 programmable calculators in
1971.

In 1974, MITS put together a microcomputer kit and
featured it in a U.S. magazine *Popular Electronics*.
The technical editor persuaded MITS to look for a
catchy name and his daughter offered 'Altair' – she
derived it from the TV as *Star Trek* was showing.

MITS sold the 8080-based Altair kit for $398 and expected 800 orders in 1975. In fact, it sold 1,500 in two months.

MITS and Altair effectively defined the home micro market. MITS was sold to Pertec two years later and the Altair name is now submerged under newer product developments.

Mnemonic

A memory aid. So mnemonic code is an assembly language code in which the instruction names are easy to remember, like MPY for multiply and STO for store – and ADD for add, too.

Molimerx

"The software works" in latin. Hmm. See *Harding*.

Monitor

The child who used to look after the milk at school. Also the most basic kind of *operating system;* we treat it as being synonymous with *executive.*

The term is also applied to a special program or a plug-in machine which will tell you what is going in inside a computer. Usually this is relevant only with the larger and more complicated machines, which are necessarily too complex in their operation for anyone to understand what's going on *without* a monitor.

More likely you will encounter the term to mean simply a display screen, or rather a display screen which (unlike a domestic TV) is used *only* as a display screen.

Motherboard

A kind of flat *backplane* – it's a circuit board with slots into which you can plug all the other printed circuit boards a system needs. Generally that will include a

CPU card, video and cassette interfaces, and memory cards.

MOS

Metàl Oxide Semiconductor. A number of semiconductor technologies are used in micros but this is the most widespread. It is a fairly obvious way of manufacturing integrated circuits by using metal for the electrical conductor and laying it on an insulating layer of silicon oxide.

The two popular alternatives to MOS are *bipolar* semiconductors and *SOS* – silicon-on-sapphire. MOS is king at the moment – cheap and simple to manufacture and to use. The availability of MOS made LSI possible.

MOSFET is an IBM version of MOS; don't worry about it, though.

MOS Technology

A *Commodore* subsidiary which makes a microprocessor called the 6502 which is used by Apple and Pet, among others. The 6502 owes some parentage to the design of the Motorola 6800.

MP/M

An *operating system* descended from the widely-used *CP/M* and designed to allow for multiple users on the one micro. It had some problems during its development but now seems much healthier, and much more usable. It's unlikely that MP/M will dominate the multi-user scene in the same way that CP/M bestrides the narrow single-user world, though; there's much more competition, notably from *Unix*.

MPSL

Microcomputer Products Software Ltd, developer of

MicroCobol.

MPU
Motorola abbreviation for microprocessor unit, now used widely to mean 'microprocessor'.

MS-DOS
A version of the *operating system* for the IBM Personal Computer which is being made available for other 16-bit microcomputers. The U.S. software developers *Microsoft* were responsible for both.

MSI
Medium Scale Integration. See LSI.

MTBF
Mean Time Between Failure. As an indication of reliability, an MTBF figure – given usually in hours – can be useful to someone who wants maximum performance, though you have to be careful about what exactly has been measured and in what circumstances.

MTTR
A much less-frequently-quoted statistic, the Mean Time To Repair.

Multi-access
A multi-access system is one which several users can access at the same time. The term usually is associated with time-sharing – organising the resources of the computer so that all users have a bite at the cherry – and multi-programming – so that several users can run different programs concurrently.

Multibus

A U.K. minicomputer from a company called Allied Business Systems. More important, it's also the name given by Intel to one of its standard *bus* schemes for interconnecting system compontents. Compare *S-100*, a rather different bus standard.

Multidrop

You probably won't ever hear this term. Generally, each peripheral – printer, disc drive, VDU – is connected to the computer by a cable. A multidrop line is something like an electricity line, in that several units can be connected to it. So several VDUs, say, can be connected to a computer but take up only one I/O port.

Of course, this requires some clever internal extras, notably an operating system which can decipher which terminal wants to do what. If you are sitting at a 'multidropped' terminal and you want to get at a file on the computer, the system will require some means of identifying *you* as the recipient of the index rather than any other terminal on the line.

Multiplex

Another term which the personal computer user will rarely encounter. Multiplexing is using one communications channel to send several messages at the same time. What happens is that individual messages are chopped-up and the pieces inter-leaved in a single long message. You need a special hardware item called a multiplexer (or multiplexor) to do this. At the other end of the link you need another to decode the chopped stream and re-assemble it into several messages. It means you can economise on transmission line charges, because if you have eight 30cps terminals you would be paying for eight 300 baud lines; multiplexing allows you to have all that traffic on one 2,400 baud line.

Multipoint

Synonym for *multidrop*.

Multiprocessor

Obviously a bunch of linked processors. There is much to be said for this, particularly for throughput reasons – each processor runs one part of the system or one part of a program, so there's no waiting; and for improved reliability, things might be set up so that if one processor fails another can take over without interruptions.

A number of the cleverer microcomputers use two processors, one to handle data into and out of floppy disc storage while the other runs programs. Normally a single-processor system has to stop executing program instructions while it looks after a transfer of data to or from disc.

In fact, most computers these days, apart from the very smallest, are multiprocessors. That may not be apparent to the user; but micros are cheap enough for computer designers to incorporate several into even a low-cost system. Typically there will be a micro looking after all the movement of data to and from a disc, for instance; there may also be separate micros controlling transfers to and from a printer; the printer may have a microprocessor inside it; if there's a free-standing VDU terminal with the computer that may well have one, too, and on the main CPU board there could be an individual micro dedicated to handling all the arithmetic functions.

So the main processor is running through a program, deciding at each step what is to happen. Anything involved with disc transfers, it shunts immediately to the micro in the disc controller; any mathematical calculations required are passed to the arithmetic subsystem; any screen interaction is given straight to the VDU controller. Since all of those can be working at the same time, things should progress much faster than if the central CPU had to do it all alone.

Multiprogramming

Multi is almost as popular a prefix as micro, isn't it? Multiprogramming is a clever way of obtaining as much work as possible from a computer. It means the *operating system* can run two or more programs at the same time, switching from one to another and giving each a few milliseconds of attention.

This takes advantage of the fact that most programs don't use all of the computer resources all of the time – so different programs may be able to use different resources at the same time.

Multiprogramming becomes very complicated, though. The operating system must be able to decide an order of priorities for programs and the actions they will want to perform. It must also watch that programs do not over-write any of each other's workspace. It has to make the best possible use of memory by detecting when one program is finishing and perhaps loading another from disc into the memory space thus vacated, and so on.

That means full-blown multiprogramming operating systems tend to be too complex, too expensive, and too big to run economically on micros. Some microcomputers allow a limited kind of multiprogramming, with an interactive *foreground* program (some use of a VDU, typically) going on at the same time as a *background* batch job (like printer output).

MUX
Abbrevation for multiplexer.

Mylar
A trade name for a polyester film used widely as the base for magnetic tape. It can be coated with magnetisable particles.

N-key rollover
Many keyboards have this facility which prevents you 'beating' the keyboard by pressing keys too fast – each key will generate the required character in the sequence in which you pressed the keys.

NAK
Ephemeral mid-60s play and film. Whatever happened to Ann Jellicoe? (She's alive and well and living in Dorset, where she runs an arts trust and organises plays which involve entire towns at a time.) Still, that one had a 'c'. This one is 'negative acknowledge', an ASCII character code sent between computer and terminal to indicate that some duff transmission has occurred.

NAND
A logical operator. The result is 'true' if at least one input is false; it is 'false' if all inputs are true.

Nanosecond
One-billionth of a second. That's a U.S. billion, which, by the way, is the one we prefer – it's 1,000,000,000, or 10^9.

Nascom
Pioneering British manufacturer of low-cost home

computers. It ceased to function three years ago but was acquired and resurrected by *Lucas Logic.*

National Semiconductor

One of the giants in the U.S. electronics business, this company makes most of its money from bulk manufacture of semiconductor components such as computer memories. It also makes some microprocessors.

Needle

Remember the discussion of *matrix printers?* Impact matrix printers build a character by firing metal pins against a ribbon, so that a dot is transferred on to the paper. Using the correct dot positions gives you a recognisable character, even if it is not in proper joined-up writing. Those metal pins are also called needles, funnily enough, and some people speak of 'needle printers' to mean an impact dot matrix mechanism.

NEC

Nippon Electric Co. This diversified electric and electronics group is already Japan's biggest producer of communications equipment and integrated circuits and has also become of the country's major computer manufacturer. Its international best-seller is the *Spinwriter* letter-quality printer; other products include a number of microcomputers, aimed mostly at business users. A recent addition is the Advanced Personal Computer, a 16-bit micro offering the *CP/M*-86 operating system. Announced in the U.S. in the Summer of 1982 at about $3,300, the APC is clear competition for the likes of the IBM Personal Computer.

The older and better-known NEC micro is the eight-bit *CP/M*-based PC-8000 and this excellent machine claims to have more than 40 percent of the Japanese market for personal computers. Good graphics; prices from about £1,850 in the U.K.

Network

A network is any system comprising a series of inter-connected points. So a TV service with local stations connected, by signals, to a central service is a good example. In computing generally, a network is either a number of terminals connected to a computer, or it is a number of computers connected together.

That second definition is the more usual one. Networks are complicated technically, since there are all kinds of traffic control and routeing considerations, apart from what is being sent. Network control usually involves add-on black boxes and complex special software, though, so that the user does not have to do too much of the network management.

A few systems are now appearing allowing interconnection of microcomputers. A more usual configuration would probably be a bunch of computers all sharing each other's local storage, or local peripherals, and this, too, is becoming possible now.

For instance, you could load a program on your computer, send it to another computer, and run it there. Or you could pick up information stored on another computer's discs or cassette files and use it in your program. You'll probably have to know the correct passwords and access codes, of course.

If you have cheap computer with no printer, you might want to dump a load of program listings quickly to give yourself a paper copy of your programs. So how about this for a scenario? You send a message to every other computer in your friendly neighbourhood network saying 'Does anyone have fast printer doing nothing?' Someone answers 'Yes', plugs-in the printer, and you can run a little code dump program which prints its output on that friendly faraway printer. The results arrive in the post next morning.

NewBrain

The hand-held (or rather lap-sized) £160 microcomputer from *Grundy*. It was announced originally by *Newbury* in 1979, and was the BBC's first choice for development as the *BBC Microcomputer*. Things went wrong, it never appeared, and the project was taken over by Grundy, which finally got the thing to the market in 1982.

The NewBrain uses a *Zilog Z-80* microprocessor with its own operating system, a 62-key calculator-style keyboard, and a built-in 16-character display. You can plug in a TV, disc drives and a printer.

Newbury Data Recording

An established British manufacturer of *VDU* terminals, Newbury Laboratories dabbled with micros (the *NewBrain*) before it was acquired by the British Technology Group and merged with a manufacturer and distributor of printers and disc drives formerly called Data Recording Instrument. Newbury Data Recording is the new name for the merged operation. You won't be able to guess in which town it's based.

Nibble

Obviously, half a *byte*. This silly word, in fact, is used by some to mean a group of four *bits* (a byte comprises eight).

NIH

'Not Invented Here'. It's a convenient label for the attitude, prevalent in many sectors of British life, which says if we didn't do it ourselves it can't be good enough for us.

NMOS
Also N-channel MOS, a type of MOS used widely in microprocessors and other electronics circuits. We're not going to tell you exactly how it differs from PMOS, an earlier technique for making MOS circuits but, in general, NMOS is faster, although PMOS can usually put more circuits on to a chip.

Noise
The otherwise indefinable and thankfully exceptional quality shared by the St Matthew Passion, Altered Images – and transmission lines, for noise is unwanted electrical signals on a cable or some other connection. Since computers work electrically, a spurious electrical effect of some kind can cause errors; an extra amount here or there will destroy the meaning of a single-character code, and misapprehension of a single character can affect the computer's comprehension of an entire message.

Noise is unavoidable in all electrical circuits. It's a property of all materials, including those used to make computers, which will generate a certain amount of electrical activity on their own. Generally, though, the signals being generated and passed around in a computer system are powerful enough, and the receiving ends sensitive enough, to separate the desired signals from the dross.

Non-impact printer
A printer which works with something hitting a piece of paper. Examples include *thermal, electostatic* and *ink-jet* printers.

Non-volatile

Some types of memory lose their contents when you turn off the power. That's because they need a permanent electric current so that they can hold information. Because switching-off loses their contents, they are termed volatile. This doesn't happen with non-volatile memory because those devices don't store information by requiring a constant source of electricity.

Examples are discs and tapes, which work by altering the magnetic characteristics of the medium; this alteration is done electrically but once that has happened, the whole thing is only encoded magnetically. This also applies to some types of internal memory, notably *core* and *ROM*. The one big advantage of core memories is that their contents aren't lost when you switch off.

By contrast, the semiconductor MOS memories used normally these days in computers are volatile. MOS has many advantages over core, though, notably its speed; reading and writing information is much faster with MOS; its heat output – MOS runs much cooler, so reliability is better, and its cost – MOS is already much cheaper and it's becoming even more so.

ROM (read-only memory) is the other significant form of non-volatile storage. These are semiconductor chips with data sealed-in.

North Star

North Star Computers is an independent Californian company which has become one of the best-liked and most succesful of the small-computer manufacturers. Its Horizon computer is a neat box packaged with Z-80A microprocessor, S-100 bus, and built-in minifloppy drives; it needs a separate VDU. The newer Advantage, which is a single unit which includes screen, keyboard and discs, is equally neat; unusually, it can display excellent graphics on the integral screen.

NOVA

The top-selling computer from the world's number two mini maker. The first Data General NOVA appeared in the early 1970s. The present version has more facilities and a much lower price but the same internal design ideas are used. A classic mini.

The DG microNOVA is a microprocessor implementation of the same design.

ns

Abbreviation for *nanosecond*.

NS

Note the upper-case. This is an abbreviation sometimes used for National Semiconductor. So is Nat Semi.

NTSC

The video signal format used for colour TV pictures in North America and Japan. The U.K. uses one called *PAL* and so do the Germans; the French (naturally) have a third variety called *SECAM*.

The point is that a particular computer (if it can display in colour) will generate video signals only for one of these formats. So if you buy a *Vic* or an *Atari* in the States, it probably won't give a good picture on the PAL-based colour TV sets we have here.

Null

An instruction meaning 'do nothing', used usually in computer-terminal communications.

Null string
A string with nothing in it and different from no string at all.

Number-crunching
Performing clever calculations quickly. In practice, computing tends to be in two flavours, number-orientated or alphanumeric, and they have very different characteristics. Alphanumeric work, as in most business applications, usually means many files, and much I/O – to and from files, to and from terminals – very little and not very complicated computation. Scientific and technical computing is generally the complete opposite – small amounts of stored data and not a great deal of I/O, but big, complicated numbers and much complicated calculation. Big numbers and sophisticated calculation is what number-crunching is all about.

A number-cruncher is a computer designed specifically for that kind of work. Usually they are powerful, expensive and very large; classic applications include meteorological calculations, NASA work, and the kind of tricky mathematics required in nuclear power.

This kind of computer frequently will use multiple processors, all operating in parallel at the same time. That way they can crunch more numbers faster. See *multiprocessor*.

Number system
Impressive-sounding reference to the numeric basis for computation and logic. Binary, octal and hexadecimal are all favourite number systems used by computer designers – they have the bases 2, 8 and 16 respectively.

Numeric
It means comprising numbers only. You knew that, didn't you?

OASIS
A derivative of the *Unix* operating system.

Object code
'Source code' or 'source programs' are what the programmer writes. The 'source language' will generally be one of the well-known mnemonics like Basic or Cobol, or it might be a low-level language (*assembler*). Anyway, before it is acted on by your computer it has to be translated into a form the computer can understand, and the results of that translation are called object code.

You won't necessarily have an object code version of your program. With an interpreted language, like most versions of Basic, each program instruction is translated and acted on directly; so there is no homogenous intermediate form. A compiler, however, always produces an object program; you write the source code, compile it, and get an object program which is incomprehensible to you.

The object program, incidentally, will almost always be in machine language. Some big and cumbersome machines produce object code which isn't exactly at the binary-digits stage of machine code; but forget about them – you'll never be able to afford them anyhow.

OCR
Optical character recognition, or sometimes 'optical character reader'; there seems to be no agreement about a precise definition. That's often the way in this business.

OCR wand

A clever hand-held device which can read characters and convert them into computer input. Recognition Equipment was the company which pioneered the technique, which obviates the need for a special separate (and usually) bulky OCR reader.

Octal

To the base 8; compare *binary* (base 2) and *hexadecimal* (16). In octal notation the numerals 0 to 7 are used to encode all possible three-bit combinations from 000 to 111; *hex* is much more popular, though – it uses 0 to 9 and A to F to encode all possible four-bit combinations.

OEM

Tricky one, this. It stands for 'Original Equipment Manufacturer', so it should refer to the people at one end of the line who make the things which other people turn into products which are then sold to the eager public. After all, the original equipment is what the middlemen buy for re-sale as assembled systems, isn't it?

In practice, the computer industry uses the term 'OEM' to mean the middlemen, who rarely manufacture anything and who only occasionally do anything original.

Pardon the repetition but I really had things the wrong way round in the first edition of the *Good Computing Book* and I still can't understand the logic of it. Let's be clear about this; an OEM is a system supplier buying components or subsystems from other manufacturers to incorporate in a product which is then sold to an end-user.

Either way, the important things to note are that OEM products are usually sold to those middlemen in quantity, at a discount on one-off prices, and with little or no vendor support. This three-pronged strategy is how mini-makers like Digital Equipment and Data General become rich; most of the business of the semiconductor giants like Zilog, Intel and Texas Instruments, is also in this vein.

As a quick summary, an OEM can usually be thought of as a company which, in practice, goes in for some badge engineering on hardware and probably adds software; you buy a standard micro, put your name on it with Letraset, and add some of your own software. Everyone's doing it.

Off-line

Not connected directly to the computer. Remember those nasty punched cards? A data preparation clerk who has to transcribe human-readable information into computer-readable information might well do that on an off-line unit called a card punch which makes the holes in the cardboard. Or you might be able to switch your printer off-line – without unplugging it – so that it doesn't suddenly start pulverising your finger with printed output while you're re-loading it with paper.

Office computer

Jargon for a computer which might be used in an office. In practice, that means a relatively cheap and fairly small computer – say between one and four VDUs, one matrix printer, an invisible processor, and file storage on floppy disc (or more likely about 10MB of cartridge disc or *Winchester* disc storage). The average 'office computer', then, would probably be a single-user, desk-style workstation driven by a micro and priced in the range £4,000 to £15,000.

Ohio Scientific

A U.S. manufacturer of microcomputers, not necessarily for scientific use – not even principally for scientists, in fact, for most sales are now being directed towards business applications. The company has recently been acquired and re-named; it goes by the snappy soubriquet MA/COM-OSI and is trying to persuade people that the 'OSI' means 'Office Systems Inc'.

Oki

Japanese manufacturer of good *dot matrix* printers for micros; and now microcomputers.

Olivetti

This giant Italian manufacturer of office equipment is active in almost every aspect of business electronic things, including small computers for business. It had a near-dominant position in that field before the arrival of the micro and its 1982 launch of a £3,000 computer called the M20 was a somewhat belated bit of catching-up. It's a 16-bit computer (compare the *Sirius* and *IBM* entries) with floppy discs, a great deal of characteristic Olivetti styling and, just for a change, an *operating system* which isn't the near-ubiquitous *CP/M*.

Olivetti says it aims to sell 83,000 of them in 1983.

OMR

Optical mark recognition, or optical mark reader – take your pick. We like 'recognition'. It is a technique which puts data into the computer by detecting the presence or absence of a mark. You need special forms and the person filling them in marks the appropriate boxes. OMR is much simpler than *OCR*, since the OMR reader has only two conditions from which to make a choice. OMR input is used widely in automating some examination marking – obviously you have examination papers which give multiple choices from which to select; and in ordering – salesmen with many product lines or a number of pre-defined selectable options usually have pre-drawn forms to fill in.

On-board
Meaning on a (or the) *printed circuit board.*

On-line
Indicates equipment connected to and communicating with a computer. The opposite of off-line.

OP CODE
Or Opcode. It's the operation code, part of an assembly language instruction which indicates the operation to be performed. Other parts might specify the memory locations, data, and/or I/O ports involved.

Operand
Someone who can still hum all of *Carmen* through a Who concert? No, it's the data used by a computer instruction; usually it's that part of the instruction which contains the address of the data.

Operating system
There are two broad categories of software – systems and applications software. The applications programs enable you to apply the computer to something – they do whatever it is you want your computer to do. Playing games, switching-off the central heating, producing invoices – all those are applications.

What we call system software fits between your applications programs and that heap of hardware on which they run. The system software takes away from you the need to know how every electronic action relates to every step in the execution of your program.

The operating system is the principal example, but not the only one, of system software. It is a complex program, or group of programs, inside the computer. There are no hard and fast rules about what it does and does not do. Here are some other attempts at definition:

"An integrated collection of computer instructions which handle selection, movement and processing of programs and data needed to solve problems". That's somewhat restricted, because operating systems also manage and control internal operations of electronic hardware.

"Software required to manage the hardware resources of a system and its logical resources, including scheduling and file management." That's better, provided you know what all the big words mean.

Operator
Disenchanted, underpaid human with aching back, bad posture, and two bad eyes. Also an operator is a symbol denoting a mathematical operation (like + for plus and ÷ for divide) or a logical operation – they vary, but check Boolean algebra for some examples if you're really interested.

Opm
Operations per minute. A measure used only by appendectomy surgeons, American dp heavies, and Glossary compilers.

Ops
Short for 'operations', as in Ops Manager – the person

who runs the day-to-day operations of the computer in a big company.

Optical character recognition

Recognising characters by looking at them (or rather the machine equivalent of that). An OCR reader scans the surface of a sheet of paper, analyses the light patterns made by anything printed or written on it, compares that information to a known set of patterns, and transmits to the computer anything it recognises. Some clever OCR systems can recognise handwriting but most can read only typescript in a particular character formation.

Each letter of the alphabet obviously must be identifiably different and this meant that the first standard OCR-readable script – it was called OCR-A – was characterised by ugly blobs and blocks on the letters. Film-makers and advertising agencies like to use this kind of script for the instant connotation of 'computer'. In fact, most OCR uses a much more ordinary, and more readable, script called OCR-B. It looks fairly normal; OCR equipment is becoming more sensitive and more discriminating, so that it can determine finer differences between one character and another.

In fact, the two typefaces represent different trade-offs between the abilities of humans and computers to recognise character shapes. OCR-A is much less legible to the human eye but it's much easier for a computer to be programmed to recognise the OCR-A alphabet. The infinitely more pleasant OCR-B necessitates a much more sophisticated character recognition program.

You can have OCR-B golf-balls for an ordinary Selectric-style electric typewriter and some printers are available with OCR fonts – including *daisywheel* units.

OCR has never really been clever enough, fast enough or cheap enough to replace the keyboard as a way of transferring information from people into computers. In any case, someone probably has to use a keyboard somewhere to create the OCR input in the first place. OCR has found a niche, however, in applications where the alphanumeric input is fairly well standardised and where there is not much of it – for forms, for instance, where many documents have to be read and input somehow. OMR is simpler, cheaper and generally more useful at this stage of the technology.

Optical mark reading
See *OMR*.

Optical wand
Hand-held device which can 'read' *bar codes*. Usually the *wand* is attached to a storage device like a cassette recorder; the information collected is processed subsequently at a computer.

Optimise
Obviously this means to amend something to make sure it performs at optimum efficiency. It's in the Glossary because you might find it being applied to computer programs. For instance, an optimising compiler is a compiler which does some automatic optimising of your carefully-produced code. There are also special programs called optimisers through which you can run your own code after you've finished writing it; they tweak your program a little so that it makes more efficient use of the internal resources available within the computer system.

ORACLE
The IBA *teletext* service.

OS
Operating system. Several manufacturers have operating systems called – with singular lack of imagination – OS. The big IBM computers are a prime example.

Osborne
Being Adam Osborne, his Osborne Computer Corporation, and its Osborne I computer.

Osborne is an interesting character. He's English but went to the States to get his PhD (chemical engineering, would you believe?) and stayed, getting involved with the micro business as it took off in the early '70s. Initially his company provided freelance programming and technical writing services. Then he started writing books, many of which are still standard references (the giant U.S. publisher McGraw Hill acquired that piece of Osborne's activities in 1979). Meanwhile, he was writing columns for the trade press, talking at conferences, and generally being prominent and influential.

He became especially well-known for putting the boot into the U.S. micro business over things like high prices and inadequate manuals, so everyone sat up when he announced a product of his own in June, 1981.

What's special about the Osborne 1? Well, it's fairly portable, designed specifically to travel as hand luggage in aircraft, we heard, though at 24lb. your arm would be a little longer than usual if the departure gate was a long way away. Inside you have two mini-diskette drives storing 102KB each, a tiny screen, a keyboard, and five free software packages. The programs are good – *Wordstar* and *Mailmerge* for word processing, *Supercalc* for financial planning, both *CBasic* and *MBasic,* and the *CP/M* operating system (naturally).

Buying the software alone would cost £800, Osborne says; in fact, most people who sell this kind of micro would give you CP/M and Basic free but the word processing and planning package would certainly top £500.

So at a basic £1,250 the Osborne 1 must be a good buy. It's not without its flaws; the 5in. screen is really too small, for instance, and you need to plug in a reasonable-sized display to use the thing in anger. Overall the design looks somewhat stark, too, but I wouldn't mind having one.

Osborne set up a U.K. operation during 1982 and sold £1 million worth of Osbornes in its first two months. World-wide the target for 1982 sales is something around 100,000 computers.

Output
As a noun, it's what you get from a computer, sometimes given the blanket term 'results'. It is also used as a verb, in which case it means to transfer information from a computer to some kind of clever device – usually a CRT screen or a printer. Less common these days are paper tape or card punches. Esoterica will include graph plotters and electronic gizmos which convert computer data into some near-recognisable representation of the human voice.

OV
Abbreviation for overflow.

Overflow
The computer has to assume that internal work areas are of a specific size. If it uses a 16-bit word, it

probably uses *accumulators* – also called *registers* –
which are eight or 16 or 32 bits long; that way it knows
that anything inside that particular string of bits is
relevant to the operation in question, and nothing else
is. What happens when the result of an arithmetical
operation needs more bits than are in that accumulator? Try dividing 22 by 7. Well, overflow is what
happens.

Your computer might not be able to handle this.
Perhaps your accumulator will contain the first eight
(or 16 or 32 or whatever) bits of the answer and the rest
will be lost. That generally happens in pocket calculators, doesn't it? Perhaps it will round-up the result.
Or it might set aside a special 'overflow accumulator'
to hold at least some of the overflowing number.
Several computers will set a *flag* to tell you that
overflow has occurred, without letting know where or
why.

Overlay

Overlaying is a popular technique used by the clever
kind of operating system for bringing routines, generally called overlays, into main memory from disc or
some other kind of mass storage during the execution
of a program. With overlaying, several routines can
occupy the same main memory storage locations at
different times. The technique is used when main
memory is not big enough to satisfy total storage
requirements of a program.

Overwrite

Another obvious one. It means to store information in
such a way that it destroys whatever was previously
stored there. Since disc, tape and internal computer
memory are all re-usable, it follows that re-using them
– by storing new information – will over-write their

previous contents. One of the virtues of ROM will be equally obvious – you clearly can't over-write anything in read-only memory.

Pac-Man

The absolutely classic video game, originally from *Atari* (which reckoned it would earn $200 million from Pac-Man alone in 1982) but now borrowed for almost every colour computer. It's the one where you control Pac-Man as he zips around a maze pursued by aliens (or ghosts, or evil blobs, or whatever) and downing 'video wafers' and 'power pills' to give him the capacity to fight back.

A U.S. business analyst recently reckoned that "Pac-Man will make more money for Warner Bros (which owns Atari) than *Star Wars* made for Twentieth Century Fox".

Meanwhile, the latest depressing development is the arrival of Pac-Woman. She has a blue bow to distinguish her from the original.

Pace

An early 16-bit micro from *National Semiconductor*.

Pack

Packing is a way of compacting information to economise on storage space inside a computer. Usually it means lopping-off zeros and omitting spaces in data to be stored, replacing them with some kind of marker which takes up less space. When the data is read subsequently, unpacking takes place and the zeros and spaces are reinstated. The opposite is *padding*.

Package

In electronics, a package is what you have when you

embed a chip in a block of plastic so that it can be used on a PCB, though that is usually called 'packaging'.

You are more likely to meet this word when it is applied to software; a package is a program developed for a particular application which is designed to be usable by more than one person.

This is normal outside computing, of course; you don't often find books designed to be read by only one person. Most applications software is custom-written to suit one user; that is because every computer user has different requirements, even in doing the same basic work.

An application package tries to be all things to all people. Or rather, it tries to be *most* things to *some* people. In theory, the user has a tried and tested program which is available more quickly and more cheaply than it would be if it had to be designed and written from scratch and if only he were bearing all its costs.

There have been problems in practice, of course. The package may not be flexible enough to cope with all the idionsyncrasies you require. It was probably written in the first place as a customised job for one user and tweaked subsequently to make its appeal more general. That might not be the best way of producing software; it has to be sufficiently general in its approach to appeal to many users. You may be paying for facilities you will never use and the software may be voluminous and inefficient when it is inside your computer.

The thinking on design of software packages usually means one of two compromises. Either you will amend your ways of doing things to suit the package – quick and cheap; or the package will be capable of amendment, perhaps by being initially a bare-bones framework on to which can be attached some custom-written routines to make it suit you better.

The critical point is economic, particularly for business programs. People who can design and develop elegant programs are not inexpensive and they are not common either. Software packages frequently are the only affordable option.

Packet switching

A clever data transmission process whereby 'packets' or blocks of data are sent on their way with an 'address' rather like ordinary mail. The alternative is more like the telephone system, where a connection has to be established first before any information can pass from one end to the other. Here we are talking about big national or international data communications set-ups, of course.

Padding

Adding blanks or some other non-significant characters to a record to increase it to a fixed size. It is usually done automatically if the programmer specifies it. Padding will be necessary if you are working with fixed-length records and some of them contain insufficient data to be processed.

Paddle

It's a knob (or 'a rotary control mechanism', if you like) which you turn to move something left and right or up and down on a computer screen – in fact, it is a variable resistor, a potentiometer or rheostat. It looks nothing like a paddle, of course; the name derives from an early use of these things to move the bats or paddles in computer games of ping-pong.

Page

Either a screenfull of characters – or rather character positions on a VDU, or chunk of storage, usually defined fairly arbitrarily – 512 and 1,024 words are page 'lengths' employed frequently.

Page printer

Compare *line printers* which print a line at a time; page printers generally assemble a page of output in a small internal memory and then put it out very quickly.

Paging

A facility on some operating systems; it is a procedure for transferring 'pages' of information between disc storage and main memory.

Memory is expensive and you may find you don't have enough of it to hold the programs and data you want. Disc storage is much cheaper and your *operating system* may allow you to overcome the problem by swopping portions of information between disc and memory – you are putting part of the current contents of memory temporarily on to disc and reading into the space so freed a piece of program or data you need. As presented, this is *overlaying;* when it is done automatically, it's *paging.*

With paging, pages of memory are moved in and out one at a time. Since this is automatic, the programmer doesn't have to know what is happening and when. To the programmer it looks as if the total memory available is the capacity of main memory plus whatever disc storage there is. That is why paging is called *virtual* memory.

PAL

One of the three main standards for displaying colour

pictures on TV; it's the one used in Britain. See *NTSC* for a little more on this.

Paper tape

Long strips of paper. Usually people mean punched paper tape when they use the phrase, though punching holes in it isn't the only way to store information on paper tape – some esoteric systems print dots on it, impregnate it with chemicals to hold data, and so on.

Punched tape is simple. A single row of holes across the tape encodes one character, rather as on punched cards. Paper tape has one big advantage over card, though – a card normally has room for no more than 80 or 90 characters. Paper tape has no such restriction and you can have blocks of characters up to any length.

You will need the software to cope with that. It is much easier to write programs which expect information in pre-defined record lengths of, say, 80 characters.

Paper tape is cheap, less bulky than cards, and can be read at speeds of up to 1,000 characters per second. No-one uses it much these days, though, because it's messy – all those hole-sized bits of paper fluff; and noisy – a paper tape punch is a fairly crude mechanical device; and you have to buy special hardware – the reader and punch. Cassette or floppy disc are much to be preferred if you can afford them, principally because they are so much faster and are more difficult to tear accidentally.

Two exceptions spring to mind. There are still hundreds of teletypes around, cheap and noisy terminals which frequently have a built-in reader/punch for paper tape: so you might as well use it. Some older high-speed printers also utilise pre-punched paper tape, typically a loop of it, this being read while the printing is proceeding and it determines vertical format – when to start a new page.

There is one largely-unexplored and extremely flippant use for paper tape, which incidentally is available in several colours. Remember those ticker-tape welcomes in New York City which no longer seem to happen? Well, ticker tape is paper tape from teleprinters and that is the same as computer paper tape.

Paper Tiger

One of the *dot matrix* printers from Integral Data Systems.

Parallel run

If you're a business and you've just bought a new computer, it makes sense to run it alongside your existing manual or computerised system for a time. This parallel running should indicate any deficiencies in your new baby before you've committed yourself fully to it.

Parallel interface

A parallel interface is one with sufficient wires for all the bits in a *word* to arrive at the interface simultaneously. So for a computer with an eight-bit word, this means both sides of the interface need at least eight wires going into and from the plug-and-socket connection – one wire carrying one bit in parallel. Compare this to the simpler, cheaper, more versatile but much slower *serial* interface in which the bits arrive one after another (serially).

Parallel interfaces are used generally for printers. This is largely because the electromechanical printer can often be the bottleneck in a system which otherwise operates at electronic speeds. Anything which optimises the performance of the printer, like presenting it with eight data bits at a time rather than one, is a good thing.

Within the broad term 'parallel interface' there are many philosophies about which wire carries what, and so on. Parallel interfaces tend to be specific to one computer manufacturer. Phrases you might hear include:

- *Centronics-compatible:*
Centronics has for some time been the leading supplier of *matrix* printers and because many of the U.S. minicomputer makers bought their printers from this company, its parallel interfaces became another *de facto* industry standard. It was adopted by several computer vendors and it is also offered by several printer suppliers, the inference being that it is a simple matter to replace a Centronics unit with another.

- *Dataproducts-compatible:*
Dataproducts has long been one of the top independent vendor of *line* printers and a similar situation obtains.

- *Digital-compatible:*
Again, several printers can attach directly to the parallel interface socket on a PDP-11 minicomputer from *Digital Equipment*. That also applies to many of the systems incorporating a PDP-11.

- *IBM-compatible:*
Check this claim very carefully. IBM has so many interfaces to so many types of computer.

Other popular parallel interface options which may be offered with printers broadly follow the league table of minicomputer manufacturers. Compatability with

Data General and Hewlett-Packard minis is common; Perkin-Elmer (Interdata) and General Automation are encountered occasionally.

More and more you'll also find interfacing compatible with *Diablo* and *Qume daisywheel* printers, though here the key question of compatability usually refers to software compatability.

Parameter

Much-used buzzword meaning an item of information which can be changed according to what you want to do. Or if you want a heavy definition, it's a constant with variable values. For instance, you might have a parameter called 'height' and you might try giving it a succession of values.

Parameter-driven

Usually in 'parameter-driven software', where it refers to an approach which allows the user to answer a number of questions about the kind of formatting you'd like in the program. It applies especially to how you'd like the output to look – which items of information you'd like where on a printed report or a display.

All this relates to a potential problem in using standard pre-written off-the-shelf software packages – they might do more or less what you want, particularly in terms of the functions you require, but they might not fit your needs exactly. The usual complaint is about the output formatting, since the basic functions tend to be the same for any user (there aren't really many different ways of doing payroll or ledger accounting). Parameter-driven software represents a compromise, in that the standard package has a number of built-in options from which the user is invited to choose.

Once you have selected the parameters you want,

the program will run with those parameters every time you start it.

The classic example in business computer systems of what some people are already calling 'parameterisation' is invoice formatting where you get the facility to decide how your invoices will look.

Parity

A clever way of checking each character as it is moved around the electronic internals of a computer. Remember binary encoding? One character is made up of a group of 0s or 1s, so if one bit is altered accidentally, somehow it's bad news. Such accidents can happen – the computer is shifting around many bits at very fast speeds with all kinds of electrical interference possible.

Parity checking is a way of making reasonably sure that the character hasn't changed in getting from A to B – usually from memory into the processor, though sometimes to and from tape, cassette or disc. What happens is that an extra bit is tacked on to the character – the 'parity bit' is set to 0 or 1 according to whether the character has an odd or even number of 1s in its bit pattern. Odd parity means that the parity bit is set when there's an odd number of 1s. Given that information, you should have no difficulty guessing even parity.

At the end of some operations the computer makes sure the parity bit is still set appropriately; if it isn't there is clearly an error and the computer will tell you. It's generally your job to correct it.

There's one obvious problem with parity checking. Clearly one troublesome bit will show as a parity error but, equally, a two-bit error will appear as a perfectly good parity check. Still, single-bit errors are much more common. If there is one chance in a million of a single-bit error, there is something like a one in one billion chance of a two-bit error.

Partition

Check *multiprogramming*. Some operating systems organise the computer memory into distinct areas, called partitions, and have different programs running in different partitions. Several micros allow you to run a *foreground* partition with one interactive program at the same time as another program, typically a *batch* job, runs in a *background* partition. They are not running at the same time; the computer gives most of its attention to the foreground partition, occasionally snatching a few nanoseconds to execute some instructions of the program in the background partition.

Pascal, Blaise

Blaise Pascal (1623-1662) was French and lived in the 17th century, at a time when Frenchmen in particular were distinguished by their breadth of vision. Even so, Pascal was an exceptional polymath – writer, mathematician, scientist, religious thinker, natural philosopher.

He also built the world's first mechanical calculator (about 1647) to help his father, who was a taxman in Rouen. It used wheels marked with digits and turning a wheel through a full revolution – from 0 to 9 – caused its neighbour on the left to move one notch.

Pascal apparently built about 50 but they suffered from mechanical problems because the interlocking cogs were not cut accurately enough. So he became bored and instead invented the hypodermic needle, the hydraulic press, the basis of probability theory, and the first public transport system in Paris.

He was as eminent as a theologian as he was a mathematician and also as an author. It was he who said: "The heart has its reasons which reason knows nothing of", which could, in itself, be sufficient to ensure his fame.

Pascal

The Pascal language first appeared in the late 1960s as the brainchild of Nicklaus Wirth and others at the Zurich Technical Institute. It is a clear descendant of the ALGOL family, which was popular in Europe before being steam-rollered by the Fortran-Cobol bandwagon from the States.

The essential idea of Pascal is to produce a structured algorithmically-orientated language which matches realistically the abilities of both man and computer. The result is an elegant language which enables long programs to be written with few errors. Pascal executes programs quickly compared to other languages, especially in comparison with interpretative languages like Basic, though that also applies to any worthwhile compiler language.

The big problem with Pascal is that its impenetrably cryptic notation and syntax rules means a hefty learning task before you can start using it.

Pascal is a good language for *structured programming*, though, and that's no bad thing; its advocates say that once you're over the initial hurdle of learning the language it becomes very easy to use.

There are three widely-available versions of Pascal. UCSD Pascal is probably the most popular. There is a British contender, the British Standards Institute version being promoted especially by Manchester University. Then there's 'Standard Pascal', which is the original flavour from Zurich. It's the UCSD version in particular which has furnished the useful and/or necessary extensions for handling any but the most simple input and output needs.

Password

This one is pretty obvious. It's a string of characters which allows you to run restricted programs or to read restricted files. Handling passwords is a function of the operating system and not all of them have it; usually a computer, or rather its operating system, will request your password; you type it in, it is checked and access is either granted or denied.

Patch

A patch is a correction, usually a group of instructions added to correct a mistake in a program.

PC

Printed circuit, as in *PCB;* or sometimes program counter – that is a memory location inside the computer which keeps track of where you are in the program being executed.

PC 8000

Reputedly the biggest-selling microcomputer in Japan, this is the pleasant machine from *NEC.* Typically it sells with two 163KB disc drives for about £2,000. Notable features include good colour and graphics display.

PCM

Plug-compatible manufacturer – someone who makes plug-compatible equipment. In practice, the term is used most often to refer to people who make IBM-compatible peripherals.

PCW

Personal Computer World.

PDP-11

The world's best-selling minicomputer family from the top mini manufacturer, Digital Equipment. The PDP-11 has more or similar internals all the way from the LSI-11 microcomputer to the six-figure VAX-11/780.

In fact, that is somewhat simplistic; there are distinct subdivisions along the way, with significant developments in the basic architecture producing four or five family groups. At one end there is the LSI-11, which is called the PDP-11/03 when it's in a box.

The 11/23 is a bigger micro, a bridge between the LSI-11 and the 11/34; the latter is the company's mainstream mini. It has its own line of development, with the small 11/10 at one end and the big 11/60 at the other. The bigger 11/70 and the 11/44 are another group, and the VAX system – a 32-bit mini, unlike the rest – is also out on its own.

PE

Phase-encoded. A way of storing data on magnetic tape. Forget it. (Some people also use 'PE' as an abbreviation for parity error, but not many).

Peach

The microcomputer from *Hitachi*.

Peachtree

On a world-wide basis, U.S.-owned Peachtree is top dog in business software packages for micros and that situation was helped along with the IBM Seal of Approval (IBM took Peachtree software as the standard offering on its Personal Computer). Peachtree products also include *Magic Wand,* one of the best (and best-selling) *word processors* for micros with the *CP/M* operating system.

In 1981, Peachtree was acquired by Management

Sciences America, one of the big boys in providing software for big IBM computers. Why 'Peachtree'? Because the company started in the state of Georgia and Georgia is full of peaches (and very little else). In fact, outside the gambling palaces of Atlanta, almost everything in Georgia reflects the power of the peach. They could hardly called it 'Gambling Palaces Software' or 'Almighty Dollar Packages Inc', could they?

Pearcom

An interesting little company which has built an Apple II lookalike. It's neater and cheaper than the Apple and it runs the standard Apple software with no modifications.

Pearl

One of the best *program generators* available for micros with the *CP/M* operating system. It's also the name of the U.K. company which supplies it.

Peddle, Chuck

Definitely one of the more interesting characters in the microcomputer game. Peddle was an engineer at a small Californian *semiconductor* company called *MOS Technology* in the mid-1970s; there he designed a microprocessor called the 6502. At the time *Commodore* was looking for a microcomputer product to rescue it from the slump in pocket calculators and digital watches; Commodore lit on MOS Technology, bought in in 1976, and gave Peddle the job of designing a computer. He produced the *Pet*.

He thought Commodore should do a bigger computer, though. Commodore's no-nonsense boss, Jack Tramiel, disagreed. Arguments followed and after a slanging match late in 1980 (Useless Fact No. 97 – this happened in a Datsun 280Z) Peddle left Commodore; he says he was fired, Tramiel says he quit.

Peddle set up *Sirius* Systems Technology, peddled the idea of the Sirius 1, received the backing he needed, built the thing, sold them like hot cakes, and became very rich.

Commodore, of course, is now launching a line of bigger computers to compete with the Sirius.

PEEK
Most Basics have a handy statement which allows you to read the contents of a specified memory address. A companion statement, *POKE,* puts a value into a specific memory address. Example: X=PEEK 18370 assigns the numeric value stored in memory address 18370 to the variable X.

Peripheral
Almost anything connected to a computer. Generally a peripheral is a discrete and physically separate I/O or storage device of some kind attached by cable to the processor. Some people legitimately use the term for almost anything which isn't the processor, including internal, invisible parts of the computer system. You will be safe if you use the term to mean disc units, VDUs and printers.

Personal Computer World
The first British magazine for the personal computing fraternity, and probably the best; certainly the best-looking, and definitely the most interesting to read.

The first edition of this book was assailed by the magazine because I remarked that *PCW* was published by the same people as *Stateboard Scene* and *Kung Fu Monthly.* (Since then it added at least two instant titles on the Falklands.) Now *PCW* has been bought for a vast sum by the Dutch-owned megalithic publishing giant VNU, which is responsible for several other British computer publications – see Chapter 8 for examples. Let's hope that neither the success of the magazine nor its move will alter it too much.

Personal Computers Ltd
The first company to sell *Apple* microcomputers in the U.K. and still a big dealer for Apples.

Pet
Just be thankful that nobody calls it the Personal Electronic Transactor any more. This is one of the world's best-selling microcomputers – *Sinclair* obviously leads the way but the *TRS-80, Apple* and *Pet* (including their derivatives) contest second place.

The Apple II beat the original Pet launch in 1977 by a few months but Commodore had designed a clever piece of consumer electronics – a pioneering, table-top design with graphics, a good clear screen, a very good Basic, and the *MOS Technology* 6502 processor among its better-liked attributes.

The calculator-style keyboard on early models and the idosyncratic use of the *IEEE* interface are probably its least-respected qualities. The newer models thankfully have dispensed with that, giving a typewriter-style keyboard (and omitting the built-in cassette because there's now no room for it).

The Pet sells best as the Commodore 8032; Commodore is keen to drop the 'Pet' appellation but it won't go away. The 8032 has a screen which displays 80 characters per line and there is a 32KB memory inside it (8032, geddit?) and it's sold principally with the separate Commodore disc drive unit as a less-than-£3,000 business computer.

The Pet is reaching the end of its marketing life. The

design now looks distinctly outdated; technology has moved on, and Commodore has announced a clutch of more up-to-date computers. They have numbers rather than names, they utilise a more advanced version of the 6502 processor chip, they are much neater in design, and they are loaded with technological goodies; they retain some software compatibility with the existing Pet lines, though, so buyers can run their existing programs and files on the new machines.

Incidentally, the name 'Pet' arose because Commodore wanted a friendly name for what it originally saw as a home computer. Pet rocks (remember them?) were all the rage at the time and that spawned the idea. 'Personal Electronic Transactor' was thought of subsequently to justify the acronym.

Petal printer

Some people use this phrase instead of *daisywheel*. They are correct, really, since it refers to impact printer mechanisms where the characters are formed on the end of a kind of stem attached at the other end to a central boss of sorts, not unlike petals on a flower. Daisywheels are just one example; others you might encounter include the *Spinwriter*.

All petal printers deliver reasonably good quality printing for word processor use.

Philips

Giant Dutch conglomerate in electrics and electronics. Philips also makes smallish office computers and word processors. It owns a Californian microprocessor company, Signetics; it has a minicomputer line called the P800, which is used principally by other Philips divisions for incorporation into its products; and it also has two U.K. companies in the *telecommunications* business.

Not much there for the personal computer interest but you'd think that all this would leave Philips well-poised to become a major supplier of *electronic office* products. There's not much evidence of that happening yet.

Philips has one microcomputer, the P2000, which it sells as a £2,000 or so business computer system. The computer features flat keys, built-in mini-cassette (that's the small size used in dictation machines), and plug-in *ROM cartridges;* a separate box holds a screen and floppy disc.

Phosphor

The inside of a cathode-ray tube is coated with a material called phosphor which illuminates when a beam of electrons strikes it. Firing electrons at the phosphor coating in an appropriate pattern produces a series of dots which look like recognisable characters.

There are several types of phosphor coating – notably P4, which gives you whitish dots, and P31 which gives green.

Picoprocessor

What is smaller than a microprocessor? The term picoprocessor, however, should be reserved for an LSI component which the U.S. company Computer Automation puts into some of its interface cables; that company thought of the word first.

What they do in the cables is organise the data moving along them so that the computer doesn't have to do it.

Pie-chart

Graphic representation of information in the form of a cake or pie with slices in it.

Pilot

PILOT is a programming language developed in the somewhat unlikely purlieus of the Medical Center at the University of California San Francisco campus. The initials stand for Programmed Inquiry Learning Or Teaching and it was designed originally to teach children how computers work.

Pilot uses many English words and programming it is really very simple, if you have the proper kind of program. It's not very useful for computation but it is satisfactory for quizzes, tests, dialogues, and other tasks involving words.

It aims to overcome the shortcomings of languages such as Fortran and Basic which are not designed to deal with text in a flexible, interactive way. Some languages with text processing features, like PL/1, are not commonly available to the teachers who need to write CAI programs, and they are troublesome to learn.

Most CAI programs have been written by professional programmers on large machines and that creates obvious barriers. Pilot is a simple language anybody can use which can be implemented on a wide variety of machines. It is inexpensive and it works.

Pins

Connector pins are the legs on a *chip*. They connect the chip to the electronic circuits on a circuit board; they fit into pre-defined holes and are soldered there, the solder making contact between the circuit and the pin.

You'll also have 'pins' inside a plug, of course. They do much the same job; as with mains electricity, the plug pin fits into a socket to make a connection.

Pixel

A 'picture element'. It's the smallest element in a graphics display which your programs can address directly. So the more pixels your computer screen can handle, the better your graphic displays can be.

PL/1

An interesting failure. PL/1 is an immodest acronym for 'Programming Language/1' and it was designed by IBM to combine the business dp virtues of languages like Cobol with the scientific capabilities of Fortran and Algol. The result is by no means a bad thing but it has never displaced the others. Big IBM installations make heavy use of it; but even there IBM Assembler, Cobol and Fortran are utilised more widely.

The trouble is that it needs a good deal of memory and plenty of re-learning, so it never appealed to the mass market of small computer users; it was never adopted over-enthusiasically by programmers who could make a living more easily with a different language.

PL/M

An *Intel* programming language designed for use on development systems. Easier to use than an *assembler* and probably qualifies as a high-level language. There is no connection with PL/1.

PL/M was largely written by Gary Kildall, who subsequently produced *CP/M*, set up *Digital Research,* and became a millionaire.

PLA

Programmed logic array. A kind of sub-microprocessor. A PLA is an LSI chip which can read several inputs to deduce which of several alternative outputs it should produce. You'll be safe sticking to PLA as Port of London Authority.

Plasma display

A microscope slide of blood? Alternatively see *gas discharge.*

Plotter

A device which draws things automatically; it could be a graph, or a picture of a man with a cloak, tall hat, beard, a fizzing bomb labelled BOMB.

Plotters are sometimes called any or all of graph, digital, incremental or X-Y plotters. They all work by receiving digital information from the computer, converting it into X-Y co-ordinates for a pen – or *ink-jet* gun, in more esoteric devices – and moving the pen across the paper in minute increments and in the direction specified.

Plugboard

Also known as patchboard – very occasionally – or patch panel, sometimes jack panel. A plug-board is simply a circuit board, which may or may not have circuits printed on to it, with sockets for removable plugs (jackplugs). Switching around the plugs can alter what the computer does, so plugboards are normally utilised only for diagnostic use by a maintenance engineer.

Plug-compatible

Something is plug-compatible if it can plug straight into something else, which in computer terms means it must meet all the electrical, logical and mechanical requirements of the 'host'. Typically an independent company will develop and sell plug-compatible add-ons – like terminals or disc drives or memory boards – which fit on to a popular computer like the TRS-80 or Pet or PDP-11 or IBM 360/370.

PMOS
Or P-channel MOS. An older alternative to N-channel MOS. A fabrication method for MOS semiconductor circuits; it's slower than NMOS.

Point of sale
This describes the locale where money changes hands in a shop of some kind. Ordinary cash registers are being replaced by clever devices which do everything the till does but also collect information about the sale – what has been sold and for how much.

This might be stored on a cassette and removed at the end of the day or the information might be passed directly to a computer. Either way the information is processed by computer to provide almost instant notification of matters like sales income and stock position.

Point to point
In computer terms it means a circuit connecting two and only two things – like a computer and a terminal – without the intermediate assistance of something else, like a computer. Compare *multipoint* connections, where several terminals attach by one line to one computer.

Pointer
It could be a *register* or *accumulator* which holds the address of the next memory location to be accessed by a program. Could be a register which effectively tells you which instruction you have searched in your program. Could be an address of part of an instruction

which defines the start address elsewhere of something else – a table of values, for instance.

POKE
An instruction available in most Basics which stores integer values in a specified memory location. For example, POKE 65,15360 places the ASCII number 65 – which is the letter 'A' – in memory address 15360.

Polish
Polish notation is a way of writing Boolean algebra so that all the operators precede all variables. There is also a backward version called Reverse Polish notation. Now forget it.

Polling
A technique used in data transmission, typically on *multipoint* networks where several terminals are sharing one line. A program in the computer interrogates each terminal in turn to find whether it has anything to say. This happens very quickly and, of course, it means you need terminals which can recognise when they are being polled.

Polymorphic Systems
Maker of the well-liked Poly-88 personal computer, it ceased operating in the 1979 shake-out.

Popular Computing Weekly
A 1982 arrival on the personal computer scene.

Port
A socket on the computer into which you can plug a terminal or some other I/O device.

POS
Or PoS. It stands for point of sale.

Power fail
Or rather, 'power-fail option' or 'power-fail/re-start' or 'power fail/auto-re-start', since it is obvious what power failing will mean. The better class of computer includes a device which monitors the power level. When voltage falls below a pre-set figure, this hardware option signals an imminent power failure and uses the milliseconds available to store the current contents of all important registers in some kind of non-volatile memory.

This could be *core* or battery-powered *MOS*. When the power can be returned, the registers are all reinstated so that things can proceed as before.

Power supply
A computer is electrical, so it needs electricity – but it can't use mains electricity direct, just as a transistor radio, calculator or train set can't. That's because your wall-sockets supply AC and the computer needs DC power. It also needs fewer volts than the mains, usually. So computers tend to include an AC-to-DC adapter, which everyone calls a 'power supply'. In fact, your computer may have separate 'power supplies' in it for the processor and memory, the disc, printer and VDU.

Practical Computing
In terms of pages, the biggest U.K. magazine for the personal computer buff. I was involved in its early days, since when it has become a moneyspinner for the publishing giant IPC (see Chapter 8 for other examples of computer-related IPC publications). It may be the biggest but that doesn't mean it's the best. I think *PCW*

looks better and it certainly claims more readers and I prefer it (not that that makes much difference).

Precision

At last here is a neat and logical definition, which makes a change. Since 'precision' means being very clearly defined, it is reasonable that in arithmetic it usually means the number of significant digits in a number.

On the other hand, there is nothing inherently clear about logic *per se*; precision, you see, is contrasted with *accuracy*. They are not the same thing. Accuracy refers generally to the number of figures following the decimal point – the more you have, the more accurate your number. Precision refers to discrimination from a number of possibilities – a four-digit numeric form allows you 10,000 possible numbers; that's exactly how precise you can be, no more and no less.

Prefix multipliers

This is a bit of maniac fun, some of the most useless information you could hope to acquire. You might have noticed that scientists and jargon generators generally like to express numbers by a factor of 10.

Here's what they mean:

deci	d	0.1
decu	D	10
hecto	h	100
kilo	k	1000
mega	M	100,000
giga	G	1,000,000,000
tera	T	1,000,000,000,000

Note the difference between 'k' and 'K'. One means 'times 1,000'; the other means 'times 1,024'. Why such an odd number? It's 2^{10}, and is handy – being so nearly 1,000 – in working decimal-to-binary conversions.

Getting smaller, you get:

centi	c
milli	m
micro	μ
nano	n
pico	p

Prestel

The pioneering British Telecom *viewdata* service. It was designed originally to make the Post Office more money by providing telephone subscribers with something else to do with their telephones. Users would have a cheap and uncomplicated *terminal* arrangement consisting of the telephone line, a slightly-modified TV set, and an inexpensive numeric keypad. With this they could dial a central computer database containing all kinds of useful information. Accessing that information would be simple, with a neat, logical, limited sequence of instructions anyone could use.

The information in question isn't provided directly by the Prestel organisers; they act as publishers. Instead, there are specialist companies called 'Information Providers' who receive a payment every time you dial their information; Prestel charges you (it appears on your telephone bill) and passes their share to them.

Wonderful idea; except that it didn't work. Early estimates suggested about 100,000 of us should have Prestel sets by now but the total is far fewer and most of them are business rather than domestic users. It transpires that most people don't want to pay the extra for information like train times or today's weather or which washing machine to buy to be presented on their TV screens. Business people, however, are finding it useful for economic statistics, share prices and other data which Information Providers can offer.

There's more to Prestel, too. You can send information to it as well as receive it; it's a little more complicated but if you have a microcomputer and a Prestel adapter board (available from several U.K. suppliers for *Apple, Commodore* and *CP/M* computers, among others) you can do it. See *telesoftware,* too.

Preventative maintenance

Things go wrong with computers and when they do they can be expensive to repair. Even small personal computers should have a regular preventative maintenance service with the aim of preventing faults before they happen (something like a regular car service, really).

Printer

Check *matrix* and *line* printers. A printer is a device which prints information sent from a computer on to paper. The principal examples are *matrix* printers – characters formed by dots when a pin strikes an inked ribbon on to paper; *chain* or band *line* printers – fast, noisy and expensive; *thermal* printers – dots formed by heating points on treated paper; *electrosensitive* printers – much the same but using electricity; *daisy-wheel* or petal printers – good-quality output; and *ink-jet* – complicated but possibly the coming thing.

Printout

What computers print-out on printers. Also the original name of a good British monthly magazine specialising in the Pet. Since then it's broadened its scope and changed its name to *Microcomputer Printout.*

Printwheel

Same as *daisywheel* when that term is used to refer specifically to the print element, the removable disc-like piece with the characters formed on it.

Private line

Also called leased line or private wire. It is possible to rent your own telephone line from British Telecom. You have to specify where it goes from and to; but once you have it, you can send data to the other end at any time.

With ordinary public telephone systems you pay by 'connect time'. You might not make contact when you want and you will suffer all the inevitable electrical interference, as well as any crossed lines and poor connections. None of that applies if you lease a private line. You will pay for the privilege, of course.

Procedure

In programming, this word will probably be used to mean a sequence of steps required to solve some problem. You might meet it in the phrase 'procedure-orientated language'; synonymous is 'problem-orientated language'.

Either way, it means a programming language in which the way you write programs reflects directly the process of solving a problem. The obvious example is something like Algol, where a statement in a program is an explicit algorithmic sequence of operations to be done. Most high-level programming languages are also procedure-orientated, some more formally than others.

Processor

Same as *CPU*. That portion of the computer which processes instructions.

To back-track slightly, a computer comprises processor, internal memory, some kind of input-output device(s), and probably some external storage. Programs are received by the processor from an input source, from memory, or from storage; they are decoded by the processor, probably with reference to system software held in memory; they are executed by the processor, which probably will involve calling information from memory or backing store on which operations are performed; and the results are despatched by the processor to an appropriate destination, like an output device or a disc store.

The terms 'computer' and 'processor' are employed usually more loosely, though, and are treated frequently as being synonymous. To some extent they are; many, but not all, of the essential characteristics of a computer system derive directly from the characteristics of the processor. Even so, it is important to realise that the processor is only one element in the system.

Processor Technology
A pioneer and an early casualty of the U.S. personal computer business, manufacturer of the Sol system which featured several novel ideas (including an operating system in *ROM*). Processor Technology was also one of the first companies to make *S-100* boards as accessories for the *Altair* computer. The company went into liquidation in 1979.

Production control
Running a manufacturing organisation is a classic case for computerisation. The problem is to meet orders placed; applying computers means that everything is so organised that the customer receives the goods on time. Other benefits might include faster delivery, less

capital tied-up in inventory, and better use of machinery.

On the other hand, to obtain all those benefits you have to integrate every possible factor. This will involve sales forecasting, planning what raw materials and other resources you will need, and when; deciding what levels of stock-holding you require; and so on. It can all become big and complex; you might need a big computer to cover it all and you might have to be a big company to derive any benefit from the outlay on your system.

Smaller companies and smaller computers can have parts of the full idealised system, of course – forecasting and stock control are the obvious examples. Anyone who can produce a flexible, full-blown production control system on a micro ought to prosper.

Production run
Like running a program, as opposed to test runs.

Program
And not programme, please God. Language is evolving; when a specific meaning is attributed by a large enough number of people to a particular bunch of syllables, let's assist the process of general comprehension.

Or to put it another way, we don't like 'programme' to mean 'program' – and the latter means a set of instructions which tells a computer what operations are to be performed to produce the desired results.

One important point is that a program is usually a complete entity which does something. A group of programs may be linked together, one working with the results from another; and within an individual program there may be subroutines which each do something which contributes to the whole. So it's not necessarily clearcut.

Program generator

A piece of software which enables the user to design a program on the computer. You tell the system what kind of input you will have, what files you want set up, what reports and other output are required, and how that output should be produced. The program generator (which is probably one or more linked programs) will then produce automatically the program *code* which would be required for the job you've specified.

Programme

A collection of advertisements and mis-spelled actors' names for which you pay exorbitantly when you make your thrice-annual visit to *No Sex Please We're British*.

Programmer

Used to be a fuzzily-bearded individual with a faded Hepworths jacket, patched jeans, a pocketful of multi-coloured ballpoint pens, and an open invitation to the girls of the local sixth form to come up and see his computer some time.

That's all changed; we're all programmers now. There's a great shortage of professionals who write computer programs for a living, though. The top-flight programmer needs a funny mix of goal-directed logical appreciation and Edward de Bono creativity; that's why they are paid so well.

Programmers aren't the same as systems analysts, though you with your personal computer will be combining the job functions. In a highly-structured world, programmers are in three flavours – applications programmers, who write programs which do something; systems programmers, who produce software which helps the applications programmers do what it is that they do: and maintenance programmers, who correct other people's work and keep existing programs up-to-date.

Programmer's Aid
A type of *programmer's toolkit*.

Programmer's Toolkit
This is a proprietary name but it is so widely-used that it's become generic. It covers a collection of additional functions and facilities which help you write programs. Usually they would be provided as *firmware* in the form of a plug-in *ROM chip* or *cartridge*.

The functions in question will be things like AUTO, to give you automatic line numbering when you are writing Basic programs; RENUMBER, to re-number lines and so tidy things when you've been making changes to the program; HELP, to indicate what went wrong when your program stopped in its tracks; and MERGE, which could enable you to merge two separate programs or to include a ready-written standard subroutine in your new program.

Some computers will provide such goodies automatically but if yours doesn't, you might want to look for a toolkit. The best-known examples are for the *Vic*, *Pet* and *Apple*.

Programming
The basic steps in the ideal version of the programming process are five. First, you think; that is usually called understanding the problem and you'll finish with a bunch of doodled notes on how the problem might be solved.

Then you draw a *flowchart* – or rather you draw several, since your first effort won't work. Well, mine don't.

Third, you write some code – and, fourth, you test it on a computer until it works. Finally, you produce the documentation which will help you and others to understand and use it (and probably to amend it in the future). In fact, you should have been keeping notes and flowcharts all along the line to help you write the documentation.

PROLOG

One of the world's newest programming languages, PROLOG stands for PROgramming in LOGic. It is based on a slightly esoteric approach to solving theorem problems which emanated from the University of Marseilles in 1975. Prolog is a halfway house towards an *artificial intelligence* language, consisting as it does of statements which define logical relationships. So you use logical statements as a way of making enquiries at databases and the like.

The language (the development of which is being done at Imperial College, London) has some way to go before it reaches what you might call maturity; it's more or less nuzzling against puberty right now. It is very promising, not least because work with schoolchildren suggests that Prolog will be a good way of teaching them about computers and a useful method of increasing their decision-making capabilities.

PROM

Storm-lashed stretch of crumbling asphalt at Skegness? Expensive opportunity to stand for five hours in the Royal Albert Hall with 37 other people and listen to the first-ever performance by 16-year-old sensation Waldemar Billings of her opus *Everything I know in*

Two Parts featuring nine choirs. J Arthur Rank on gong, and a Newcomen beam engine? Programmable Read-Only Memory? Answers on a £10 note, please.

You'll find a discussion of PROM in the *memory* section. It's a type of read-only memory which can be programmed individually by the user (ordinary ROM is ready-programmed from the factory). You'll need a special device called a PROM programmer, which is what puts the bit patterns into a PROM chip. Some PROMs are erasable; they are called EPROMs and they can be re-programmed.

Proofread

To check text for mistakes. Some of the so-called *spelling checker* programs are described optimistically as 'proofreaders' but that just highlights one of their major deficiencies. They can ensure only that the words are spelt correctly; proofreading is also concerned that the word is the correct one to use ('beech' may be spelled correctly but it's not the word you want in the phrase 'hey gang let's go down to the beach') and that the grammar is also correct.

Proprietary software

Programs for which the legal title is held by someone other than the user. The point is that in law you are not allowed normally to copy, re-sell, or amend someone else's program. The question of who 'owns' software is still in the air, though you would have to change someone else's programs very thoroughly to claim them as your own.

Protocol

As in diplomacy and elsewhere, it's a collection of rules which govern intercourse. Stop sniggering at the back there. A communications protocol is a set of formal conventions for the exchange of information, essentially so that both sides (a computer and a terminal, say) know what's supposed to be happening and when. Otherwise the stream of bits passing down the link would be more or less meaningless to the recipient.

Prototype

Prototyping is the development phase in a microprocessor-based product. We tend to see only the man-machine end of computing, with people creating and running programs as the normal use of a micro system. Most microprocessors are used in products where they are almost invisible, like sewing machines, ovens, cars, automatic manufacturing, and even pocket calculators.

To develop the software for them you need a prototyping system, which is a programmable version of your chosen micro configured with a terminal and some storage. You will probably have a *PROM* which will be buried eventually in the end-user product along with your micro.

Obviously the first fruits of this process will be a prototype; because you will be expecting errors, you will produce only a few and you will spend a good deal of time checking them.

PSN

Witty and much-needed abbreviation for PSTN.

PSTN

Public Switched Telephone Network. The ordinary public telephone system, as compared to *private lines*.

PSW

Processor Status Word; some computers call it the Program Status Word. It's a reference area within the processor which is updated automatically with useful information – like what is going on now. It is used by clever programmers and operators to alter some detail of the execution of the program.

PTP

Paper tape punch.

PTR

Paper tape reader. It detects the presence or absence of punched holes. Usually it does so optically, by picking-up light shining through the holes. Electrical sensing has also been used.

Pulse

Black-eyed beans qualify. So does a short and sudden burst of electrical activity. It's important because a computer system can easily be designed to accept information transmitted as pulses – after all, the pulse/no pulse condition is a binary state, exactly like the off/on 0/1 internals of the computer.

'Pulse code modulation' or PCM is a fairly simple data transmission technique which uses this; an alternative is frequency modulation, where information is represented not by pulse/no pulse but by the frequency of signals.

Punch

Apart from the obvious impact this can have, a punch is an ingenious mechanical device constructed cleverly for the purpose of putting holes into punched cards. Obviously a punched card isn't a punched card until it has been punched with a punch. See *card*.

Q-bus

For some reason *Digital Equipment* seems to be trying to suppress this name but it's still widely-used to refer to the *bus* system on its LS1-11 microcomputers.

Qume

The major rival at present to *Diablo* in the *daisywheel* printer business but there are many up-and-coming Japanese and Italian contenders.

QWERTY

The traditional typewriter keyboard layout, which starts with these letters. In Europe you'll find most start AZERTY.

Rack

Same as *chassis*.

Radio Shack

A line of home electronics stores in the States bought a few years ago by leather goods company Tandy. Today Tandy retains the name Radio Shack for its direct selling in the U.S., which is why TRS-80s still have Radio Shack stamped on them, even though you might be buying them in a Tandy shop.

Rair

Founded in 1975 as a computer *bureau* and vendor of computer *terminals,* Rair has become a likeable and independent-minded British manufacturer of micro-computer systems at the £2,000-plus level. Its first *Black Box* appeared in 1978, since when it has sold more than 1,000 of them — not bad for a small and largely self-financed firm.

RAM

That husky Hemeling drinker with the MGB who gets the spotty *au pairs*. It's also random access memory, which is the kind you load programs and data to and from. The other kind is already there ready-loaded with programs or data; that's ROM. See the extended exposition on *memory*.

RAM is sometimes called read/write memory, because that's what you can do with it — and this distinguishes it from read-only memory (ROM). RWM doesn't make a neat acronym, unlike RAM. That's life.

RAM might be qualified as 'dynamic' or 'static'. This is getting into heavy electronics but, in essence, a RAM chip stores information as bit patterns (qv) in electrically-charged cells, one cell to a bit; so when a charge is present, that bit is read as '1'. In static RAM, information is retained until power is interrupted. In dynamic RAM, the storage cell must be re-charged continually to maintain an 'on' state.

RAM memory chips are sometimes called simply RAMs. Use this if you want to appear sophisticated and knowledgeable, or perhaps if you need to save your outlay on breath. One of the hot areas in memory technology at the moment is just how much information you can store on RAM chips — obviously the greater the capacity the more compact and cheap the overall system.

It should also be simpler and more reliable, too, for reducing the number of components required (the 'chip count') means that the electrical requirements and heat dissipation are easier for the designer; and less heat means greater longevity in electronics.

The original RAMs stored 1,042 bits (1 Kb). They were displaced by 4K RAMs, then by 16K chips — which is what most minis and micros use now. 64K

RAMS are becoming available on a few systems and soon there will be 256K-bit memory chips.

RAMP
You might never see this acronym but it stands for 'Reliability Availability and Maintenance Performance'. These are what you need to keep your computer up and running. U.S. manufacturers, in particular, put together 'RAMP kits' or 'RAMP courses' to help you and/or their engineers to obtain the maximum working life from your purchase.

IBM has a similar slogan, RAS, for Reliability, Availability, Serviceability.

Random access
See *RAM.* The term 'random access' really means that it takes just about the same length of time to get at any information, no matter where it is in the particular storage device.

Random number generator
A *program* or hardware component whose sole purpose is to produce (would you believe) random numbers. That's a number which can be repeated only by chance. Random numbers are handy for games, being more or less the equivalent of throwing dice.

RCA
Radio Corporation of America. This company was one of the pioneers of computing, though it sold its computer line to Sperry Univac in the 1960s. It has also done a great deal of work on raw electronics, including the early R&D on *CMOS.* It had a microprocessor line called the RCA 1800, packaged under the name COS-MAC if you want a working version; a few hobbyists rate it highly.

Read

Extract information, usually from *memory* or *external storage*.

Read-only memory

See *ROM*.

Readout

A displayed or printed message.

Real time

Once a popular buzzword, now heard rarely. It has various esoteric definitions but 'fast' is a generally appropriate synonym.

Real-time clock

A component provided in most computers which acts essentially as an electronic timer. Usually it can provide both *clock time* (the time of day) and *elapsed time* (how long a particular internal job is taking).

Record

Many esoteric concepts are available for a full formal definition but practically a record is a bunch of related information or items of data. A collection of records is a *file*.

Redundancy

Provides extra and/or duplicated equipment or programs for use in an emergency when the main lot fails. There is also 'redundancy checking' which is a technique for ensuring against data loss when information is being transmitted or passed around inside the computer. It involves adding one or more redundant *bits* on to each *word* which is being moved and checking at the other end to make sure they're still there.

Re-entrant code

Clever programming technique provided on some computers to minimise memory occupancy when two users want to run the same *program* or use the same *subroutine* at the same time. Instead of each user having his or her own copy of the code, re-entrancy means one copy can reside in memory with users sharing it. Problems can result, of course, if users want to run precisely the same block of code at precisely the same time; but the *operating system* will be fancy enough to include prophylactic measures.

Register

Same as *accumulator*.

Research Machine

Likeable Oxford-based microcomputer company whose 380-Z computer is being well-accepted in the educational market.

It's a little expensive and looks uncompromisingly boxy; but it has some good facilities, especially a good graphics package. It uses the *CP/M* operating system.

Reset

Same as *initialise,* except that the word 'reset' usually appears on a button on the keyboard. You press it and everything returns to its start state — which, among other things, means you jump out of any program you happen to be running at the time.

Response time

How long it takes the computer to respond to something — which in practice is usually you typing-in something at the keyboard.

RFP

Request for Proposal — what a business user would send to a would-be supplier.

RFQ

Request for Quotation — much the same thing.

RGB

You might meet this in reference to video *monitors*. It stands for the highly-untechnical 'red-green-blue'.

You see, those are the three basic colours used to build a picture on a television set or a computer's colour screen. There are three electron 'guns' inside the TV or the display, each of which handles the production of only one colour.

There are two types of colour display in terms of the way a picture reaches the screen. All TVs and some monitors use what's called 'composite' video and here all the information about colour and shape arrives at the screen as a single stream of data; translating that into the three colours to work the three electron 'guns' takes some time and the distinctions between colours become a bit fuzzy.

RGB monitors require a special piece of circuitry in the computer which sends the signals for the picture in three separate streams of data, one for each colour and therefore one to drive each 'gun'. The result is infinitely more crisp.

The RGB circuitry adds to the price and you also need a special RGB monitor; both of those increase the total price, which is why most computers and most screens stay with composite video. A few micros incorporate RGB (like the NEC PC 8000, IBM Personal Computer, Cromemco and Apple III) and for others, notably the Apple II, you can obtain plug-in RGB boards.

Robot

Not easy to define, though most of us know one when we see it. Broadly, a robot is a physical computer — it can be assumed to have a memory for programs and a computer to control it, input coming from various *sensors* and output including physical actions.

ROM

Read-only memory — see *RAM* and *microcode*. Because the supplier doesn't have to include any ways of changing the contents of this kind of *memory*, those contents being fixed at the manufacturing stage, it is very quick to access ROM. So it's widely-used for non-alterable programs which are used frequently and for which fast access is desirable — all or part of the *operating system*, for instance.

Rosetta

Small U.S. software supplier responsible for *SMALL-TALK*.

Routine

A few lines of *code* which perform a particular function as part of a program. Same as *subroutine*.

RPG

Report Program Generator. Interesting programming *language* invented by IBM for small business computers. It's much simpler to use than Cobol and is based on the fact that most business computing really involves little more than collecting together previously stored pieces of information into reports of one kind or another. RPG never really caught on, though — it's too simple and takes up a good deal of memory.

RS232

A type of *interface*. See *serial* and *IEEE*, too.

Run

Execute one more *program*.

Savvy

Some speculative flag-waving. Savvy is going to be big, you will to hear a great deal about it, it's the best thing since sweet 'n' sour gherkins. It's a kind of novel programming language from New Mexico, courtesy of a company called Excalibur Technologies; and, in effect, it provides a low-cost method of allowing a microcomputer to respond to English language commands.

It's a plug-in circuit board which functions as what's called an 'adaptive pattern recognition processor'. This means it will look at a phrase you've typed-in and ask itself whether it's ever seen anything like that before (so you don't have to worry too much about typing-in commands in exactly the same way every time). If it doesn't recognise the input, it asks you to define what you want.

Savvy will then translate your English-like input into something the computer can understand, thus acting as a kind of robot programmer.

Savvy costs about £1,000, which isn't bad. It has been demonstrated working on an Apple II.

SBC

Small business computer — same as SBS.

SBS

Small business system — which is a somewhat vague term. Let's take it to mean a computer costing less than £50,000 (probably less then £20,000, in fact) which can be used by a business; that means it has the appropriate I/O, *memory* and *programs*.

There is also a U.S. venture calles Satellite Business Systems which is abbreviated to SBS. This company is putting communications satellites into orbit and will be selling telecomms facilities based on them; IBM has a stake in SBS, which is one reason why it's so interesting — IBM computers and other clever devices can be used at the ends of the communications link.

Satellites are likely to be big business soon and a number of ventures are putting them up there, among them a consortium of European *PTTs* which includes British Telecom.

Scheduling

A way in which several users can share one computer — providing the *operating system* will allow it. There are two methods of scheduling system resources. 'Time-sharing' typically involves a 'round-robin' schedule, where all users are given a fixed time-slot — typically about 100 milliseconds — and they get it in strict sequence.

'Priority scheduling' is more complicated — each possible event has a priority level and system resources are given over to the job with the highest priority awaiting execution. That job keeps executing until a task with a higher priority wants to run or until the current task reaches a point at which some input or output is called for.

Most interactive commercial applications obviously perform plenty of input and output, with system and user talking constantly to each other. Consequently, the switching between tasks is very fast and only rarely will a particular task be able to monopolise system resources for more than a fraction of a second.

Scratchpad
Same as *workspace*.

Scriptsit
Popular, low-cost *word processor* package for *Tandy* computers.

Scroll
Refers to the action of moving the contents of a display screen up or down. There are two methods of getting new information on to a screen — scrolling (it's sometimes called *roll* mode) or paging. In page mode the new information just over-writes the existing display from the top, often without wiping the screen clean first; but scrolling means that the information to be displayed isn't split into 'pages' like this. Instead, the screen is treated as a kind of window which can be moved around memory — so the effect is very like unrolling and reading a Hear Ye Hear Ye scroll. New information appears at the bottom of the screen and everything moves up one line. Some screens can scroll the other way, too — new information appears at the top and the text already there moves down.

SECAM
One of the three main standards for displaying colour pictures on TV; it's the one the French use. See *NTSC* for more on this.

Sector
Part of a disc — the term is also used as a synonym for for the data held in the *sector*.

The disc has concentric tracks; it also has radial divisions, so that the disc surface is also organised into wedges.

These divisions may be physical, in that the magnetic material on the disc is not physically there, or notional in that the data is written in these patterns. The two kinds are called 'hard'- and 'soft'-sectored respectively.

One of those triangular sections is a sector, and location of a block of data usually is addressed by reference to its track and sector numbers.

Seek time

What happens after you have counted to 100 with your hands over your eyes. It's also the time taken by a disc unit (could be a floppy disc drive) to position its read-head over the specified track on the disc.

Seek time is a good measure of comparison — a disc drive which can get to the information quicker than another disc drive should be better. There's more to it than that; it may also take some time for the disc to get up speed, and there'll be a few more microseconds taken by reading or writing the data. So total *access time* involves more than just seek time.

In any case, there are many other blocks, bottlenecks and other pitfalls for the computer to negotiate before it can translate your program into information delivered back to you. So seek time isn't necessarily a useful indicator of overall computing throughput. In which case you may wonder why I included it in the Glossary. Well, so do I — now.

Segment

A variable-sized portion of program used in *paging;* see *swapping,* too.

Seikosha

A Japanese maker of *dot matrix* printers. If you want a printer which can do 80 characters to a line, which approximates to normal A4 paper size, I don't think you'll be able to find a cheaper printer than the Seikosha GP80A. True, you'll have to be satisfied with a modest print speed (60 characters per second if you're lucky); it can't do true below-the-line descenders and, frankly, it screeches, but for less than £200, who's complaining?

Semiconductor

Malcolm Sargent when he was still a church organist? Oh, well, never mind. A semiconductor is a material whose electrical conductivity is between that of metal and an insulator.

Semiconductors have many exceptional and usable attributes in computing, which is all you need to know about them.

These days computer memory tends to be semiconductor, which means data is stored in a bunch of miniature semiconductor circuits.

Serial

Serial means things happen in sequence rather than at the same time. So serial transmission or serial I/O is a method of communication in which each bit of information is sent sequentially on a single channel; serial access means getting at records in the order in which they occur.

Serial-access storage devices are typified by cassette; they are cheaper than *random-access* systems like floppy disc, but it takes much longer to reach a given piece of information on a serial medium like tape.

Serial interfaces are widely-used to connect terminals to computers; they are technically simpler than *parallel* interfaces and can be used over longer distances.

There are three well-known serial interfaces, defining which pin in the plug relates to which wire and which electrical signal.

RS232C, a specification also known as CCITT V24, was laid down originally by an American standards body (the CCITT is a European organisation). It is probably the most widely-used interface; almost all microcomputers and many peripherals — especially printers and terminals — have RS232C connectors. If you're thinking of hooking on to a RS232C socket, check carefully what the wires mean — the 'data in', 'data out' and 'common return' pins are usually standard, but others, like 'printer busy' (very useful for stopping the flow of data while a printer gets on with things) can vary.

20mA current loop is still popular. It was first used on the Teletype terminal, and the Teletype 33 was for much of the 1960s the dominant computer terminal. It became a *de facto* standard but these days RS232C is more popular. The 20mA current loop design cannot operate normally as quickly as RS232C, so it cannot be used for the faster printers.

IEEE is described fully in a Glossary entry of its own. Designed originally for attached scientific instruments to a computer, it was adopted by Commodore for the *Pet* and then the *Vic*.

Set
Usually means giving a particular *bit* the value '1'.

Sharp
One of the major Japanese manufacturers of most things which qualify as advanced domestic electronics, especially stereo sound systems and calculators. Sharp has a number of small computers. The MZ-80K, was one of the first personal computers from Japan, and to some extent it shows; you have screen, keyboard and

built-in cassette for about £460. There's already plenty of software for it now, though. The MZ-80B is a much more pleasant unit, with a much-improved design, better keyboard, fine graphics, and a price tag of more than £1,000.

You knew the company originally got its name from a self-sharpening pencil, of course.

Shift
Moving data to the right or left. In practice, the term applies to operations deep inside the assembly-language level, and a shift consists of moving the contents of a register left or right by one (or more) bit. The bit falling out of one end would go into carry area somewhere; the bit coming in is usually '0'. The left shift of a binary number by one place is equivalent to multiplying by two.

Signal
Any conveyor of information — 'the physical embodiment of a message', says one dictionary. In practice, in computers it means a desirable electrical event — undesirable electrical happenstance is called *noise*.

Silicon
A non-metallic chemical element widely-used as the semiconductor in modern *semiconductor* circuitry.

Silicon Valley
The area around Sunnyvale in California where most of the semiconductor manufacturers are installed — and where Fairchild and Hewlett-Packard, the two major progenitors of the modern electronics business, are located. Also called Silicon Gulch.

Simplex

You won't often meet this word but it means communication in one direction only. Compare *duplex,* which allows you to transmit in either direction down the same link.

Simplicalc

A *spreadsheet* calculator for the Pet and Vic.

Simulate

Often confused with 'stimulate' but you'll get used to the difference when you get older. Simulate means to represent some aspects of one thing by setting-up a symbolic analogue of it. Usually this means running a mathematical model of something.

This simulating is typified by something like the Club of Rome's *Limits to Growth* scenario; the computer is given a set of base data and a collection of variables. Those can be frankly wrong and, more important, you might well have missed some of the more important considerations when you set up your model.

Sinclair

Clive Sinclair is an entrepreneur in the classic mould, one of the great (though not always successful) innovators in British electronics. A pioneer of good design and compact packaging in audio equipment, he seems to have given the world much of the electronic gadgetry which characterises our times — the first pocket-sized pocket calculator (that was in 1972 and it cost £79), low-cost digital watches (circa 1975), the world's first miniature television (1977 originally).

In 1980 he had another first in the shape of the £100 computer, ZX-80. Since then he's produced the £70 computer, too, (ZX-81); and the Sinclair Spectrum at £125 again has very definitely set new standards for price-performance in home computers. The man probably is some kind of authentic genius, an electronics engineer with a most unusual flair and the ability to translate his skill into real products; they are products which are always priced attractively, which always look good and which always earn themselves a great deal of publicity.

Sinclair products have not necessarily had an entirely favourable press. Some have not withstood prolonged use; the calculators and the 'Black Watch' in particular racked-up more than a few complaints. Sinclair's company was in trouble in the mid-1970s following component supplier problems with the watch at a time when Japanese imports meant the bottom suddenly fell out of the calculator market. The NEB put in some money in the expectation that the miniature TV would take off, and it didn't; and Sinclair was probably lucky to get out with a £10,000 golden handshake and some of his top design people to set up his own company to make the ZX-80.

What's more, the promotion of Sinclair products has occasionally been over-enthusiastic. Early in his career Sinclair recognised the virtues of mail-order marketing and he has always opted for glossy fill-in-the-coupon promotions. The advertisements for the ZX-80 were somewhat misleading in the suggestion that you could run your business with one of the computers. You can't.

The ZX-81 and Spectrum are promoted much more accurately as 'personal computers'. In other words, they are computers for the individual and can be justified only in terms of what they will do for the individual.

Sinclair is now riding high. The ZX-81 works and it's selling well — more than 300,000 at the last count, and it's only just starting to get under way in the States.

Sinclair isn't pausing for breath: his projects now include a flat-screen TV the size of a cigarette packet and due to retail for £50, an electric car, and a new compact computer with built-in flat screen and micro-floppy discs.

Makes you proud to be British, doesn't it?

Sirius

The company is called Sirius Systems Technology and it's one of the fastest-growing U.S. microcomputer manufacturers. The computer it makes is the Sirius 1 and it looks like one of the best business micros to have appeared in many moons. It's a 16-bit computer, which means it can have a good deal of memory, which in turn allows it to run relatively complicated and sophisticated programs.

The Sirius, which is distributed in the U.K. at a basic £2,400 or so by *ACT,* also has a remarkably good, clear display and an excellent keyboard. It uses the *Intel* 8086 microprocessor and the 16-bit enhancement of the *CP/M* operating system CP/M-86 (*Unix* is also promised). For the starting price you get a desk-top computer with two mini-floppy disc drives and 128KB memory.

Chuck *Peddle* set up the company after he left *Commodore.* The (probably apocryphal) story behind the name was that he wanted to be taken seriously. Do you believe that? Well, that's what he said, I think.

SMALLTALK

Here's a bit of propheteering — this novel and little-used programming language is both important and likely to become a big thing. It's been around for a time, in fact, but has suffered from being bottled-up in a Xerox Corp research laboratory in Silicon Valley. A company called Rosetta Inc is trying to popularise it now.

Another reason for its lack of acceptance is its unusual structure — basically, it's just not like any other computer language. This is hardly the place to go into detail but if you're interested in programming keep an eye open for it. The language is really simple to use, features plenty of readily-understood graphic interaction, and generally looks an excellent choice for really 'personal' computing.

SNA
Systems Network Architect rivals DNA in the complexity stakes. SNA is the latest of IBM grand designs for specifying how its computers and other hardware can be plugged together. Look at *network*.

Software
Programs. In strictly literal terms, you also ought to include program documentation and programming procedures.

Sol
RIP. This pioneering home computer had wooden sides and a neat flat PCB layout inside it. Made by Processor Technology, which ceased to operate in 1979.

Solid-state
This is the branch of physics which concerns itself with the essential properties of semiconductor materials. All you need to know is that 'solid-state' and 'semiconductor' are used loosely as synonyms to refer to the wonders of current computer technology.

Sony

Sony had dabbled in just about everything else a self-respecting Japanese electronics company might contemplate, so it was only to be expected that it would announce a microcomputer, too. It's the SMC-70, a very stylish business microcomputer with the *CP/M* operating system and a mid-range price.

The other notable Sony participation in the microcomputer game is probably the more important activity, really — its development of very small and fairly cheap *floppy disc* drives. These 'microfloppies' measure 3.5in. in diameter and record something between 280KB and 440KB of information per disc. The SMC-70 uses them but Sony is also selling them to other manufacturers.

Sorceror

The microcomputer from *Exidy*. An *S-100*-based system, it was one of the first micros to use the *CP/M* operating system as standard; it was one of the first to incorporate a reasonable keyboard (and it still has one of the best typewriter-type layouts); and it was one of the first to feature the idea of plug-in *cartridges* containing games, languages and other functions in *firmware*. Despite that, it never achieved the early success it probably deserved.

It is promoted principally as a business computer. In its basic form it costs £700 but business installations with discs and screen are more likely to start at around £2,750.

Sorcim

U.S. software company with a number of good packages for *CP/M* microcomputers, including the Supercalc *spreadsheet* calculator. Great name, isn't it?

Really redolent of magic and mystery but it's just 'micros' spelt backwards.

Sord

Sord is a Japanese company which claims to have about one-fifth of its home market for personal computers. Outside Japan it's relatively unknown, though it takes Europe seriously enough to have a new factory in the Republic of Ireland. It has several micros but the one which will probably be pushed in Europe is the M-23 business system, priced around the £2,000 mark.

Sort

A helpful function whereby items in data file are re-arranged in some specified sequence according to some *key* which each record in the file has. There are dozens of sorting techniques, none of which you need to know anything at all about. A sort package is usually provided among the *utilities* with a computer.

SOS

Several microcomputer vendors have confusingly adopted these initials for their *operating system.* Among them are *Sord* for the M-23 and *Apple* for the Apple III.

Source, The

An information service available to people with personal computers. The Source maintains a good deal of information, games and other things a subscriber might want; you pay them money, you get a *modem* or an *acoustic coupler,* and you dial the Source computer whenever you want to access its databases. See the entry for *Compuserve,* which is a head-on competitor.

Source code

This is a *program* written by a human programmer. It compares to *object code,* which is the *machine code* into which a source program is translated.

Spec

Short for specification. If you're a company buying a computer, you should receive several specifications at different levels of detail as part of the system's documentation.

Spectrum

It has to be on your short list if you want a home computer, doesn't it? At £125 the *Sinclair* Spectrum has set a fast pace in the price-performance stakes at this level of computing. Styling is better than with either of the ZXs and the keyboard in particular is a real improvement; it still doesn't give typewriter-type keys, which is one definite plus for Spectrum competitors, but at least there is a positive feel to them. Anyhow, at this price that is probably quibbling; the Spectrum offers good colour and graphics, a good version of Basic with helpful graphics commands, and the promise of economical extension from Sinclair (forthcoming goodies include a low-cost floppy disc drive) and from numerous independent vendors of software and hardware add-ons.

Spelling checker

A program which (wait for it) can check your spelling. Spelling checkers have a dictionary of words at their elbow, though in fact it's not a dictionary, it's a lexicon (a list of words). When you run the program it reads through the specified piece of text you have stored previously on the computer. Each word of your glowing prose is checked to see if it's in the dictionary. If it isn't, you are informed somehow; usually the word is marked or highlighted if the spelling checker does not recognise it.

Words picked up in this way might be mistakes, in which case you can correct them. Or it could be that they're not in the dictionary, in which case most spelling checkers will give you the option of adding them automatically to the dictionary.

Sometimes these programs are called 'proofreaders' but they aren't. See the Glossary entry for *proofreader*.

Spinwriter

The letter-quality printer from *NEC*. It's fast, robust, and compares well in quality to *daisywheel* printers; but then it uses a very similar print mechanism, which resembles a daisywheel whose spokes have been bent upwards to form a kind of cup. NEC calls it a 'thimble'.

Spellbinder

A good *word processing* package for microcomputers with the *CP/M* operating system.

Spellguard

A fine *spelling checker* for *CP/M*-based computers.

Spooling

A technique of saving data temporarily on a high-speed device for output by the operating system to a slower peripheral. This overcomes the irritating fact that some parts of the computer work faster than others. Usually it's the disc versus the printer.

Say the printer outputs at a respectable 150 characters per second. If you have a large amount of output, you may find this a real bottleneck when your floppy disc is delivering data to be processed at more than 12,000 characters per second – and the CPU can process data even more quickly. Of course, there are natural gaps in the workflow when the printer can catch up a little, but even so it's clear that the system could often have to stop everything to deal with the printing.

Spooling overcomes that because everything destined to be output can be dumped on to disc and printed later.

Spreadsheet

There are at least 22 programs of which I know claiming to be *spreadsheet* calculators, which must mean there are several more. A spreadsheet is a sheet of paper ruled into a grid of rows and columns on which you can do numeric (usually financial) calculations. A spreadsheet calculator program does exactly the same thing on the screen of your computer; with at least 22 such packages available there's almost bound to be one which works on *your* computer.

Usually the program allows you to set up a spreadsheet which is wider and deeper than the screen, so you can scroll horizontally and vertically to get around the sheet. Into each of the boxes you can put numbers and words which are displayed. Or you can put a formula there, in which case the computer remembers it, works it out, and displays the result in the box. When any of the figures in the formula are changed, it is re-calculated and the new result displayed.

Because of that capability, spreadsheet calculators are exceptionally good at doing 'what if' assessments. You can try a forecast with one set of figures, then change them and see how the result alters.

The craze for spreadsheets on small computers began with the 1979 arrival of *VisiCalc,* which now is approaching 500,000 sales. Several other packages are referenced in the Glossary.

Sprocket holes

Holes along the edge of *continuous stationery*. They engage the sprockets on the printer platen which pull the paper around.

Punched tape (nasty) also has sprocket holes, though in this case they run down the middle of the tape.

SS-50

An interface *bus* with 50 wires along the *backplane*. An early starter in the *de facto* standard stakes, it was developed for M6800-based systems by SWTP; the S-100 bus had a head start, though, because it applies to the more popular 8080-based micros.

SSI

Small-Scale Integration, with only a few logic circuits on one chip (typically four or five). This is now old-style IC technology; much more common is MSI (up to 100 circuits per chip) and Large-Scale Integration (more than 100, often more than 500 or 1,000 per chip).

Stack

Don't bother with this one if you don't feel like it – it's really esoteric. Some computers use a small area of main memory as a temporary data store called a stack; it works on a last-in, first-out basis and it is essential for keeping track of subroutines – the stack typically holds the return address.

The assembly language will provide instructions for getting data in and out of the stack, often the amiably-named PUSH and POP commands.

Systems which use stacks generally do not require

the programmer to keep track of the locations into which data is being stacked. This is done automatically through a stack 'pointer'. To keep track of the last item added to the stack, a register may contain the memory address where the last item is stored in the stack; on some systems, all but one or two registers may be used as a stack pointer.

There's also an outfit in Liverpool called Stack Computer Services with knowledge about *Commodore* products and several add-on goodies for the Vic and Pet.

Starwriter

One of the *daisywheel* printers from *TEC*.

State of the art

About the most extreme possible compliment a computer vendor can use to describe the computers it vends. It means something like 'technically the most advanced possible within the constraints of today's technology and today's knowledge'. Or in other words, 'very good'.

Static RAM

See *RAM*.

Stepper motor

Sometimes called a *stepping motor*. It is found frequently in electro-mechanical devices like printers. It rotates by a fixed amount every time it accepts an electrical pulse. Stepper motors are generally the best solution where designers want precise, economical movements with minimum wear.

Stimulation

Easily distinguished from 'simulation' by being much

more fun (usually).

String

A sequence of records, words or characters – usually arranged in some specific order.

Stringy floppy

A curious but apt name for a device which tries to give you the benefits of floppy disc storage at the price of tape cassette storage. In fact, it's a high-speed continuous tape loop cartridge; it can operate at speeds similar to those of a mini-floppy, and the storage capacity also compares well – but it is half the price. So why don't you see more of them? Good question – I don't know.

The name is a trademark held by a manufacturing company called Exatron but it might become a generic term.

Structured programming

The trouble with *Basic* is that it's too easy. You don't have to do too much thinking before you can start writing your program; this means it's tempting to do your thinking while you are writing. So you can add new steps as they occur to you. If they don't fit in the sequence of instructions which you happen to be working at the time, you always have the mighty GOTO statement; that can switch the program away to some other point where you can put the addition. Then you use another GOTO to return to where you were.

So what's wrong with that? Well, the seductive GOTO can produce a real mess. If things aren't proceeding in a tidy, natural sequence, there is a very good chance that confusion and error will be the result. The program may run but with all that jumping about it will be extremely difficult for anyone to understand what is going on; and it's likely that one day you or someone else will want to amend the program somewhat, so you'll have to be able to figure it out.

GOTO is the prime example but it isn't the only statement in Basic which encourages such sloppy and dangerous programming habits, and Basic isn't the only language to include them.

What's the alternative, then? Let's hear a big hand for 'structured programming'. Massive textbooks have been written on this subject but, to put it simply, structured programming is the desirability of applying some forethought and some method to your programwriting.

For a start, almost all programs can be separated into functional sections, different portions which each do something even though they also fit together. Structured programming advises you to develop your program in those terms. So first you decide on a description of what the different sections will do.

Then for each section you put in a little more detail and you'll find that there are identifiable subsections within each portion. You continue like that and eventually you will reach a level of detail where you can start writing program code. It's sometimes called 'topdown programming', for obvious reasons.

Put like this, structured programming doesn't sound like a big deal. Indeed, if you have a Vic with only 3.5K memory, you won't be able to write programs long enough to have many sections and subsections. Even so, the general approach is well worth it; you will have programs which are more likely to work, which are simpler to amend and adapt, which are easier to understand, and which may even operate more efficiently.

Back to the much-maligned GOTO and Basic. Structured programmers abhor GOTOs and would advise you never to use them; well, why not try to reduce the number of them? If your programs have been zigzagging around under the influence of over-indulgence in GOTOs, they won't be any worse if instead you apply some discipline and logical sequencing to them. See the Glossary entry for *GOTO*.

Don't believe *all* that rubbishing of Basic. True, there are some programming languages (notably Pascal, on small computers) which are much more conducive to structured programming but it's by no means impossible to write neat, sensible, and reasonably well-structured code in Basic. Try it. If you want some advice, check the book called *Basic With Style* in Chapter 8.

STX
Start of Text – a communication control character used to signal the start of text transmission. Note that some of the message will have preceded STX; there will be *header* or control characters before the text.

Subroutine
Some operations will be repeated frequently in a program, like passing the results of something to the printer. You could write a program which repeats the printer call every time, or you could write a short piece of code which does the same thing, so that your program can just call this up every time it needs to. That's a subroutine – a sequence of instructions which perform an often-required function and which can be called from anywhere within the body of the main program. Getting into a subroutine is generally done by a *jump* or *branch*.

Subset

An identifiable bunch of things which belong to an identifiable but bigger thing. You'll probably meet language subsets – which are programming languages with some but not all the features or a well-known language. So Tiny Basic is a subset of Basic though as yet there is no agreed formal definition of what Basic should comprise; perhaps the bigger Basics are really a superset of Tiny Basic. And so it goes.

Suite

My mum has one in lavender moquette. A suite of programs is generally a collection of separate but inter-related programs run after one another to do a single big job.

SuperBrain

The highly-successful business-orientated microcomputer from *Intertec*. It's now starting to show its age; newer computers seem to have better designs and in some quarters it has a poor reputation for reliability (though mine's been satisfactory, touch wood). At prices from £1,600, or so, however, it is reasonably cheap. The unit is a single cabinet with a good keyboard, screen, and two *floppy disc* drives built into it; the *operating system* is, of course, *CP/M*.

SuperCalc

One of the best-liked *spreadsheet* calculators for *CP/M* systems.

Superset

Something which is an enhanced version of the standard thing. A superset of Cobol, for example, might have all the facilities laid down for the language in the latest *ANSI* specification – and then some.

Swapping

Or 'page swapping'; see *multiprogramming, partition* and *overlay*. This term usually applies only on a very large and/or very clever computer. It is one of the ways an *operating system* can handle more than one program in memory.

The simplest organisation is the *foreground/background* split – this defines two areas of fixed size in memory. Such areas are called *partitions* by some vendors. Fixed-size partitions might be an uneconomical use of memory: operating systems with the facility for variable partitions can allocate the exact amount of storage, and no more, to each program.

A multi-programming system usually cannot keep all applications in memory all the time. Some can and they move around memory from one program to another as each program gets into its time.

Most systems do not have sufficient memory space available for that and so maintain part or all of the active programs on backing store – a disc file. When the time allocation comes round, that program is copied from disc into memory and run. When its allocation is over, the next program is brought in. That is called 'swapping'; the term 'roll-in/roll-out' is synonymous.

More sophistication and more efficiency calls for 'paging', in which the operating system will organise memory as fixed-size pages, usually about 512 bytes in length. Programs and data are also moved around in page-size quantities. So the operating system does not have to load a whole program into memory – just that page which needs to be executed. This speeds the process, of course.

SWTP

Or SWTPc. It's South West Technical Products, the

best-known manufacturer of microcomputers to use the *Motorola* M6800 family of microprocessor chips. SWTP also developed the *Flex* operating system and the *SS50* standard.

Sybex

Interesting Franco-American publisher, microprocessor consulting group, and seminar organiser. Its books are mostly by Rodnay Zaks, who runs the organisation.

Symbolic

Programming languages are sometimes described as symbolic – programs refer to storage locations and machine operations by symbolic names and addresses which are independent of their literal hardware-determined locations. A symbolic name is a label used in programs to reference data peripherals, instructions and the like. In practice, 'symbolic' just means representing something by the everyday alphanumeric symbols.

Synchronous

Often abbreviated to 'sync'. It means two logical processes or parts of a system are kept in step because they are controlled by the same central timing mechanism.

In synchronous transmission the sending and receiving instruments are operating continuously at the same interval between successive bits of characters which are sent and received.

Compare *asynchronous* operation, in which the sender and receiver are not in phase. This means any transmission has to include start-stop commands so that both ends know what is happening.

Syntax

You can avoid this by getting espoused and thus qualifying for the Married Person's Allowance, which is tough on gays.

Really syntax means the rules which decide how programming language *statements* must be constructed – in other words, the grammar of the language. So if you try to key-in a program and computer comes back with the derisory message SYNTAX ERROR, you can look for these kinds of faults:

● duff composition – like typographical errors, incorrect punctuation, not following the specified form for statements or parts of statements, misuse of variables.

● inconsistencies – especially statements which are satisfactory in themselves but which conflict with other statements.

● incompleteness – like GOSUB 9000 when there isn't a subroutine to go to at line 9000, or a FOR-NEXT loop with a FOR statement but no NEXT statement.

System

Oh dear, this one's tricky. The word is used so often and so loosely that an exact definition is very difficult. A practical one might run along the lines of 'a collection of parts united by some form of regulated interaction'. We might say 'parts and procedures', in fact, for the methods of using components are sometimes almost indivisible from the system elements.

How about this: 'an organised whole'. Yes, that should suffice – a complete assembly capable of functioning according to its defined intention. Wow, that's good.

System software

Look at the entry on *applications*. Software in general

is in two varieties – applications software and system software. The former does something for the user; the latter comprises the tools which enable a programmer to develop and then run applications. So a basic set of system software generally includes a debugging program, operating system, a text editor, assembler, and an I/O system.

Systems analysis

The job of work which involves analysing all phases of the activities of an organisation and developing detailed procedures for collection, manipulation and evaluation of all associated data.

A systems analyst is a person who defines the applications problem, determines system specifications, recommends equipment changes, and designs dp procedures. He or she probably progressed through programmer training, but systems analysis work doesn't involve writing programs. It will mean producing *block diagrams* and record layouts from which the programmer can prepare *flowcharts* and subsequently write the programs.

Systime

One of the success stories of British computing, a company which boomed during the 1970s from one man and a dog to multi-million pound status by selling minicomputer systems to business. Originally it bought the hardware, in particular basing its systems on minicomputers from *Digital Equipment;* it still does so to some extent but it's also developed its own extremely classy microcomputer; it's called the Systime 500 family, and you might buy one for your business for upwards of £6,000.

S-100

Another success story. S-100 is probably the most popular *bus* layout for microcomputers. It involves 100 pin connections, it first appeared on the pioneering *MITS* Altair systems, it works on the Intel 8080 and its many derivatives, and now most people who sell things which plug into home computers using this micro will follow the S-100 connection scheme.

Things have been helped along mightily by the *IEEE*, which has developed a modified and much-improved standard version of the S-100 bus.

Be warned – there is still scope for interpretation by manufacturers of the S-100 specification. So an S-100 peripheral may not plug straight into an S-100 microcomputer.

Table

A collection of data items stored in memory, organised so that individual items may be referenced by specifying *keys* which are part of each item. The 'key' may be very simple – it may just be the position of the data in the table.

Tandy

Originally a leather company, then a mass marketeer for hi-fi, now a pioneer of the mass market for personal computers and its leader in terms of total shipments (Tandy is tops in the States, *Commodore* is No. 1 in Europe). It sells in the States under its Radio Shack label, which indicates the home and hobby electronics field through which Tandy approached the micro.

Tape

Magnetic tape is basically the same as audio reel-to-reel or cassettes, though manufactured to rather higher tolerances – the fast idiot computer lacks the sensitivity and the ability to compensate for faulty recording which the hearing human can boast. Tape is cheap, so it's good for the low-cost computer and for large archive files but it must be accessed sequentially.

Tape head

That portion of a tape deck or cassette unit which reads to and/or writes information from the tapes. These days many tape units have two separate heads, one for reading and one for writing; among other things this allows a wonderfully logical read-after-write check on some decks which ensures that some meaningful information has been put on to the tape.

Tarbell

A U.S. microcomputer components manufacturer, best-known for the Tarbell Cassette Interface. At 187cps, this is the fastest of the standard cassette interfaces for personal computers – compare *CUTS* and *Kansas City*.

TEC

There's a TEC which makes *VDU* terminals in Texas but microcomputer users are probably more likely to see the initials on a line of very good daisywheel printers; they're cheaper than most, look flatter and generally neater, and are reported to represent a good buy. The initials stand for Tokyo Electric Company, by the way.

Telesoftware

Programs which can be loaded from *teletext* or *viewdata* services. In other words, the programs are held at the central computer and can be sent to you via a telephone line (viewdata) or via a TV signal (teletext). In the latter case, you'd just take a copy of what appeared on the screen; with viewdata the program could go directly into your computer memory or on to cassette.

The BBC is experimenting with teletext broadcasting of programs for the BBC Micro, and the Council for Educational Technology is trying a Prestel service.

Teletex

An imminent alternative to Telex which many European PTTs (including British Telecom) are preparing to offer. Teletex will provide faster transmission and more flexible text editing than Telex.

Teletext

A method of broadcasting information which utilises the 'spare' lines on a TV signal (the picture you get on your TV set doesn't take up all of the signal lines which are transmitted to you). People with slightly-modified domestic TV sets thus can receive and display 'pages' of information, one page being a screenful of information.

See *telesoftware*, too.

Tektronix

The major manufacturer of specialist *graphics* display terminals; it also makes various instruments.

Telecommunications

The transmission and reception of data over radio circuits or telephone lines by means of electromagnetic signals.

Teleprinter

Really it's just the typewriter-like device at one end of a telegraph line but the term is used more generally to

refer to any printer-plus-keyboard device on any telecommunications link – which is more acurately described as a teletypewriter.

Teleprocessing
IBM invented this word to describe systems in which
remote locations are connected to a central computer
by data transmission circuits – usually telephone lines.
So teleprocessing by that definition involves some
remote terminals linked to a central computer. The
term is also used more broadly, for instance to refer to
data transmission between computers in different locations.

Teletype
Used loosely for any keyboard/printer terminal, rather
as 'Hoover' and 'Kleenex' have passed into the language. In fact, it's a registered trademark for an AT&T
subsidiary called Teletype Corp, whose terminals
dominated computing in the 1960s and early 1970s;
their operating characteristics were widely-copied and
their specification became a *de facto* standard for
low-cost input-output devices – even when VDUs
started becoming cheap and common in the second half
of the 1970s.

The simplest and most inexpensive *VDU* terminals
still feature Teletype-compatibility.

Meanwhile, Teletype is still among the big boys in
the terminal business.

Teletypewriter
See *Teleprinter*.

Televideo
A U.S. maker of *VDU* terminals originally, but now

the manufacturer of some good business-orientated microcomputer systems.

Telex
A world-wide subscriber network for teleprinters. It is often a feasible alternative to data links using telephone lines – you can send and receive messages on both kinds or service but the Telex is cheaper and simpler, though slower. It uses the *BAUDOT* code.

Terminal
Specifically it's the end of a communications link, more helpfully defined by one dictionary as the point at which a user communicates directly with a computer'. So in theory the keyboard and screen on a TRS-80 or a Pet are 'terminals'.

In practice, you'd be better thinking of a basic unit comprising keyboard, screen, and/or printer connected to a computer by a cable and/or telephone line. That's the simplest terminal.

More clever are the so-called 'intelligent terminals'. They incorporate a microprocessor and may give you local programming facilities – which means the terminal user can develop and run programs without communicating at all with the central computer. In that case your terminal will probably have a cassette or floppy disc attached.

Going on a little, there are purpose-built industry-specific terminals which are really very complex. Banks and supermarkets, for instance, typically have whole terminal systems with the 'terminal' involving several types of device – special printers, cash registers, those hole-in-the-wall bank dispensers, various kinds of automatic credit-card checkers, and so on. All can be linked to a small mini or microcomputer; this in turn passes the data collected to the central computer.

Text editor

A special program which allows you to input alphanumeric text and modify it without you necessarily having to be aware of how and when it will be printed. The output side may be looked after by a second program called something like 'print formatter'; together the two programs constitute a word processor. On its own, a text editor is a dramatically useful tool for program entry and correction – it can greatly simplify the time-consuming chores here.

Thermal printer

A type of *non-impact* printer which involves building-up a character on the sheet by scorching dots on the paper in the appropriate shape. It sounds clumsy but thermal printers are neat, silent and reasonably fast. One disadvantage, though, is that they're not cheap; and they tend to need special coated paper, because trying to put a black dot on to ordinary paper by heat doesn't work too well.

Thimble

The printer element on a *petal* printer from the Japanese company *NEC.* I suppose it looks a little like a thimble; small stalks with characters on the end rise from around the edge of a central boss.

Third-party

As the buyer you constitute one party; the vendor is another. So anyone else is a third party. The term is encountered usually in reference to third-party suppliers of maintenance services, software, or peripherals.

Thoughput
Results of Montezuma's Revenge? 'Throughput' is one of those words which sound really good at parties given by advertising men, teachers, or sixth-formers about to go to university. It's usually defined in some all-embracing fashion like 'the total useful information processed or communicated during a specified time period by a machine, system or procedure, measured in some terms meaningful to the process under consideration'. For example, a payroll system may deal with 50 employee records per minute; you might get through 5,000 enquiries from an information retrieval system.

Tic-tac-toe
The American name for noughts and crosses.

Time-sharing
A method by which one computer can service several users more or less all at the same time. In fact, the computer services each user in sequence; its high speed makes it appear that the users are all handled simultaneously – while each is really getting a few milliseconds of the computer's attention in turn.

Tiny BASIC
A subset of Basic devised by a mini-genius called Tom Pitman. It allows only integer arithmetic and limited string operations but the more useful Basic facilities are there. Tiny Basic fits into only 4K bytes and that made it eminently satisfactory for sub-£250 microcomputer kits like the Elf II.

Since those early days the memory restriction has become less of a problem, because people have discovered how to put software like a Basic *interpreter* into *ROM* chips. That way it doesn't take up any of the

RAM, so it's all available for the user's programs. So a 3.5KB computer like the basic Vic-20 can run a very full version of Basic.

Tiny C
A popular microcomputer version of the *C* programming language, available from the memorably-named Tiny C Associates.

Toolkit
See *Programmers' toolkit.*

TP
Teleprocessing – though sometimes it abbreviates to 'transaction processing'.

Track
The channel on a disc along which data is stored – called a cylinder by some. The term is also used with magnetic tape to refer to the longitudinal paths on which bits can be placed – so nine-track tape can have up to nine bits in a character, and a character is read by picking-up a particular combination of bits horizontally across the tape from whatever is in the nine channels at that position.

Tractor feed
The mechanism which moves *continuous stationery* through a printer by engaging toothed sprockets into the holes down the side of the paper and dragging it through.

Train printer
Type of *line printer.*

Transaction

This term is bandied about a good deal in business computing. A transaction is any event (like receiving a bill or despatching an order) which requires a record to be generated in the system – that's all.

You may see the term 'transaction processing'; it's impressive but ill-defined. Usually it means that each transaction is processed as it happens – which makes transaction processing the opposite of *batch* processing in the commercial environment.

Transam

A likeable, independent British micro manufacturer, whose *Tuscan* machine sells well as an expandable *CP/M*-based system to schools, personal computer buffs, and (less enthusiastically) to business users.

Transfer rate

Speed at which a footballer changes clubs. Also the rate at which data is transferred from a peripheral device to main memory; you'll usually see it in reference to cassette or floppy disc units. The transfer rate quoted so blithely is the theoretical maximum; in practice the performance will generally be constrained by many other factors. Transfer rate is usually given as characters, bits or bytes per second.

Transistor

You don't really need to know anything about them but this electronic device was absolutely critical to the development and design of today's computers. So there.

Transmit

Send information from one place to another via a data

transmission circuit – which usually means a telephone line.

Trap

A method of detecting program errors when illegal instructions are executed or illegal memory locations are accessed. Usually what happens is that the program branches briefly to a special *subroutine* when some unusual condition occurs during the running of a program. Then the operating system may assume control automatically and correct the condition or notes the cause of failure; trapping is also a feature of certain diagnostic routines.

TRS-80

The Tandy microcomputer family is in three basic flavours and constitutes one of the three top-selling personal computer lines in the more than £500 field. As announced originally, the TRS-80 adopted a rather different approach from the *Commodore Pet,* which appeared at about the same time (circa 1977) even though both use the same elements – keyboard, screen, cassette, graphics, Basic. Tandy chose the Z-80 rather than the 6502 (Intel derivative versus Motorola parentage), opted for a real keyboard rather than the original Pet choice of calculator-style keys, and decided to sell three cable-connected boxes rather than one integrated unit.

As a result it's difficult to weigh these two similarly-priced computers against each other. Both manufacturers are now going for 'business' versions of their computers, floppy disc systems at the £2,000-plus mark.

The TRS-80 Model I dominated early sales of the three prime contenders for the personal computer world. Now selling for about £450, it includes cassette, display and keyboard (a good one) which also houses the processor and memory. A huge volume of software is available for it. The Model II is a £2,000-plus business computer with 8in. floppy disc drives built into the display unit. The Model III fits between the two, and it's a single unit containing screen, twin mini-floppies and keyboard for about £1,400.

The 'TRS' stands for 'Tandy/Radio Shack'; the '80' is there because the computer uses the *Zilog* Z-80 microprocessor.

Truth table

When I was a child our gang used to have a Truth Table where recalcitrant members were tied while the rest of us dropped worms on to his face. Ah, the joys of youth. We never discovered what David was doing with Janey behind the bike sheds ...

These days you may meet the term as applying to a table which describes a logic function by listing all possible combinations of input values and indicating all the logically true output values. This is all associated with the heavy esoterica of Boolean arithmetic, so most of us can safely forget it.

TTL

Stands for transistor-transistor logic; it's one of the standard design approaches to semiconductor integrated circuits. Standard TTL provides the lowest component cost of conventional logic. It is relatively fast and is unsurpassed for variety of functions but it has at least four disadvantages – high power dissipation, limited noise immunity, inadequate speed for some applications, and limited complexity.

TTY

Abbrevation for Teletype – and sometimes by extension for teletypewriters in general.

Turnkey

Traditional preference to chicken or goose at Christmas? A turnkey system theoretically is complete and ready to go; the user need only turn a key to start work. In practice, most small business systems are indeed started by a key – though some just have an on-off switch.

The essence of turnkey is that the purchaser has minimal involvement in the protracted and technical process of designing, developing, testing and implementing the computer system he will use. So the product sold to the customer should consist of a ready-programmed computer complete with operating instructions and training, as well as all relevant manuals. This is the way most computers are sold today – after all, you don't have to understand how a typewriter or a car works to use them.

In practice, it is rarely as simple as that, of course. The user has to be sure that the all-in system on offer matches all his requirements; and that there will be no contractual hassles when the software writers start bickering with the hardware supplier. Still, it works reasonably well.

Tuscan

The microcomputer from the independent British manufacturer *Transam*. It uses the *CP/M* operating system and the *S-100* standard for its internal structure, and both of those give it a good deal of versatility; there are now many options available for it. Like most British micros, however, the external appearance won't win it any Design Awards.

Twisted-pair

Cable with one wire twisted around another (would you believe). This is usually what is used for telephones around the house or the office, so its plentiful and cheap. It can be used for connecting computerish things and it is all that you need, in terms of the physical connection, for the least expensive *local networks*. (The other inexpensive option is to use *co-axial cable*.)

Turtle

Funny word, really, isn't it? Just try saying it a few times. Anyhow, a turtle is a kind of simple robot. It's a glass dome on wheels with a retractable pen pointing down underneath it, so that when it moves it can draw lines. It receives its instructions via a lightweight cable connecting it to the computer; those instructions will be provided at the keyboard in the Logo langauage. It's wonderful.

Two's complement

This is another esoteric idea; it's a method of expressing binary numbers where the negative of a number is generated by complementing the number and adding 1. The effect is that you can then perform signed arithmetic with binary numbers. Forget it.

Typesphere

The real generic name for the 'golf-ball' print element on some electric typewriters.

UART

Universal Asynchronous Receiver/Transmitter. It's a serial-to-parallel and parallel-to-serial converter.

UCSD

The San Diego arm of University of California. It's here because you might see the phrase 'UCSD Pascal'; that is a version of the Pascal programming language which was developed there. It has become widely-used on small computers.

UNIBUS

A trademark of *Digital Equipment,* the top maker of minicomputers. The Unibus is the single high-speed *bus* in the PDP-11; it's a classic approach to minicomputer design, especially good because it really simplifies the connection of additional peripherals, more memory and upgraded processors.

It has limitations and it's somewhat complicated for micros. This type of bus can't cope with very complicated systems, so bigger Digital computers don't use it, either.

Unit record

Normally means a thing which holds a whole record – the 'thing' typically being a punched card or a ledger card. A 'unit record computer' is a little-used term to refer to a visible record computer, an outdated type of business computer which stores its information on ledger cards.

Unix

Unix is widely-touted as 'the *operating system* of the future', though in fact it dates from 1969 (it was developed originally by Bell Laboratories, which runs most of the telephone systems in the States). Since then it's been under continuous development; so it's not so much an old operating system as a fairly mature one, if you see what I mean.

Unix gets brownie points straight off because it was

conceived by a user of computers rather than a software specialist or some kind of computer designer. So it is relatively easy to use; with much other software the prime goal often seems to be to make money, or to sell more hardware and software, or whatever.

In brief, Unix is a general-purpose, multi-user operating system with a clever method of holding files. It's a complex system, which means both that it is rich in facilities and difficult to get to grips with.

A number of microcomputer versions are available. Because Unix is here, proven and ready to use, there's a good chance that up-market 16-bit micros with multiple users will be adopting it as a standard operating system – in much the same way and for much the same reasons as CP/M became the standard on single-user 8-bit micros.

Univac

Today it's Sperry Univac, part of the big Sperry group and one of the top four computer manufacturers in the world. The original UNIVAC was the world's first commercially-produced stored-program computer, bought by the U.S. Bureau of the Census in 1951. The word is an immodest acronym for UNIVersal Automatic Computer. You'll note that these days few people are prepared to describe the average computer as really universal *or* fully-automatic.

USART

The Universal Synchronous/Asynchronous Receiver/ Transmitter is an improvement on the *USART* in that it may be programmed to operate as a synchronous communications link.

USASCII

More poularly known as *ASCII,* though one stands for

USA Standard Code for Information Interchange and
the other is the American Standard Code for Information Interchange. Well, no-one said it would be
simple.

Users' group

It's obvious that a users' group is a group of people
who have computers from a particular supplier, or who
have some other kind of common computing interest.
This entry is here to emphasise how valuable this kind
of association can be, even when it's a manufacturer-
inspired mouthpiece designed primarily for marketing
purposes. Users can discuss problems, swap solutions
and programs, band together to get discounts on bulk-
buying consumables like paper and discs and, if necessary, present a coherent front to get some action
from the supplier. Buy a computer which has a good
user group; then join it and use it. Or start one
yourself.

Utility programs

These are a collection of programs for routine tasks –
some systems offer utility *subroutines* as well, helpful
functions which can be called-up by a user program.
Utilities which typically will be provided include source data editors, debug programs, copy utilities, sort
functions, and I/O control.

Validation

Checking input data to make sure that it's logically
correct – that language syntax is correct, and so on.
Compare *verification*.

Value

Basically it's a number assigned to a *variable*.

Variable

A symbolic unit which can take a variety of values. In practice it's anything which can be altered, measured or controlled – and which can therefore have different values at different times. That's all.

VDU

Visual (or sometimes 'video') display unit. It's a screen-plus-keyboard *terminal*.

Vector

An address given to the processor which will direct it to a new area of memory. A 'vectored interrupt' is an *interrupt* which causes a transfer to a particular interrupt-handler routine starting at the location specified – rather than leaving things to some generalised interrupt routine.

Vector Graphic

This U.S. microcomputer manufacturing company has an active U.K. distributor called Almarc. Its computers all use the *S-100 bus* and the *CP/M* operating system; they sell principally to business and can start at about £2,200, though most users users will pay something between £4,000 and £10,000 for a multi-terminal system. Among standard software is an excellent word processor.

Vector Graphic is distinguished by making computers which don't have graphics and which don't do any processing in terms of vectors. The company originally had plans for an X,Y graphic display but they came to nothing.

Verification

Checking input data to make sure it was entered correctly.

Vic

The best-selling home computer from *Commodore,* a versatile £165 machine with a good version of Basic (taken from the *Pet*) and fine colour display possibilities. The keyboard is of better quality than you might expect and the on-screen editing of programs is excellent. The Vic uses plug-in *ROM cartridges* for expansion of facilities, addition of memory, and some games. A large body of add-on hardware and programs on cassette is available for it, too.

So what's the catch? Well, there's the competition for one thing; the *Spectrum* is cheaper and is a little easier to use for graphics; colour and graphics are superior on the more expensive *Atari.* The Vic has a definite restriction in the size of its display (only 23 lines of 22 characters, with a big unused border permanently mocking you on the TV picture). Commodore has busily been announcing forthcoming products, including one computer smaller than Vic, one larger, which may be a better bet. At the moment, though, the availability of so many add-on options and ready-to-use software makes the Vic very attractive.

Vic Computing

A British magazine devoted to the *Vic.*

Video Genie

A microcomputer built in Hongkong by a company called EACA and distributed in Britain by Lowe Electronics. Its full title is the Video Genie EG 3003. It is compatible with the *TRS-80* Model I, which means you can use the vast range of programs available for the Tandy computer. Naturally, it's cheaper than the TRS-80; you can buy a starter system from less than £300.

Videotext

A term used to cover both *teletext* and *viewdata*; any form of transmitting and displaying textual information, in fact.

Viewdata

This is now a generic term for an information-dispensing service utilising telephone lines, one or more central computers holding the databases of information, and low-cost receivers based on the simple technology of TV sets. Prestel is a public viewdata service; the basic principle also holds for 'private systems' which provide similar facilities on an in-house computer. Though originally an information retrieval service, viewdata can make use of the two-way capability of the telephone lines to permit a number of interactive applications. All of this is possible with conventional 'on-line database systems', where every user has a VDU and connection to the computer's files; but viewdata offers an essential simplicity and low cost.

One day it will be easy to use any personal computer as a terminal for viewdata and the Prestel-type service will provide all the data we need plus a cheap (free?) method of passing messages and sharing information. Then perhaps we'll see a significant step towards the global village, an electronically-based information-using society rather than merely an oil-based energy-using one. End of today's lesson.

Virtual memory

This is a really clever *operating systems* technique whereby the programmer appears to get a much larger memory space to work in than is available.

What happens is that the operating system extends the possible addressing range to some or all of the disc backing storage. It does so by transferring automatically portions of programs between disc and main memory; in theory the program can address the whole address space without having to worry whether memory or disc is being referenced. The problems are such that virtual memory is feasible only on large computers. The super-clever operating system needs a good deal of memory for a start; the disc transfers usually have to be fast and the processor has to be speedy.

Visible Record Computer

A small computer designed for a smallish company – sold as a *turnkey* system for something between £5,000 and £12,500. The name is derived from the use of the special but familiar-looking accounts ledger card. Information is stored by typing it on to the ledger card and simultaneously it is stored on a magnetic strip attached to the top or side of it; you read the typescript, the computer reads the strip.

Ledger cards and the visible record computer have, of course, been outdated substantially (and out-priced) by the arrival of microcomputers, floppy discs, and good-quality business software which runs on them. Two manufacturers cling to the ledger card, principally to service the more conservative business areas which for some reason still want them; but most of us are better off without the inelegant and restricted VRC.

VisiCalc

The classic example of *spreadsheet* calculators, a massive seller and one of the main reasons why people in business started to regard microcomputers seriously. The program was unveiled only in 1979 but it is reported to have sold something approaching 500,000 copies, if you can believe that. It's available for *Apple*, *Commodore* and *CP/M* computers.

VisiCorp

The people who sell *VisiCalc* (and several add-on programs which extend VisiCalc capabilities). It used to be called Software Arts but since the only software it was selling was VisiCalc and its derivatives it thought it might as well reflect that in the name of the company.

Voice input (and output)

Frankly, the idea of being able to hold an intelligent vocal conversation with a computer will probably have to wait until the year 2001 – well, perhaps not so long, but the problems are immense. The technical side isn't so difficult, it's the business of getting the computer to say something you haven't pre-programmed into it; see my notes on *electronic brain* and *artificial intelligence*.

Still, some small computers can now have voice input and output attachments. Voice output is technically easier; instead of directing a message to the printer or the VDU screen, the processor will probably send it to a special voice output unit which may contain a microprocessor. This looks at each word to be output and either assembles the relevant sounds electronically into a more or less accurate word-sound, or it plucks out a pre-recorded word-sound from a library of them. The sound is usually created by an electronic gismo called a tone generator. Since there aren't really that many different sounds in the standard human vocabulary, the tone generator can provide most of the noises we understand as language.

There are other ways of getting the computer to talk to you. We have seen a clever £25 system for the Vic which samples the wave forms of your voice when you speak sample words into a microphone; it converts those wave patterns into digital values and stores them on disc. When the computer wants to output a word, it fetches the relevant pattern and uses the digital values to drive an analogue converter which causes sound to emerge from a small loudspeaker. Of course, the sound you hear is your voice – much more pleasant than those tinny artificially-constructed words.

Programming the thing may be a little difficult if you want it to do more than throw a few words or numbers at you through its loudspeaker; but at least it's not just a silly toy for providing sound effects on computer games; there are many occasions on which spoken output is better than printed or displayed messages, not least for error warnings. Much more could be made of this in off-the-shelf systems, particularly those for business use.

Audio input is fundamentally trickier, because the computer has to be able to recognise all the possible words you'll input in all the possible accents and inflections you might use. That can be amazingly complicated; at the moment you probably can't get even a simple voice input system for less than £5,000 – and that's without the computer.

Such a system may recognise only 10 or 20 words, too. Commercially-available voice input systems go to 200 or 1,000 words but they cost more. Generally these devices work by being taught – a particular user says each word several times and the device stores the resultant sound pattern in code in its memory. When any user with an equivalent sound pattern speaks, the machine compares the newly-spoken word against memorised words until it finds one which matches. So the computer must be trained to recognise each word and how to respond to each word, or defined phrase, individually. Vocabularies larger than a few hundred words are too large for even a medium-sized commercial computer; but much can be done with a limited vocabulary, such as the letters and numbers.

Considering the growth rate of technology, computers may well be able to understand what words we are saying before we are able to prepare these computers to respond meaningfully to them. Beat that for a heavy concept.

Volatile

Non-retentive, usually applying to memory – MOS *semiconductor* memory loses its contents when you switch-off the power: that's the biggest problem with it. *Core* is non-volatile, which means it retains its data; some of the newer (and more expensive) memory technologies are also non-volatile.

Volkswriter

An independently-sold *word processor* program for the *IBM* Personal Computer.

Voltage regulator

Despite the presence of a *power supply* your computer may still need another gismo to convert the mains electricity supply before it gets to your new toy.

The mains power is subject to voltage fluctuations: it's rated at 240V here, but the actual current can be higher or lower. If everybody in the country switches on *Match of the Day,* eight fan heaters and the oven all at the same time, there's a sudden drain on the electricity system and the people in the power station may take some time to push some more volts into it. Similarly if we all switch off at the same time there is a sudden excess.

Well, on a smaller scale this is happening all the time; and computers become a trifle sensitive to these sudden peaks and troughs. They can cause memory misreads, blown fuses, and perhaps even over-heating of wires which causes permanent damage.

Enter the solution – the voltage regulator; these just even-out the voltage flow. You may have one built into your computer already but if not they cost only a few pounds to buy – you plug one end into the socket, the other has a socket for your computer. (They are satisfactory for stereo systems, too – no more nasty clicks when the refrigerator switches on.)

VSLI
Very Large Scale Integration; the next step up from *LSI*, usually taken to mean more than 10,000 circuits per chip.

Wafer
A lump of silicon is cut into thin slices on which semiconductor chips are fabricated; those slices are also called 'wafers'.

WAIT
A condition in which the processor has suspended program execution, usually while waiting for data from memory or a peripheral.

Wand
See *optical wand*. Sounds good either way, doesn't it? It's a hand-held device for reading coded labels or tags, typically in a supermarket; most work by detecting bars across the label (*bar codes*) but some non-optical wands pick up other encoded data like magnetic dots.

Wang
One of the leading independents in the *Electronic Office* stakes, Wang has an advanced line for this

market – small and large computers, word processors, electronic mail, photo-composition.

Watson
Thomas J. Watson died in 1956 but deserves a mention because he invented IBM – he fostered its growth around World War II, epitomised the hard-sell go-getting U.S. salesman, and filled the company offices with THINK, a distinctly over-rated and somewhat daft slogan. (Later imitations included ACHIEVE! and GRASP! reports our U.S. correspondent).

His son, Tom Watson Jr, became president of IBM in 1952 and guided the company solidly into its present dominance of the computer business. He stepped down a few years ago and started an ambassadorial career for the U.S.A.

WCS
Writeable Control Store.

WHICH COMPUTER?
Good question. In fact it's a magazine, started in 1977 by the company which originally set up *Practical Computing*. It's an interesting phenomenon, because the magazine exists only because business computers suddenly started becoming cheap and readily available; technology drove down prices at the end of the 1970s, and more people found they could make more use of computing. WHICH COMPUTER? attempts to provide objective comment on computing and independent assessment of smallish business computers. There's no connection with the Consumer Association *Which?*, incidentally.

The magazine is now part of the EMAP publishing empire; see Chapter 8 for other examples of computer-related EMAP publications.

Which Micro?

One of the 1982 crop of microcomputer magazines, another entrant from the EMAP publishing combine.

Winchester

This is the latest type of disc technology for small computers – though in fact the first Winchester was the IBM 3340, circa 1973. The IBM code-name stuck for the technology which uses discs hermetically-sealed inside a plastic casing.

The 3340s were definitely big-machine storage devices (more than 300MB) and featured big-machine prices. In the small business computer sector it was IBM again which took the initiative in popularising the idea, as it had done in the early '70s with floppy disc; the first System/34 with a Piccolo drive was shipped in January, 1979.

The Piccolo was the classic small-computer Winchester drive – sealed, non-removable, backed up on to floppies. Today there are at least 28 other companies building and/or selling Winchesters.

There are five main reasons for a small-system builder to look at Winchesters – access speed, reliability, cheapness, compact size and quiet operation. All are important virtues in a small office computer. Broadly, the demand towards the end of the 1970s was for inexpensive high-capacity discs to minimise costs and floorspace requirements. The floppy disc provides cheap and compact storage but not sufficient of it; the upper limits are around one megabyte. The new 3MB diskettes are, to say the least, unproven. At 5 to 12 megabytes the cartridge disc stores enough data but it is relatively bulky and expensive.

Microcomputers at that time were maturing rapidly in terms of their system software, particularly with multi-programming for spooling and multiple users. Disc-hungry database managers, query languages and report generators are now fairly common; so are Cobol compilers, multi-programmed word processing and integrated ledger systems — applications which need multiple files on-line simultaneously for instant updating.

So storage capacity and access speed are becoming key requirements – but so are environmental considerations. A large disc is frequently noisy and usually demands special air conditioning and/or electricity supply. By comparison, the smaller Winchesters in particular have simple electrical needs and are very quiet. They are also very compact, a significant point for the system builder designing something which will hope to fit unobtrusively into an office. Reliability and cheapness go hand in hand; minimising the cost of buying and owning the system obviously increases its appeal in the market.

The latest Winchester-type models are also overcoming what was formerly the Achilles heel of this technology – the back-up problem. You generally need to be able regularly to take copies of the work you've been doing on the computer, so that you'll have some relatively up-to-date information when some unforeseen disaster occurs. You just load your latest copy and you're computing again with not too much lost.

Now removable Winchesters are appearing, giving all the benefits of Winchester technology (relatively low price, relatively large capacity, relatively high speed) without the significant disadvantage – the disc unit includes a slot-in cartridge disc as well as the fixed non-removable Winchester storage.

These are also proving less than perfectly acceptable, though, and backing-up to floppies or to tape will probably become the norm.

Wordcraft

One of the two good *word processing* packages for the *Commodore* 8000 line; this is the British one and, as it happens, it's the one I prefer (but don't let that influence you). It's also available in a slimmed-down version for the Commodore *Vic*, would you believe?

Wordpro

The North American contender for *word processing* packages for the *Commodore* 8000. Wordpro has the better facilities for doing arithmetic on columns with a text document.

Workspace

An area of memory set aside for short-term working storage but otherwise without pre-determined use.

Windfall

A British magazine dedicated to the Apple microcomputers.

Word processing

The buzzword of the later 1970s is likely to be surpassed in the 1980s by terms like 'office automation' and 'the electronic office'. For the moment, however, word processing is still a meaningful concept.

Basically the phrase covers the processing of *text*–which in practice equates to alphanumeric information organised in variable-length files. Those are two important contrasts with data processing, where most information is numeric and most files contain groups of records of the same length – you know exactly how many characters you need for an invoice, a zap-the-

Klingons game, or an inventory record, but you don't really know how long a letter, an article or a whole book will be. That has major implications for the type of software which will have to manipulate the records and that's why special WP software has appeared.

You can now buy a word processor package for most micros. There are two parts to WP – the text editor, which edits text (you guessed it) and an output program, which formats and prints it.

Purpose-built word processors still dominate the scene, of course. The IBM screenless typewriter-plus-memory systems had a head start – they appeared in the 1960s with text being stored on a tape unit connected to the typewriter. Later IBM produced a funny kind of magnetically-sensitive card with a reader unit also connected by cable to the typewriter.

In the 1970s came screen-based word processors using microprocessors and floppy disc storage, which changed this radically. These screen/keyboard/printer/disc combinations are really dedicated microcomputers in a purpose-built package; most are software-driven, which means you load the WP program from floppy disc at the start of the day, but a few can also be programmed by the user.

That's partly because the WP systems are programmed only in assembler, partly because the vendors don't want to have to provide any user support other than operator training, and partly because the typical end-user (like a secretary or converted typist) won't want to program. All this makes excellent sense.

So does the counter-argument, which is that you might as well make the most of the small computer. So more and more systems are appearing in the middle ground between DP and WP – microcomputers are acquiring WP packages, word processors are getting Basic.

WPM
Words per minute – not a measure encountered frequently.

Write
To put information into memory or on to disc or tape.

Writeable Control Store
A special type offset-access memory into which the user can put specialised instructions or repetitive routines. These would be written in *microcode*.

WCS is expensive and difficult to use; it is generally provided only on the more sophisticated minicomputers. Most of us don't need this capability (and few of us can afford it).

Xerox
Xerox Corp is a big multi-national, joint owner of Rank Xerox in this country and best-known for its photocopiers – through its brood of subsidiaries and acquisitions includes several prospects for the forthcoming *electronic office* markets. Among them are Diablo (*daisywheel* printers and office computers) and Shugart (the top maker of *floppy* disc drives).

Xerox (and Rank Xerox) also has a *CP/M*-based business microcomputer, the 820, which sells at the £2,500–5,000 level.

Your Computer
The British hobby computer magazine which the publishing giant IPC spun off from *Practical Computing*.

Zaks
Rodnay Zaks is a Frenchman who became an electron-

ics engineer, went to California, and is now riding the microcomputer wave as an author (see bibliography) and owner of *Sybex*.

Zenith Data Systems
The microcomputer arm of the *Heath* electronics kits organisation. It sells (ready-assembled) a neat but slightly over-priced micro which looks a little like the *SuperBrain*.

Zeuse, Konrad
The good professor tends to be overlooked in histories of computing, partly because he was a German in Germany during World War II. He studied mechanical and then civil engineering and while fretting over the calculations involved he evolved one of the best possible reasons for automation: "I could not accept that human beings should waste a substantial part of their life-time with a work that is empty and demanding at the same time". And so say all of us.

So, in 1936, he built a real computer in his front room. The Z1 was program-controlled and featured binary arithmetic; it used many second-hand components, though, and kept breaking-down. The Z3 followed in 1940, by which time he was working as a statistician for an aircraft company; it wasn't patented because they said it wasn't technical enough, but it was the first programmable relay-controlled calculating machine. After the war came the Z4 and subsequent machines; taking-over Zeuse KG in the 1960s gave Siemens its first steps into computers.

Zero
Oh; come on, you don't really need a definition for zero.

Zilog

Interesting would-be success story. Three of the designers of the 8080 left *Intel* in 1974 to set up their own company with funds from the oil giant Exxon. Their company is reported to be only just starting to make money, but its micro – the Z-80 – is definitely one of the milestones of the business.

In fact, the Z-80 has now overtaken Intel micros as the world's most popular eight-bit microcomputer.

The Z-80 is faster than the 8080 and the other pioneer of eight-bit microprocessing, the Motorola M6800. It has more machine instructions (158) and it needs a simpler power supply (one +5V source). Programs can be shorter, execution is quicker.

And every single 8080 instruction is supported, which means if you want to upgrade to a Z-80 you can retain all those programs you wrote for your 8080.

Zilog isn't standing still, of course. As well as many support chips it packages the Z-80 into a working microcomputer configuration (the MCZ line); and it has a 16-bit micro, the Z-8000. It also has one of the funniest examples of industry paraphernalia in the shape of its amazing comic-strip hero Captain Zilog.

As a name, by the way, Zilog means something – 'Z' stands for 'the last word', 'I' denotes 'integrated', and 'LOG' is 'logic'. So Zilog is the last word in integrated logic. Ah well, we can allow it *some* licence.

8 NOW READ ON

If you want to get yourself an appreciation of computers, an obvious and economical starting point is to buy yourself an introductory book of some kind. When you come to look for your swift introduction to computers, though, you'll probably find that your local bookshops and W H Smiths are starting to fill up alarmingly with alternatives.

Inevitably, some are bandwagon riders, commissioned by publishers out to make a fast(ish) buck and written hurriedly by journalists or academics who are less than qualified. A few will be imported from the States; both their high cover price and the effusive and confusing use of U.S. examples should make you think twice before investing.

But there are several introductions which we can recommend. Read on.

If you have problems getting any of these you could try giving the details (as many as possible) to a local bookshop. Book ordering is notoriously slow, though, so your first step should be one of the specialist bookshops. Biggest, best-stocked and friendliest of those which deal only with computer publications is:

Mine of Information
1 Francis Avenue
St Albans
Herts AL3 6BL
Telephone 0727-52801

- **Introducing computers and computing**

The *Good Computing Book* hopes to provide a basic introduction, but there are several alternatives if you want more facts (or fewer).

The Personal Computer Book
by Robin Bradbeer
published 1982 by Gower
price £5.95
ISBN 0 566 03423 9
Second edition of a best-seller. I am less than enthusiastic about it; a degree of self-indulgence and no
little logorrhea permeate the book, and though suppos-
edly written for the beginner it includes a good deal of
technical jargon. There is also a misleading equation of
'computer' with 'computer hardware'; the book has
little mention of software or programming. But it does
contain much useful information, it is widely available,
and Bradbeer ought to know what he is talking about
(an early convert to the mighty micro, he lectures in
electronic engineering, consults and generally behaves
in man-about-the-microcomputer-market mode). Runs
over more or less the same ground as the first five
chapters of the *Good Computing Book,* pitching at a
rather more technical level, with several appendices
and a summary of most of the personal computers
available here when it was published (59 of them).

The Computer Book
by Robin Bradbeer, Peter de Bono and Peter Laurie
published 1982 by BBC Publications
price £6.75
ISBN 0 563 16484 0
Part of the BBC computer literacy project and designed to be read in conjuction with the 'Computer
Programme' TV series. There's a slightly earnest feel
to it, a desire to set the scene and explain and perhaps
even educate; but in general it's a worthy 'introduction
to computers and computing', which is the subtitle (an
excellent section on programming, for instance). Certainly it is one of the better-produced books in this list.

But as well as that collection of writers there was "additional material and editing" by Susan Curran and David Allen; and the 'thanks to everyone who helped' bit is signed by Allen, not by the authors. Sometimes the book does feel like a Project for a Team ("you handle this, I'll do that"): and no committee-written book will have the bounce of a good effort by a single author.

The Usborne Guide to Computers
by Brian Reffin-Smith
published 1982 by Usborne Electronic World
price £1.85
ISBN 0 86020 542 8

This paperback does not have many pages (32), but they are used extremely well to produce a cheery, cartoon-style introduction – 'a simple and colourful introduction for beginners', as the subtitle has it. The target audience is obviously kids, but in fact this would be the starter-level book which we would recommend to anyone.

Micro-computing: everything you ever wanted to know
by Rose Deakin
published 1982 by Sphere
price £2.25
ISBN 0 7221 3010 4

Ms Deakin's biography gives her Cheltenham Ladies College, Oxford University, "no science and little maths", a career initially in social research, and a first encounter with microcomputers in 1979. All of those attributes are reflected in greater or lesser measure in this paperback; so, too, is her current connection with one of the smaller British manufacturers, whose products get prominence. That apart, the book is a worthy (if wordy) attempt to introduce micros – though the promise in the subtitle is rank optimism.

The Microelectronics Revolution
edited by Tom Forester
published 1980 by Basil Blackwell
price £4.95
ISBN 0 631 125728
A beefy compilation of articles, supported by the DoI Microprocessor Applications Products scheme (which is why there are 589 pages for only a fiver) and biased towards micros as controllers rather than an general-purpose programmable machines. The subtitle is 'the complete guide to the new technology and its impact on society'; that claim is decidedly optimistic. Still, while the book sometimes feels like a summary for students, there is something for everyone in its pages. Especially interesting on the historical background.

- **More words**

If you want more definitions, here's one serious dictionary and one entirely frivolous one to try.

Dictionary of Microprocessors
by Anthony Chandor
published 1980 by Penguin
price £2.25
ISBN 0 14 051100 8
Dull, worthy, not all that comprehensive, and filled with terms you'll never need to know. But it's cheap and it's better than nothing.

The Devil's DP Dictionary
by Stan Kelly-Bootle
published 1981 by McGraw-Hill
price £5.95
ISBN 0 1405 1039 7

The author is a Liverpudlian who has written songs and worked in computers for more than 20 years. This is an entertaining and definitely silly collection of jokes, puns, comments which had me rolling on the floor (but then it's my kind of humour, and it may not be yours). Example: auto-eroticism – 'computer generation of best-selling novels'. To get most of the jokes you have to know something about the computer industry, though.

• Food for thought
The idea of lying in the bath or drowsing in bed with a book on computers (rather than say the latest Jackie Collins) may not appeal to you. But if you want to open your eyes a bit, try one or more of these.

The Mighty Micro
by Christopher Evans
published 1979 by Gollancz
price £5.50
ISBN 0 565 02658 8
(paperback 1981 by Coronet, price £1.50)
Readable, popular explanation and discussion of the impact of the micro from the late Dr Evans – a psychologist who worked on the ergonomics of computers and human-friendly uses of them. That concern to make technology acceptable illuminates his book. Not much technical exposition, but a good deal of explanation and interesting speculation – which is one reason why it made a TV series. Despite its relative age, the book is wearing well.

The Electronic Office: a management guide
by Dennis Jarrett
published 1982 by Gower
price £12.50
ISBN 0 566 03409 3

Written by me. The book covers what I see as the key technical developments which will affect offices in the next ten or fifteen years, but it also goes into the way offices might change and what the likely stumbling-blocks will be.

The Micro Revolution
by Peter Laurie
published 1980 by Futura Publications
price £1.50
ISBN 0 6588 1794 7

Despite the publication date (1980 was a long time ago in the micro business) this book is still good value, not only because you get 278 fact-packed pages. Laurie is a professional journalist and technically competent (most recently associated with *Practical Computing* magazine); this book is a substantial meal of microcomputer information, but it is readable – and features excellent use of practical and comprehensible examples.

Computers and Social Change
by M Laver
published 1980 by Cambridge University Press
price £3.25
ISBN 0 5212977 10

Murray Laver is a fine writer on computers (though his big-computer background shows through) and he is at his best on the effects of computerisation. This book is very good on the wider, unintended effects.

The Silicon Chip Book
by Peter Marsh
published 1981 by Sphere Books
price £2.50
ISBN 0 349 12286 5

Another readable though more general introduction,

again written stylishly by an informed and authoritative journalist *(New Scientist)*. A good explanation which incorporates sensible, thought-provoking (and not over-long) comment on the wider social and economic issues.

Running Wild
by Adam Osborne
published 1979 by McGraw-Hill
price £2.95
ISBN 0 931988 28 4
How and why to cope with the micro – and thus the next industrial revolution. A neat little book, written in the author's best journalist/columnist style.

Mindstorms
by Seymour Papert
published 1980 by Harvester Press
price £12.95
ISBN 08 5527 163 9
Papert is at MIT and is identified closely with turtles and Logo, so the book's subtitle 'Children, Computers, Powerful Ideas' should give a clue to its content. Ostensibly about teaching maths, it is in fact an imaginative and stimulating discussion in entirely practical terms of how computers and kids (or anyone, really) can get together. By the time this book is printed there should be a paperback version available at around £3.95.

The World Challenge
by Jean-Jacques Servan-Schreiber
published 1980 by Fayard
price FF64.40
ISBN 6 30617 9
French author who is a well-known politician and a journalist – unusually this qualities him to write about

politics with some style. The book is about the quality of life and the way we will live in the future, which sounds vague enough. Servan-Schreiber argues the case for a massive technology transfer from the industrialised world to the developing nations, which is more specific at least. He links the microelectronic revolution and the power of petrodollars as two key factors in our future, and though his vision of technology is somewhat uncritical his views are really interesting.

The Third Wave
by Alvin Toffler
published 1980 by Pan
price £1.95
ISBN 0 330 26337 4
Mind-bogglingly comprehensive work from the polymathic author of *Future Shock* – there are 20 pages of small-type index alone, and another 80 pages of notes in the total of 544. The book describes nothing less than the civilisation which is emerging from the influence of the new technologies; the book's reviewers found it difficult not to go in for words like "blockbuster" and "dizzying" to describe it. The book's sheer size is a deterrent, and so is the author's amiably hectoring tone. But it can repay persistence.

The Soul of a New Machine
by Tracy Kidder
published 1982 by Allen Lane
price £7.50
ISBN 0 7139 14823
The inside story of how one U.S. company (Data General) designed one high-technology minicomputer (the 32-bit Eclipse line). Written by a professional writer rather than a technologist, it's frankly a good read – but it also includes some insights into the design

process, and along the way there's some good (and very necessary) explanations.

• Getting technical

Peering inside the computer is something you might want to do. These books offer a heavier dose of electronics and how computers work.

Illustrating computers (without much jargon)
by Colin Day and Donald Alcock
published 1982 by Pan
price £1.95
ISBN 0 330 26599 7

Unreservedly recommended as the best introduction you will find to what goes on inside the computer – but you must accept the restrictions in its subtitle; this is 'a beginners' guide to how computers work' and it's nothing more than that. It's very clearly for the layperson; true, it is easy to find fault with the generalisations, but in general the style is excellent. The content, organisation and style all work effectively to the desired end – for a start, it gets off on the right foot with a chapter headed 'why bother about them' (computers). This paperback follows the same path as Alcock's *Illustrating Basic;* his personal attitudes shine through, which makes a pleasant change. He also hand-wrote and hand-illustrated both books (copious drawings in them) ... which sounds zany, but really works very well.

Introduction to Microcomputers: Volume 0 – The Beginners' Book
by Adam Osborne
published 1982 by McGraw-Hill
price £5.95
ISBN 93 198864 0

Despite the book's somewhat oppressively American

bias, this introduction is recommended – especially in its new second edition – for quality of the information, the author's style and the sensible organisation of the content. All help to make Osborne's classic introduction and the following books in this series the best way to get any further into the micro.

• Writing programs

Most micros will come with some kind of programming reference book, but they may not be too well-written or too easy to use – especially if you're a beginner. Here are some alternatives which will provide you with a general, machine-independent basis for programming. They cover the two languages recommended for starters in *The Good Computing Book*.

Illustrating Basic
by Donald Alcock
published 1978 by Cambridge University Press
price £3.50
ISBN 0 521 2170 040
Personally, my favourite introduction to Basic, spiral bound to lay flat and hand-written (and hand-illustrated) to allow the author's personality to get through the facts. A Good Thing – and a good introduction to the language.

Basic With Style
by Paul Nagin and Henry Ledgard
published 1978 by Hayden
price £5.80
ISBN 0 8104 5115 8
Exellent advice on how to proceed, mercifully compact and leavened with humour. Subtitled 'Principles of Good Programming with Numerous Examples to Improve Programming Style and Proficiency' and based on the premise that "Programmers can and

should write programs which work correctly the first time". This book is part of Hayden's 'Programming Proverbs' series, which now includes a similar title for most programming languages.

30 Hour Basic
by Clive Prigmore
published 1981 by National Extension College
price £5.50
ISBN 0 86082 269 9

A self-teaching book which can be used as part of the College's mail-order tuition on computers. It has what I regard as some quirks of organisation (like DIM being covered before FOR/NEXT loops and GOSUB being dealt with only towards the end of the course). Not many jokes, either, and some erratic printing with misaligned green highlighting in the text. But quibbles apart, this is good, meaty stuff. It teaches the variety of Basic employed on the BBC computer, but there are conversion sheets available for many other micros to indicate any differences which affect the text.

Pocket Guide to Basic
by Roger Hunt
published 1982 by Pitman
price £2.25
ISBN 0 273 01685 7

Not exactly a book, more an instant reference. It's small (pocket-sized, in fact), has a spiral binding along one of the short sides, and its card cover folds around so that the book can stand up on your desk with the pages being flipped over. It's neat, accurate, and reasonably comprehensive.

Pocket Guide to Pascal
by David Watt
published 1982 by Pitman

price £2.25
ISBN 273 016490
Comments as for preceeding title.

A Practical Introduction to Pascal
by Tony Wilson
published 1982 by Macmillan
price £6.95
ISBN 0 333 333403
Concise, genial, recently updated and genuinely practical. It's British, too.

• Particular computers
You might also want to supplement the vendor's manuals with a more specific overview. There are a number of independently-produced books on particular computers; here's a selection.

Using CP/M: a self-teaching guide
by J Fernadez and R Ashley
published 1980 by Wiley
price £8.75
ISBN 0 471 08011 X
Not a book about a particular computer, to be sure, but still specific enough to merit inclusion here. The title says it all; the book succeeds in covering the principal usage of CP/M.

The CP/M Handbook
by Rodnay Zaks
published 1980 by Sybex
U.K. price around £12.20
ISBN 0 89588 048 2
A best-seller on the CP/M operating system, with some coverage of the multi-user upgrade MP/M as well; despite it's relative age it's still a good reference to CP/M – though a more critical approach would have

made it a better one. It could also have included some of the tips and tweaks with which any serious CP/M user has to get acquainted. Still, it makes a solid starter for newcomers to CP/M.

The Acorn Atom Magic Book
by Mike Lord
published 1981 by Timedata
price £5.50
Not great value for an 80-page opus, but stimulating as a bagfull of programs and pointers.

Apple II User's Guide
by Lon Poole, Martin McNiff and Steven Cook
published 1981 by McGraw-Hill
price £10.95
ISBN 0 931988 46 2
Probably covers everything the average user might want to know.

Basic Programming on the BBC Microcomputer
by Neil and Pat Cryer
published 1982 by Prentice-Hall
price £5.95
ISBN 13 066407 3
Solid, practical introduction. But why doesn't the BBC provide such a book with the computer?

Pet/CBM Personal Computer Guide
by Adam Osborne and Carroll Donahue
published 1981 by McGraw-Hill
price £10.95
ISBN 931988 55 1
Substantial, accurate, and clear.

Beginning Basic on the Commodore Vic
by Don Munro
published 1982 by the Tiny Publishing Co

price £4.95
Good little introduction for the Vic.
Cartoons by Bill Tidy.

Programming the Pet/CBM
by Raeto West
published 1982 by Level
price £14.90
ISBN 0 950 7650 0 7
Excellent value, really; more than 500 A4-sized pages
and packed with good information. It covers all software aspects of Commmodore 2000, 3000, 4000 and
8000 computers – it's comprehensive, accurate, and
British, too. If you have trouble getting it, send £14.90
(inc p&p) to Level Ltd at PO Box 438, London
NW3.1BH: same-day despatch is guaranteed.

TRS-80 Basic: a self-teaching guide
by R Albrecht, O Inman and R Zamora
published 1980 by Wiley
price £7.50
ISBN 471 06466 1
Something of an object lesson in providing a comprehensive grounding in one version of Basic (albeit one
which is nearly a standard in the micro business) on one
microcomputer (albeit the world's biggest-selling
micro). All the authors are notable independent com-
mentators, activists and propagandists on the West
Coast.

The Explorer's Guide to the ZX-81
by Mike Lord
published 1982 by Timedata
price £4.95
Many programs and ideas. Mike Lord has been in and
around the home computing world for a long time and
knows what he's talking about.

The ZX Companion
by Bob Maunder
published 1981 by Linsac
price £7.95
ISBN 0 907211 01 1
Successful and deservedly applauded for Sinclair owners who have got beyond the first stage with the ZX-81. Price includes p&p: send to Linsac at 68 Barder Road, Linthorpe, Middlesborough, Cleveland TS5.5ES.

The ZX-81 Pocket Book
by Trevor Toms
published 1981 by Phipps Associates
price £5.95
ISBN 0 9507302 2X
A chirpy introduction, easy to read and easy to use.

- **Personal computer magazines**

Most of these can be ordered through your newsagent, but the better way is buy your first copy somewhere (a railway station?) and then send for a subscription. You're likely to get your copy before everybody else; and the publishers (some of whom can do with all the help they can get) will make more money that way at no extra cost to you.

Acorn User
monthly, £1
annual subscription £15
53 Bedford Square, London WC1B.3DZ
01-631 1636
New magazine dedicated to this machine. Also covers the BBC Computer.

Commodore User
10 issues per year

annual subscription £12.50
19 Whitcomb Street, London WC2
01-839 2846
Commercial development of the sponsored magazine
for Commodore's 'official' user club. Relatively technical and biased towards the Pet/CBM 8000, but with
coverage of the smaller Commodore computers,
too.

Computer and Video Games
monthly, 75p
annual subscription £10
8 Herbal Hill, London EC1
01-278 6556
The title says it all. A mixture of news and information
about video and computer games, plus many readers'
games programs for popular micros (mostly Vic and
ZX-81 at the time of writing).

Computing Today International
monthly,
145 Charing Cross Road, London WC2H.0EE
01-437 1002
One of the earliest micro magazines, rooted originally
in a home electronics publication and still displaying a
hardware bias.

Microcomputer Printout
monthly, 95p
annual subscription £11.40
9 Harpton Parade, Yateley, Surrey
0252 878748
Amiable, usually authoritative monthly which has long
since left behind its original bias to the Pet. Bought by
a substantial publisher in the summer of 1982 from its
original progenitors, but hopefully the formula won't
change.

Personal Computer World
monthly, 75p
annual subscription £11.50
62 Oxford Street, London W1
01-636 6890
First, broadest, liveliest and best-designed of the U.K.
personal computer magazines. Acquired for a mind-
boggling sum from a smallish independent publisher by
the giant VNU concern in summer 1982.

Personal Computing Today
monthly, 65p
annual subscription £11.65
145 Charing Cross Road, London WC2H.0EE
01-437 1002
Launched summer 1982 as a stablemate of *Computing
Today International* and claiming to service "anyone
with an interest in the subject of microcomputing".
Started well in editorial terms – early issues carried a
good deal of 'which computer should I buy' information and the magazine employs at least one genuinely
competent technical expert.

Popular Computing Weekly
weekly, 30p
annual subscription £19.95
19 Whitcomb Street, London WC2 7HF
01-839 1855
A brave attempt to do a weekly journal in a market
populated (over-populated, in fact) by monthlies. Not
as good on the news side as a weekly should be, but at
the time of writing it's still early days for the magazine.

Practical Computing
monthly, 80p
annual subscription £10

Quadrant House, The Quadrant, Sutton SM2 5AS
01-661 3500
Biggest of the U.K. personal computer magazines.
Very wide range, but often it's heavy going.

Sinclair User
bi-monthly, 60p
annual subscription £9
30-31 Islington Green, London N1
01-359 7481
First (and currently the best) of the Sinclair-only
magazines.

Sinclair Programs
bi-monthly, 95p
annual subscription £6.60
30-31 Islington Green, London N1
01-259 7481
Explicitly-titled spin-off from *Sinclair User*.

Vic Computing
bi-monthly, £1
annual subscription £6
39-41 North Road, London N7.9DP
01-607 9489
First of the single-micro magazines. I have to declare
my interest, but it's probably the best single source of
information about the Vic (in editorial and the advertisements) – though orientated more towards the beginner than the experienced Vic-tim. Will expand its
coverage to include the newest micros from Commodore, the Max and CBM 64.

Which Micro?
monthly, 85p
annual subscription £5
57A Hatton Garden, London EC1N.8JD
01-242 6552

One of the 1982 crop of magazines for the home computer buff – still finding its feet when this book went to press. Subtitled '. . . and software review': most of its content comprises product reviews (descriptive rather than analytical, on the whole) and low-level introductions to different elements of micro systems (which generally include lists of relevant products available).

Windfall
monthly, £1
annual subscription £12
68 Chester Road, Hazel Grove, Stockport SK7.5NY
061-456 8353
Substantial magazine devoted to the Apple and apparently written in a reasonably knowledgable style by enthusiasts (two characteristics noticeably absent from most of the British microcomputing magazines).

Your Computer
monthly, 60p
annual subscription £8
Quadrant House, The Quadrant, Sutton SM2 5AS
01-661 3500
Spin-off from *Practical Computing* specifically for 'home' micros. As good for the advertisements in it as the editorial, which mostly comprises users' programs.

ZX Computing
quarterly, £1.75
145 Charing Cross Road, London WC2H.0EE
01-437 1002
One of the 1982 crop of magazines for the Sinclair fraternity, a spin-off from the *Computing Today International* stable.

• The 'straight' computer publications

These titles are aimed at people who buy computers for their business or who work in the computer industry. They're included for the sake of completeness, but writing to their editors is also a useful expedient if you have some complaint about a particular micro or a particular supplier – I don't guarantee success, but all journalists love a scandal.

Business Information Technology
Business Publications Ltd
109-119 Waterloo Road
London SE1 8UL
Monthly on computers and other 'new technology' for business.

Computer Bulletin
British Computer Society
13 Mansfield Street
London W1M 0BP
Monthly official journal of the professional body.

Computer Confidential
27 Blatchington Road
Hove
Sussex BN3 3YL
Monthly newsletter for business users.

Computer Management
30-31 Islington Green
London N1 8BJ
Monthly for people who run big computers.

Computer Systems
Walton House
93 High Street
Bromley
Kent BR1 1JW

Monthly mostly about industrial and non-office systems.

Computer Talk
Quadrant House
The Quadrant
Sutton
Surrey SM2 5AS
'Controlled circulation' weekly for computer industry employees.

Computer Weekly
Quadrant House
The Quadrant
Sutton
Surrey SM2 5AS
'Controlled circulation' weekly for computer industry employees.

Computing
53-55 Frith Street
London W1A 2HG
'Controlled circulation' weekly for computer industry employees.

Data Business
53-55 Frith Street
London W1A 2HG
Weekly covering computers for accountants.

Data Systems
198-200 Keighley Road
Bradford
West Yorks BD9 4JQ
Monthly mostly covering big computers.

Datalink
53-55 Frith Street
London W1A 2HG

'Controlled circulation' weekly for computer industry employees.

Educational Computing
EMAP Computer Publications Ltd
8 Herbal Hill
London EC1
Computers-for-schools newspaper-style monthly.

Electronics and Computing
67 High Street
Daventry
Northhamptonshire
'Home and hobby' monthly for people with soldering irons.

Infomatics
53-55 Frith Street
London W1A 2HG
'Controlled circulation' monthly for computer industry employees.

Irish Computer
Birchdale
Cherrywood Road
Loughlinstown
Co Dublin, Eire
General business-orientated computer monthly.

Micro Decision
53-55 Frith Street
London W1A 2HG
Monthly about micros in business.

Practice Computing
Paradox Publications
39-41 North Road
London N1 1JT
Monthly on computers for GPs.

Systems International
Quadrant House
The Quadrant
Sutton
Surrey SM2 5AS
Monthly for people who build or assemble computer systems.

What to Buy for Business
11a Kings Road
London SW1
Wonderfully aggressive no-advertising subscription-only monthly which includes coverage of computers.

Which Computer ?
EMAP Computer Publications
8 Herbal Hill
London EC1
Monthly on computers for business.

Which Word Processor ?
EMAP Computer Publications
8 Herbal Hill
London EC1
Monthly on word processing for business.

9 HOW TO BLUFF YOUR WAY IN COMPUTERS

Computers are hip, so why not make the most of it? As with most areas of life, a little terminology easily beats a great deal of knowledge; so here's a Complete Conversation Kit for Beginners, a bluffer's guide to micros.

Anyone can play. As the blessed Stephen Potter wrote, quoting with approval the unpublished remark of Rilke, "if you're not one up (Bitzleisch) you're one down (Rotzleisch)". By the by, Potter recommended Rilke along with Kafka as OK names for 1945–50; but times move on. OK names for the 1980s are Samuel Palmer, any non-American writers of science fiction, any feminist author (preferably dead) — and Steve Wozniak, Adam Osborne and Chuck Peddle.

The new technology is today the way to be one-up. And, fortunately, it is entirely possible to achieve that state without any in-depth knowledge of the stuff at all. All you need is in this chapter, which contains:

Lesson One: Four Types of Keywords (most of which are easily-remembered)

Lesson Two: Only Two Rules (compare other kits, most of which have many more)

Lesson Three: Six conversational Gambits (all guaranteed successful).

Lesson One: Computerbluff Keywords

This is the only difficult part of the course; in computer bluff there are certain Keywords to be learned. Some of them are definitely to be used at every possible opportunity, because they constitute the essential method of saying not very much at all with the self-assured air of a competent insider.

Other Keywords are to be avoided at all costs, either because they mean something or because non-OK people use them.

The OK words are in three grades. They are distinguished in the present text by one, two or three asterisks. Three-star words carry most weight but they should be used sparingly, since several of them almost mean something and you might fall into the dangerous quicksand of imparting information. Still, nearly all the OK Keywords are basically unnecessary and esoteric terms for which there are perfectly adequate but definitely non-OK equivalents in normal English.

You should aim for a modest total of at least 15 stars in your average Computerbluff conversation. Any more than that and you can start doubling the star-value of Keywords until you reach a total of 50 stars per conversation, at which point all Keywords from any category automatically carry a value of 10 stars.

As for the maximum target at which you should aim, the English record is held by Al Julianson of Berkshire (2,457 stars in a 23-minute conversation held at Reading, December, 1981) and the All-Comers' record for the Asterisk Sprint is in the possession of Kay Guano, London N5 (clocked at 129 stars per minute during a June, 1982 training seminar for would-be computer journalists).

They are exceptional figures, of course. Unless you are aiming for one of the records, you should aim for a balance in your Computerbluff conversations. Julianson advises the 50:30:10 split. "Ideally 50 percent of the terms you use will come from the one-star list, 30 percent will have two stars, and 10 percent will be three-star words. This is the way to success, I have found".

Of the balance of your conversation, five percent of the content will comprise non-OK words (well, you can't win them all); and five percent should be new multi-star words invented by you on the spot.

It is recommended that you cut out the Keyword lists and paste them somewhere discreet. Practise using them while waiting for trains, brushing your teeth, waiting for the coffee to percolate and so on. You will then be able to call on them instantly as required.

NON-OK KEYWORDS
(do not use)

electronic	databank
integrated circuit	on-line
core	real-time
disc	punched cards
programme	firmware
personal computer	operator
electronic brain	Cobol
tape	assembler
data	"chips with everyting"

OK WORDS

	One star	Two stars	Three stars
I	16-bit	32-bit	
N	chip	code	bit-twiddle
T	bit-slice	response time	
E	resource-sharing	network	
R	memory		
N	ROM		
A	RAM		
L	machine-code		
S			

	micro	database	Osborne
E	end-user	terminal	Peddle
X	system	application	Wozniak
T	machine	buzzword	buzzphrase
E	program	microcomputer	micro
R	terminal dialogue	package	computer literacy
N	word processing	spelling checker	electronic mail
A	microprocessor	Pascal	mini-Winchester
L	diskette	mini-floppy	mini-Winny
S	Basic	artificial intelligence	workstation
	CP/M	MP/M	Unix

A			
D	programmable		
J	intelligent	micro-miniaturised	
E	interconnected	top-down	optimised
C	modular	configurable	structured
T	flexible	networked	ergonomic
I	integrated	top-down	
V	expandable		
E			
S			

Lesson Two: Rules of the game

"In conversation play", writes Potter, "the important thing is to get in early and stay there." This, of course, goes without saying. Life being what it is, that ploy may not always be possible. So as an addendum to the main strategy, here are the Only Two Rules of Computerbluff.

Rule One — the one-m k-not-c principle

You should always spell 'program' with one 'm' and 'disk' with a 'k', especially in conversation — the adept bluffer will practise this in front of the bathroom mirror, and will also be alert to detecting 'mme' and 'c' in other people's speech.

The point is that it gives you an opening to show your class. Here are some appropriate gambits you might use:

"I think it's important that language evolves ..."

"New concepts should require new language ..."

"Americanisms? No, no, micros make for a new Internationalism ..."

"It seems a bit silly to talk about 'diskettes' with a 'k' and 'disc' with a 'c', doesn't it ..."

Rule Two — the Instant Get-Out

No-one knows everything about computers. People who know a great deal about one aspect invariably know very little about any other.

For instance, you may meet an expert in systems software. So you should emphasise the practical. "Theorising and bit-twiddling in the nuts and bolts of the machine is all very essential, of course. But I like to look at computing from the point of view of the user. What do *we* get out of it?"

Note that 'bit-twiddling' is a three-star Keyword and 'machine' is also on the list. Bit-twiddling [***] is a particularly important term in Computerbluff; it can be used derogatively, to suggest that the said twiddlers are either ivory-tower theoreticians or mere mechanics.

Such conversations will normally be reinforced by multiple Keywords like response time [**], terminal dialogue [*], and ergonomics [***].

'Bit-twiddling' can also be used to refer to oneself with self-deprecating charm. Say your conversation is with an expert designer of software which does something for the user. Then your ploy would involve a shy smile and "I'm afraid I am just a bit-twiddler myself. My interest lies in the nuts and bolts of the thing ..."

You might continue: "We're putting together some novel ideas for *optimised* [***] *bit-slice* [*] *micros* [***]" or "*multifunction* [**] *networks* [***]" or "*re-

source-sharing [*] *interconnections* [*]" ... and so on.

Lesson Three: Actual conversation

Armed with your new-found knowledge and your crib sheets, you may repair with equanimity to the pub, cocktail party or user group meeting.

You will there search for Openings. They are distinguished by (a) affording the opportunity for you to optimise three-star output and maximising from the one- and two-star lists, while you (b) adhere to Rule One and (c) seize opportunities to go one-up via Rule Two.

Your major chances will come, however, (d) in non-competitive situations. These you enter by first making sure that the target group contains no other Computerbluff graduates. You can then drop your computer-awareness casually into the conversation.

Recommended gambits are:

... "Funnily enough, something similar happened with me and my computer ..."

... "Just as well I have the computer; I'd never have been here on time otherwise ..."

... "I really had to tear myself away ..."

Someone in your audience will then pick up the ball and run with it. You may, however, have to do some more groundwork. Either way, you will find that one of six standard conversations will invariably start.

1. *The gas-bill story.* This perennial tale of final demands for £0.00 has now been joined by the Book Club Boob, a situation in which it is impossible to prevent the computer sending you unwanted and unrequested 'on approval' material.

Your response should be a sorrowful shake of the

head, a wry smile reflecting on the vagaries of the human race, and a comment to the effect that computers only do what they're told. (You can slate programmers at every opportunity during Computer-bluffpersonship, if you want, so long as there are none present.)

2. *The 'How do they work' enquiry.* Modify your answer according to your ultimate sexual intentions vis à vis your questioner; in all cases, however, you'll have to side-step. Fortunately, no-one has ever explained satisfactorily how a computer works.

That in itself is one suitably dry riposte. Or you can switch back into lovable self-deprecation — "I don't really care how they work; I just like to use them."

If pressed, you can resort to incomprehensibly basic electronics. The important Keyphrases here are UNIQUE to this situation and should NEVER be used elsewhere. They are "switching", "streams of electrons", "the presence or absence of pre-specified voltage levels" (best remembered via the memonic TPOAOPSVL), and "combinations of these."

3. *The "my cousin/husband/aunt/next-door-neighbour has just started a programming/systems analysis/word processing course" remark.* This is usually produced as the speaker's most intimate contact with computers, so you have a clear field.

Again, choose your response according to desired effect. On the one hand you can shake your head sadly again and comment on the inadvisability of committing one's career to the decaying branch of the industry (e.g., big computers which need systems analysts) rather than the sex-drugs-and-rock-'n'-roll liveliness of the micro market.

Alternatively you can commend the farsightedness of that career choice, with approval for the idea of entering a growth industry on the ground floor. Either way, don't get involved in any discussion of what exactly a systems analyst *does;* not even systems analysts know the answer to that.

4. *The "will they take over my job?" paranoia,* the fear of personal and then mass unemployment; will computers replace people? Yes, they will. Or at least, they'll replace some people. Frankly (you can say knowledgably) computers can get rid of the duller, more mechanical jobs which people do; and indeed that will mean fewer people employed on production lines, copy typing, and the like.

At this point you should look earnest. Start musing about the need to change people's views about work and leisure, about the lack of political will, about the importance of re-distributing the workforce for the good of the country, about the opportunities to change life for the better.

5. *The "Bet they can't write novels, ho ho" syndrome.* That's correct, they can't. Still, you can't tell them that, so one correct reply would use the two-star term 'artificial intelligence' in some expression like "well, the Americans/Japanese/Swedish are doing amazing things with computer-based artificial intelligence . . .".

If that doesn't work, ask them if they've read *Into the Morning* by Martin Eyre. It was published in 1982 to critical acclaim – *The Sunday Times* said something like "It is really refreshing to discover that the art of the novel is not dead". The book is about a young man's dawning awareness of his emotional strength; and it was written entirely by a computer. The machine was fed the Oxford English Dictionary and of rules of grammar and syntax; it then produced a synopsis, expanded it into a first draft, and polished it until one of the big publishing houses accepted it. Only after the book was published did it emerge that 'Martin Eyre' was a computer at Harlow.

That'll shut them up, ho ho. It's all a pack of lies, of course.

6. *The "Don't you have to be good at maths?" ploy.*
This enables the speaker to feel artistic and therefore superior to the more boring and probably numerate technophile. This is because the follow-up is always: "I couldn't do it; I'm no good at figures – I think I'm too sensitive/emotional/sensuous to get on with computers."

This one is extremely tricky, since you are clearly vulnerable to accusations of non-sensuousness – and who wants to be non-sensuous? So your response should be airy: "No, actually, that's an old fallacy. I don't understand science and maths myself, and look at me".

From there you move quickly into something like "When it comes down to it, there really are too many fallacies surrounding computers. The educational system should be changed to improve 'computer literacy' [***]..."

Go to it

That's it, the rest is up to you. Let us know how you get on; a full report on all letters received will appear in the next edition of the book (assuming there is one).

NOTES

NOTES

NOTES

NOTES

NOTES

NOTES